*Unamuno*
AN EXISTENTIAL VIEW OF SELF AND SOCIETY

# Unamuno AN EXISTENTIAL VIEW OF SELF AND SOCIETY

*Paul Ilie*

THE UNIVERSITY OF WISCONSIN PRESS
*Madison, Milwaukee, and London* 1967

PUBLISHED BY THE UNIVERSITY OF WISCONSIN PRESS
*Madison, Milwaukee, and London*

U.S.A.: Box 1379, Madison, Wisconsin 53701
U.K.: 26-28 Hallam Street, London, W.1

Printed in the United States of America by
Kingsport Press, Inc., Kingsport, Tennessee
Library of Congress Catalog Card Number 67-25944

*To*
PROFESSOR MAIR J. BENARDETE

*of Brooklyn College*

# PREFACE

*If Unamuno* were to see the mass of scholarly publications devoted to his works, he would be appalled as well as amused. Once, in 1902, he wrote complaining about the excessive number of periodicals accumulated in the Madrid libraries. With irascible humor, he said that he was constantly distracted from whatever review he would pick up to read by the lure of some other review sitting next to it on the shelf. Thus, he explained, his eye caught sight of one volume after another, and title after title, until he became so entangled in the wealth of material that he ended by reading nothing. "And so," he concluded, "starting out by reading books, one goes on to read reviews, then reviews of reviews, and finally, catalogs."[1]

Today, the bibliography on Unamuno is so extensive that one wonders how prophetic Unamuno will prove to be. We are not as yet reduced to scanning catalogs of works about him, but the critic's only justification for adding another title to the list is the hope that he will make a relatively new contribution. I have written the present book with this hope, for it seems to me that of the many areas worthy of attention in Unamuno's philosophy, his existentialism still remains rather neglected. Much energy and space have been given to his biography, theology, and metaphysics, but there remain at least three substantial aspects that have not yet been studied. These are his concept of psychology, his theory of value, and his methodology for cultural analysis. Each of these topics covers a significant area in itself, and yet as a group they comprise a unified perspective for defining his existentialism clearly.

[1] *Obras completas*, III, 541.

If there is any distortion in the lens of that perspective, we will find that it is due to the confusion that plagues Unamuno's writings. He was as unsystematic in devising a total philosophy as he was disorganized in composing individual essays. It will be necessary, therefore, for us to have accurate techniques of analysis that will organize the massive tangle of ideas left in his works. This is not too difficult to accomplish if we bear in mind the special disposition of the existentialist mind. Being so sensitive to people and to ideas, Unamuno was capable of adopting many points of view, and he could argue for or against them as he pleased. Moreover, he was highly self-conscious, and he remained constantly alert to his own ideas and emotional reactions. Therefore, what we might believe to be Unamuno's contradictory positions is actually the result of a shifting intellectual detachment. Exactly how this happens and what it means emotionally will be taken up in Part One. The point is that in Unamuno we find at work a psychology of paradox which has its roots in a self-conscious division of personality, and this permitted him to adopt many divergent viewpoints. Since Unamuno could not change his personality even if he had wanted to, he continued to make digressions and parenthetical remarks throughout his essays. The result was an ostensibly inconsistent philosophy. However, an internal analysis of these textual divergences reveals a completely coherent and often unvaried statement on a given question. My approach, therefore, in this book will be to consider the entire body of writings as the expression of an intellect at war with itself. And within the specific issues, Unamuno's remarks will be examined in relationship to each other, as well as in the light of their given contexts.

If I avoid mentioning the work of other scholars, it is not because their contributions are unimportant. But there are so many approaches to Unamuno that it will not be feasible to relate them to this study. My purpose is not to evaluate or to refute other theories of Unamuno's thought, but to present in as undistracted a fashion as possible my own approach.

I would like to express my gratitude to the Horace H. Rackham Foundation, whose generous support made this book possible.

P. I.

*Ann Arbor, Michigan*
*October, 1965*

# CONTENTS

*ix*

x    *Contents*

# NOTE ON DOCUMENTATION

Parenthetical references in the text to Unamuno's works are by volume and page number to Manuel García Blanco's definitive edition, the *Obras completas* (Madrid: Afrodisio Aguado–Vergara Editorial, 1958——). Page numbers are cited in the order of their importance. See the Appendix for the titles of works cited from this edition. Translations of Unamuno in the text are mine.

Parenthetical references in the text to Nietzsche's works are to the *Werke*, edited by Karl Schlechta (Munich: C. Hanser, 1954–56), except those to *Der Wille zur Macht*, which are to the edition by Alfred Bäumler (Leipzig: A. Kröner, 1930). Translations are from the *Complete Works*, translated and edited by Oscar Levy (London: T. N. Foulis, 1909–14). Abbreviations are:

| | |
|---|---|
| A | *Der Anti-Christ* |
| EH | *Ecce Homo* |
| FW | *Die Fröliche Wissenschaft* |
| G | *Die Götzen-Dämmerung* |
| GM | *Zur Genealogie der Moral* |
| J | *Jenseits von Gut und Böse* |
| M | *Morgenröte* |
| MA | *Menschliches, Allzumenschliches* |
| NCW | *Nietzsche contra Wagner* |
| UB | *Unzeitgemässe Betrachtungen* |
| W | *Der Fall Wagner* |
| WM | *Der Wille zur Macht* |
| WS | *Der Wanderer und sein Schatten* |
| Z | *Also Sprach Zarathustra* |

*Unamuno*
AN EXISTENTIAL VIEW OF SELF AND SOCIETY

# INTRODUCTION

*Miguel de Unamuno* (1864–1936) was a Spanish philosopher with a profound love for mankind and truth. His insight into human nature was as deep as it was compassionate, and he used it to inspire the most extraordinary corpus of writings that can be found anywhere in modern Europe. This is no exaggeration, for Unamuno's accomplishment was prodigious. His complete works run into the tens of thousands of pages, and they embrace genres as diverse as the philosophical essay, poetry and the novel, religious polemic, theater, philological studies, and literary and social criticism. Taken singly, any one of these categories would have sufficed to thrust Unamuno into the foreground of Spanish letters. Collectively, they have made a place for him among the first-ranking intellectuals of twentieth-century Europe.

This fact, of course, is generally admitted without much question. But outside of the Spanish-speaking world, it is a fact conceded somewhat negatively, in a kind of vacuum rather than on the basis of the full evidence that ought to support judgments of this sort. The truth is that the heart of Unamuno's writings, his philosophical essays, are little known to the English-speaking public. To anyone familiar with these essays, which make up two-thirds of his total production, it is incredible that Unamuno's current reputation as a leading existentialist could have been made without them. Not that such well-known titles as *The Tragic Sense of Life; Saint Emmanuel the Good, Martyr; The Life of Don Quixote and Sancho;* and *The Agony of Christianity* are unrepre-

*3*

sentative of their author's thinking. But, taken together, they comprise a fairly unequivocal statement of what is really an elusive, paradoxical philosophy. Moreover, their intent is heavily religious. This does not falsify matters for the general reader, but it does prevent him from getting more than a two-dimensional view of a spiritual universe that must be seen in all of its four dimensions.

Fortunately, the two dimensions that have been visible reveal Unamuno's profile quite accurately. Written all over it are the passions and yearnings of a sincere religious searcher. It is, at the same time, clouded by the doubts and anguish of a rational mind too sophisticated for the simple faith of ordinary men. But this profile is only half a face, and here is where the difficulty begins. For when we turn Unamuno's full countenance toward us, we must be prepared to decide whether it is indeed one face that we see or many, or whether, as some suggest, it is a two-faced Unamuno that we find. This is one aspect of the problem, to know where hypocrisy ends and ambiguity begins, and where philosophical relativism emerges from apparent ambiguity.

There is also a second aspect, which, for those of us who are not interested in judging Unamuno's sincerity as a man, is the more fruitful issue. This involves the originality of his thought. Once again, a reading of his translated works is likely to recall, and quite accurately, the spiritual fervor of Kierkegaard and the raging humanity of Nietzsche. We cannot question the peculiarly Spanish form which Unamuno's philosophy took with respect to his predecessors. But the fact remains that, within the history of ideas, his religious and ethical positions would seem to offer little that is radically new. Many scholars would debate this point, yet granted that they are right, it is possible to find still firmer grounds on which to base Unamuno's originality. Without doubt, the issues that he raised concerning consciousness, anguish, death, transcendence, and personality anticipate the more systematic—and less vital—analyses of Heidegger, Buber, Jaspers, and Sartre. Although the latter have been recognized as the leaders of modern existentialism, Unamuno wrote well in advance of their philosophies, and specifically enough to be considered more than just a precursor.

Be this as it may, the nature of existentialism is sufficiently diffuse to make questions of influence and chronology immaterial. Its precise definition continues to evade us because many of its characteristics have already appeared in previous intellectual movements. At the same time, there are metaphysical, theological, psychological, and axiological features to existentialism that distinguish it from other philosophical schools. Having lived with these features for one or two generations, we have reached the point where our reaction is much the same as it has been to the term romanticism: the word is hard to define, and yet we all know what it means. There is little doubt, however, that existentialism has stated the problem of life and of philosophy in a way that is more personal and conflictive than any other philosophical position prior to it. This is not a matter of emotional or of subjective approaches, but rather of how the questions are asked. The issues are no longer formulated as, What is man? What are values? What is the nature of the universe? Instead, the existentialist's questions are, Who am I? What do I believe in? What is my relationship to that which is not me?

It is here that the originality and greatness of Unamuno lie. For these problems, as they are lived and experienced, are each inextricable from the other, and Unamuno was incapable of separating them for the purposes of philosophical discourse. This did not make him an incoherent or chaotic writer, but it did prevent him from approaching those issues systematically. There are, of course, exceptions, the most notable being *The Tragic Sense of Life*. But in general, his ideas and feelings spilled over onto the pages of an essay as they were conceived and lived, without ever resolving the question that the essay had originally proposed at the beginning. Thus, Unamuno is closer in method to Kierkegaard and Nietzsche than he is to Heidegger, Jaspers, and Sartre. And yet while he recapitulates the ideas of the former two, he anticipates the concerns, if not the actual solutions, of the latter three, and this, unfortunately, is what we tend to forget.

The general outline of Unamuno's existentialism can be seen by a few comparisons. He demonstrated that the rational mind shatters the foundation of Christian values, as did Dostoyevsky; he suggested that man's will dictates to the imperative of moral judgments, as did Nietzsche; his need for God resulted in agonistic faith, as in Kierkegaard; the fear of death revealed to him the most authentic feature of existence, as in Heidegger; his self-realization consisted of acting upon the world, as in Sartre. And so the list

continues. It is not my intention to establish influences or antecedents in Unamuno's thought vis-à-vis other philosophers. It is clear
that their common preoccupations are part of a *Zeitgeist*, however
old-fashioned this explanation may be. But I do want to point out
how unique this Spaniard was in synthesizing those concerns as a
thinker even while he was experiencing them as a man. The emotional pattern of Unamuno's life was intimately involved with his
attitudes toward religion, an interaction which is reflected in his
writings. Moreover, his theory of value and culture was rooted in
his condition as a Spaniard, so that by discoursing about society he
objectified his personal problems, and, conversely, while speaking
subjectively he developed ideas that can stand on their own as valid
concepts.

The fact that Unamuno's intellectual expression of his existence
mirrors his life experiences has been commented on by most critics.
In biographical studies, as well as in discussions of his metaphysical
and religious thought, the extent of his existentialist leanings has
also been adequately shown. This is not, however, the entire story.
There is also the question of what other values and principles
central to existentialism are present in Unamuno's thought, and
how they are related to the individual and to society. Here, indeed,
is the basic existentialist issue, perhaps more so for the mid-
twentieth century than the religious question ever could be for the
nineteenth. It concerns the theory of values, including ethics, as
determined by individual personality and by patterns of culture. A
major sector of Unamuno's philosophy can be included under these
headings of axiology, psychology, and sociology, but what is more
significant is that they are existentially bound to each other and
mutually dependent. It is Unamuno's unique personality structure
which influences the formation of a value system, thus committing
him to the latter's tenets. It is within Spanish society that these
values must be tested and put into operation. And it is that society
which molds the personality which formulates the values.

My point, therefore, is that the existential conflict of Unamuno
the Spaniard is transformed into a self-sufficient existentialist philosophy, just as the problems of existentialism as a philosophy are
recognizably operative in Unamuno the Spaniard. In order to un-
tangle this tight network of interacting elements, we have to distinguish the three forementioned categories: psychology, axiology,

and culture. If we can determine what psychological factors Unamuno believed to be involved in thought and action, we will begin
to understand the value system behind his view of human behavior.
If we can establish Unamuno's concept of personality, we will be
able to discern the origin and development of moral values. And
finally, if we can see how psychological and moral attitudes are
acted out in society, we will perceive the relationship between
culture and the individual. All three of these categories, taken
together, comprise a major and modern statement of Unamuno's
existentialist philosophy. They also represent three basic areas of
human participation: the private self, the realm of ideas, and the
cultural context. Clearly, each realm partakes of the other, and,
indeed, culture is little more than a collective private self, just as the
latter is a condensation of the culture at large.

We will, consequently, be speaking of existential psychology,
although the term has little meaning as a doctrine or school of
thought. Rather, it is a method of looking at the self and asking
certain questions. Whether we apply the term to Nietzsche or
Husserl, Dostoyevsky or Sartre, Kierkegaard or Frankl, the procedure is the same, although the conclusions differ. In every case,
Unamuno's included, an individual self sets about to explore its
own structure, its feelings, and its position with regard to everything that is not itself. Fundamentally, this is a phenomenology of
consciousness. Beginning with a desire to know himself, the individual comes to adopt a more analytical view of the self and its
mechanisms. In this solitary dialog—or monodialog, as Unamuno
called it—a number of basic questions arise. If one part of the self
can contemplate another part, which self is the authentic one?
What, indeed, is the real nature of personality? If the self "out
there" that I am watching is merely an actor, am I responsible for
the values which it is acting out? Is it possible to talk about sincerity and hypocrisy, or even commitment, when one part of the self
can be so easily alienated from another? In fact, is not the social self
some "other" self that shares my body with me, but is otherwise no
more than an extension of my self, a property, so to speak?

These are some of the issues which arise as soon as the individual
undertakes to know himself seriously. For Unamuno, the situation
is as deeply disturbing as it is inevitable. Whereas he once had an
integrated personality, he is now faced with a self that has suffered

a differentiation of parts. One part of him is a contemplator—a *cogito*, let us say technically—and the rest of him is a set of ego fragments that carry out different roles. He finds that he can be divorced from the emotions, and even the ideas, of another fragmentary self. Indeed, he learns that much of life is a charade, with masks and myths often substituting for realities. But even worse, he discovers that man can live a private farce, creating the self-deception of a secret legend that corresponds neither to the social self nor to the naked private self. At this point, it seems as if man is reduced to nothingness, that man is an essential hollow—the void of pure consciousness—around which he has built the fragile shell of existence.

It is this confrontation with the empty core of reality which thrusts Unamuno back into an affirmation of selfhood and life. He admits that the cogito can contemplate everything except itself. He also accepts the fact that his knowledge about other parts of the self may be unreliable. But he realizes too that to have remained without a self-contemplative attitude toward himself would have been to live in a brute animal state. He might possess individuality in this state, but not personality. Self-awareness, with all the doubts and alienations that it produces, is still the only humanizing faculty that can knit him into a social fabric and provide him with inner spirituality. Of course, there are times when a satanic self emerges to whisper insinuations into the ear of the contemplator. But this only means that at some point everyone withdraws psychologically from his role in life and sees it dispassionately. This disaffection would, for Sartre, mark the end of a commitment to that role. For Unamuno, however, to adopt an ironic attitude toward the social self need not detract from the sobriety of that self or its role. Such irony or disaffection poses many difficulties, as we will see, but ultimately the self-in-the-world must be affirmed.

As a result, self-alienation may be a blessing in disguise. Since this condition comes about after a desperate effort to know ourselves, the anguish that we suffer during the experience can help us to understand the suffering of others. The pain of our own sorrow may well induce us into a compassion for the sorrow of our fellow man. As Unamuno puts it in one of his magnificent metaphors, "when by submerging you enter into yourself, and advance along the dark inner galleries of your soul, you never know when you have left your own spiritual underground and have entered your neighbor's" (IX, 842). Alienation, therefore, is admittedly the last psychic state before utter disintegration of the self. But it is also the means for fulfilling an ethical imperative, the commandment of loving our fellow men. And in the fulfillment, we regain our self.

One might surmise that there is more than just a trace of religious feeling in Unamuno's psychological analysis. This is indeed true. Personality for him is the instrument of spirit in man's existence, and spirit is the consciousness of self, of mortality, and of God. Without going into the theological aspects of the problem, it should be clear that a certain psychological condition must exist before the individual can be suitably prepared for a spiritual life. The steps involved in this preparation are detailed, and will be examined in Part One. It is enough to say here that the final result is a harmony of all the elements of personality. In other words, the divided self is resolved into a spiritually whole man, a man who has found his real, permanent self and has reconciled it to his role in society. By this means, he maintains a bond of communication between his private world and external reality. But, by being aware that his life is bound by time and limited by death, the spiritually whole man finds his ultimate substantiality in his consciousness of time. Or rather, he learns that his real, permanent self is at one with his temporal awareness: the continuity of himself in time even as he changes from day to day, from role to role. This is what I will call the *psychochronic self*, a neologism which I hope will not obtrude in a discussion that necessarily must be more conceptual—and less compelling—than Unamuno's own metaphorical language. Nevertheless, the basic point remains. The key to Unamuno's general philosophy is to be found in his psychology.

We may state, therefore, the following principle of Unamuno's existentialism. Reality consists of realms of being whose value is determined by the conflicts of consciousness. This idea is easily illustrated. Any object or animal can have being (*ser*) by virtue of appearing in the world, by existing phenomenally. Human existence rises above the animal level of phenomenon when it has a psychological experience rooted in the drama of self-awareness. But, full being in the existentialist sense of a meaningful human condition (*serse*) is achieved only in the larger drama of social engagement. It is not enough for man to have a private consciousness and a public mask. He must also transcend his private being (*ser*) by a reflexive act. By watching himself project a personality into a social situation, he reintegrates himself, his innermost self, with the external world. We will see exactly how this is done later on. What is important for us to remember now is that such an act binds the individual to other people. He thus becomes responsible not only for himself but for his social condition as well. Here, then, is a second principle of Unamuno's existentialism: the values that men live by are embedded in the psychology of consciousness.

It is in this area of valuation that Unamuno stirs up the most trouble. Were he to assume a practical sense of life, there would be no need to question men's actions or motivations. As long as events turn out well and social order is maintained, why dig into the secret places? But, as we learn from *The Life of Don Quixote and Sancho*, Unamuno cannot be practical. He therefore points out the inescapable truth that as long as we watch ourselves as if we were someone else, we cannot behave sincerely. Or, to state this positively, the fact that we are spectators to our own role in life makes us hypocrites. But, the term hypocrisy must be understood in the original sense that Unamuno meant for it—as playing a theatrical part. What does this imply in ethical terms? Primarily, that all our ideas, thoughts, and values are fraudulent, because they are conceived during the state of self-contemplation. Every value that we construct is the formulation of some other self, a self alienated by the contemplator. There is always an ironic perspective within us, so that seriousness—or sincerity—is only possible when the reflective process itself is suppressed. As Unamuno put it, "insofar as man speaks, he lies, and insofar as he speaks to himself, that is, insofar that he thinks, he lies to himself" (II, 901). Which is to say, only animals, with their pure reflex actions and unconscious state of bring, are sincere. The point here, of course, is not that thinking is bad, but that knowing that we think, being conscious of it, makes us actors.

This psycho-moral problem inevitably brings Nietzsche into the picture. His life and thought seem to reflect a similar conflict between animal health and intellectual sickness. Despite Nietzsche's many infirmities, which kept pace with his extensive erudition, the philosophy he developed exalted strength and joyous living. He conceived of an ideal man who would be far from the cultural hero or protector of society envisioned by traditionalists. On the contrary, his superman could come into being only after one essential truth were grasped: that the meaningful core of existence—and the triumph of life—lies in the will to power. Since this vitalistic value is the supreme good, there can be nothing wrong with subverting conventional morality whenever the latter gets in the way. Conversely, no traditionally evil value is really immoral if it enhances individual power and the affirmation of the self. In fact, if we were to examine Christian ethics, we could demonstrate it to be the means by which certain people—the weak ones—themselves dream of power and ultimate self-vindication. Consequently, all moral systems are the rationalizations of a will to power, and this truth can be seen in the lives of saints and ascetics as well as transgressors. Thus, by placing himself beyond good and evil, the superman simply recognizes that morality is a projection of psychological attitudes, and hence a matter of personal criteria. Everything, therefore, is permissible, and nothing can be condemned if it serves the ends desired by us.

Even if Unamuno had never heard of Nietzsche, he still would have made the Nietzschean statements we find so frequently in his works. Unamuno was not an immoralist by any means, but his commentary was as devastating in its psychological analysis as Nietzsche's was in its critique of Christianity. Of course, it was this very hostility to Christian ethics that alienated the Spaniard from the German. But willingly or not, Unamuno met Nietzsche at the gates of consciousness and entered with him inside. There, he learned that evil is a useless concept whose meaning is altered by many influences. Good and evil are relative criteria, depending on whose interests are strengthened or threatened. Even more, good and evil are related to each other, each relying on the opposite quality of the other for its definition. Indeed, may it not be said that every situation is a composite of opposing principles, where one value is understood by its opposite, just as we understand light because we also know the nature of darkness? Moreover, can we really expect those abstract principles to guide men's actions when there are concrete motives at work in the heart and mind? Probably not. What, then, is the true basis of determining value judgments? It would seem that there are two choices. Either we consider morality to be a behavioral science, or we regard morals as having a psychological genealogy. Unamuno elects, with Nietzsche, the second alternative.

We see, therefore, that the basis of all valuation exists in consciousness. However, once inside its gates, Unamuno and Nietzsche proceed along different paths. For Nietzsche, consciousness is an obstacle to the development of the superman because it inhibits his healthy impulses. Self-awareness acts to repress instinct, and instinctive action is the will-to-power made manifest. On the other hand, Unamuno thought consciousness to be more than just a condition that leads to alienation. He felt that eventually it enables us to reintegrate ourselves in a socially productive way. True enough, at the beginning it permits moral ambiguity among the conflicting selves that divide the mind. And, also true, we cannot know whether we are good, because we don't know which of those selves is the real one. But in the end, consciousness begets conscience, and moral conscience is governed by love.

Here, then, is the emotional axis around which the worlds of Unamuno and Nietzsche turn. At one pole is Christian love and the repudiation of egoism, and at the other pole is self-love and the repudiation of Christ. How did these philosophers get to such opposite ends of the scale when their moral psychologies were so closely linked? The answer is not easy, but it will be found in the notions of the superman which each of them propounded. In Nietzsche's exultation over the physiological impulse, even destructive acts were praised when they were carried out with spontaneity and animal innocence. Such conduct was healthy because it kept man free from the crippling effects of intelligence. And it was only by these acts of unconscious freedom that the superman might evolve.[1] As we shall see, Unamuno was also capable of forgiving harmful acts if they were committed with "purity of intention." But his reasons were quite different, and involved the exercise of Christian love. His idea of a superman was formed in the image of a terrestrial Jesus, and he saw Don Quixote as a Christlike hero. In contrast, Nietzsche's superman was not only an Antichrist, but an antisocial being altogether. It was not simply Christianity's denial of the flesh that repelled Nietzsche, nor even its self-sacrificing

---

[1] I am aware of the oversimplification here. Nietzsche's concept of artists and certain philosophers is an important factor, but it involves larger, controversial issues, such as reconciling the early and late Nietzsche.

demands. Basically, he hated the limitations on freedom which the
Christian ethic imposed. Thus, the superman would be absolutely
liberated, bound neither by moral obligations to his neighbor, nor
by civic duties to his society, nor even by cultural allegiance to his
intellect. Indeed, neighbor, society, and intellect would be neutral
elements in his existence.

In all of this, we cannot doubt that Nietzsche held the salvation
of mankind to be the highest goal of human life. In the superman,
he saw the fulfillment of that condition. Since Unamuno also
shared Nietzsche's objective, as well as his hero-worship, the presence of anti-Christian values posed a formidable stumbling block
for the Spaniard. Unamuno did not look upon God as the obstruc-
tion that Nietzsche imagined to be standing in the superman's path.
On the contrary, Unamuno wondered whether God was not really
the supreme and absolute Superman. If so, then the superman's
aspiration as described by Nietzsche was nothing less than the
desire of mortal man to acquire God's immortality. And if this
were true, then there was little difference between Unamuno's
deepest wish and Nietzsche's. Both God and superman were the
projections of man's image into the infinite.

Needless to say, Unamuno could never have made this identification with Nietzsche's ideas consciously. In Part Two, I hope to
show how reasonable the comparison is. If Nietzsche eliminated
God for his own purposes, Unamuno certainly used God for similar ends. Together, the two thinkers shared a desire for a perfect
human condition in which Nature would be a state of grace. And if
their concepts of social progress were mutually exclusive, their
insights into the psychological origins of social values were quite
close. It should not surprise us, therefore, if we find Nietzschean
categories to be useful in understanding Unamuno's moral philosophy. As a matter of fact, we would do well to pause and remind
ourselves of how much alike Nietzsche and Unamuno were, since
critics tend to gloss over the resemblance.

Indeed, the number of characteristics which these two men have
in common is startling in view of their reputedly antithetical ways
of thinking. Both were poets, classical philologists, and teachers
who despised pedantry. They both reacted against the rationalism
of their epoch. They wrote philosophy without regard for organi-
zation or logic, and cultivated vehement, lyrical styles. Both were

concerned with mortal weakness, and with man's final destiny. Each emphasized the voluntaristic nature of existence, and maintained a certain optimism in the face of anguished self-doubt. And both utilized a dialectical technique for their subjectivism, turning metaphor and paradox into philosophical methods. To the end, they remained dedicated admirers of Goethe and Don Quixote. The two men differed fundamentally in their evaluation of Christianity, as I have said, and Unamuno did not share Nietzsche's passion for music, but in all other respects they coincided in temperament, subject matter, and egocentric value formations.

Given these factors, it was inevitable that Unamuno and Nietzsche should delve into psychology and moral valuation with comparable attitudes. When they parted company, it was in the intermediate zone which linked private experience with social action. Once Nietzsche devised a set of values that would lead to self-fulfillment, his problems were over. For Unamuno, they went on and on. He had to deal with the larger reality in which that set of values would operate. In other words, he faced the problem of the cultural and historical reality of Spain. This, of course, was a lifetime preoccupation for Unamuno and his contemporaries. The idea of "Spain as a problem" had been a perennial topic for Spanish writers, and it reached its peak of interest during the period dominated by the Generation of 1898. Essentially, the issues involved the revival of national prestige, prosperity, and progress, all deceptively self-evident goals, and all fought over without solution by patriots whose plans for regeneration differed radically.

For Unamuno, social questions of this kind were not new. He had often written about the two antagonistic Spains: clericalism against secularism, conservatism against liberalism, monarchy against republicanism, orthodoxy against heterodoxy, oligarchy against masses. But what brings him into the mainstream of European existentialism is one special methodology that stands out among the many approaches he used for writing social criticism. He discovered that the Judaic tradition could serve as a basis for comparative culture, thereby helping to elucidate the Spanish problem. As part of this method, the Hebrew myths of the Old Testament were of particular value. The use of mythology—Biblical or pagan—is a notable characteristic of virtually all existentialist philosophers, and the works of Kierkegaard, Jaspers, and Buber are foremost in this respect. It is difficult to recall any other period in the history of ideas when myths were depended upon to such an extent. Equally difficult to explain is the phenomenon as a whole, although in Unamuno's case many answers will be thought of.

For us, however, what is important is that Unamuno's use of Judaism be kept in perspective. He was just as fond of quoting the New Testament as the Old. Furthermore, he treated many of the cultural issues in conventional ways, although his interest in Semitic culture focused these issues in a new light. Nor was he interested in Biblical studies for their own sake, but as an instrument for social analysis. Thus, his disposition toward Judaism tended to adopt an anthropological view, utilizing Biblical material without much of its religious significance. Generally speaking, we will find that Unamuno's approach to the Old Testament was to consider it as a literary springboard that would initiate more precise discussions of Spanish civilization. He did not regard the Bible as a source book for divine revelation, nor even as a guide for theological discussion. But it did provide him with a great deal of flexibility in examining cultural themes which required few religious suppositions.

The role of the Hebrew myth in Unamuno's existentialism is fresh, original, and unique. This role was created in three steps, as we have seen. First, as a psychologist, Unamuno was concerned with the individual as a universal man. Second, as a moralist, he had to modify this view by considering man in a social context, although no specific context was needed. But third, as a social critic, he would now have to deal with Spain as a culture. And this in turn would involve Spanish values, as well as the psychology of Spaniards both as individuals and as a collectivity. In handling such complexities, he saw the myths of Jacob, Cain, and the Garden of Eden as profoundly symbolic structures. The Jacob-Esau myth, especially, cannot be overemphasized for the far-reaching implications it uncovered in illuminating the conditions of Spain and the Spaniard. For the moment, I will say briefly that by means of it, Unamuno managed to integrate the major problematic areas of existential man: self, standards of value, society. The elaboration of this idea will be left for Part Three.

No complete view of Unamuno's existentialism can ignore his metaphysics and religious ideas. Since there are some excellent studies of these topics, I will not cover the same ground here.

However, Unamuno's religious existentialism touches upon the Judaic tradition, and in this respect there is something to add. If we recall the conflict between reason and emotion in *The Tragic Sense of Life*, we realize that its crisis of faith made ordinary religious feeling impossible. All that was left for people like Unamuno was a dynamic tension of belief and doubt. When he turned to the wanderings of Israel in the wilderness, he thought he saw a parallel. The forty-year exile of Moses and his people was actually a test of that nation's faith, and it was a test that they failed. The fact that the children of Israel demanded proof of God's existence and were punished for it, suggested to Unamuno that blind faith was expected of them. His question, therefore, was whether this showed a defect in the Jewish people or in their God instead. How significant was it that the notion of God had evolved among Jews from Jehovah to Jesus? That is, was it significant that the concept of divinity had evolved in man's awareness from fear to forgiving love? Unamuno found it to be meaningful indeed, and he judged the Mosaic God to be humanistically useless. Since man has intellectual doubts as well as religious needs, a deity should be considered Godlike when it overlooks those doubts. God was valuable only to the extent that He reflected man's existential needs. For this reason, Jehovah rises in esteem as He becomes Jesus. And by the same token, religion declines in esteem as it hardens into Pharisaic formalism, be this Jewish or Christian.

Here, then, is an outline of a three-sided problem which this book will undertake to examine. As I have said, the door to Unamuno's general philosophy—metaphysics included—is opened by the key of psychology. Hopefully, that key has been forged here, but the reader will be the best judge of this.

# PART ONE
# *Existential Psychology*

# 1 SELF-KNOWLEDGE AND THE SUBCONSCIOUS

*Unamuno once* said that people often appear to be "automatons who produce in us the illusion that they are living beings" (III, 755). By this he meant that many people seem to lack the kind of self-awareness and emotional depth that we usually consider the mark of "sensitive" men. Whereas some have a great capacity for self-knowledge, the majority fail to display the sort of insight into the self which Unamuno called "reflexive consciousness." He therefore urged that everyone gain as much knowledge about himself as possible, and thus enrich his experience within the self as well as in society. To do so would be to reach a fulfillment in life which went beyond a sense of mere well-being. It would involve a "plenitude of plenitudes," a condition in which the act of knowing would be the most perfect way of feeling oneself to be truly alive.

Self-knowledge was an important capacity for Unamuno, and he classified men as spiritual, intellectual, or natural according to their reflexive consciousness or self-awareness. He found the condition of the spiritual man to be most worthy, because of the latter's ability to integrate his experiences in both the physical world and the realm of intuitions. Here, Unamuno established no dichotomy between matter and spirit. He regarded the highest spiritual condition to be the plenitude just mentioned. Moreover, it represented the ultimate reality of mortal life, precisely because no fuller mode of existence is possible.

We must conclude, therefore, that for Unamuno self-knowledge is an existential problem and not a metaphysical one, and indeed, his language reveals this quite pointedly. When he refers to knowledge, he means knowledge of *something*, of our spiritual substance. Thus, he writes that he who "touches his soul with the soul itself" has, at the least, "the intuition of his own substantiality," and at most, a "full possession of himself" (III, 755). Self-knowledge is inherently charged with an almost tangible reality. It is quite possible, then, to follow Unamuno's urging to "look for your soul with the very arms of the soul and embrace it, and rub yourselves against its contact, and feel how substantial and warm it is" (III, 754). All of these steps leading to the possession of the self's substantiality are welcomed by Unamuno. Together, they afford the prospect of a higher, more intense, and subtler way of life. And in a colorless world of everyday activity, this kind of life offers the hope of discovery and vitality.

However, once that embrace is consummated, an unforeseen danger suddenly appears. After the individual is spiritually conscious of himself, he wants to know his personality in a more analytical way. But the more he examines his tangible sense of self, the more elusive he finds its substance. The fullest moment of plenitude cannot be grasped in a rational way. Thus, at the peak of contact and warmth, he glimpses the hollow core which lies within the self. What was substance becomes emptiness, and knowledge turns into an intellectual void. Unamuno explains the experience as he looks into a mirror: "at once my eyes leave me and go after my eyes, after their portrait, and from the moment that I gaze at my gaze I feel myself grow empty of myself, lose my history, my legend, my novel, return to unconsciousness, to the past, to nothingness" (X, 865). During this moment, the various components of the self are met and pushed aside as Unamuno penetrates deeper, behind his body and his sensations, behind his reputation, and even behind his image of himself. But in the end, his efforts to know himself are futile. The very fact that he can detach each attribute from himself, one by one, means that none of them belongs to him essentially. He is left with an "unknown and unknowable self."

Thus, Unamuno is of two minds regarding the value of self-contemplation, especially when it is extensive. His experience with the mirror raises the question of whether the self can ever really be known. Furthermore, there is the suspicion that no "permanent base" or essential bottom exists in the human personality at all. That is, after a man is stripped of the characteristic layers which we usually consider personal, he is left only with his "own nothingness" (*propia nadería*), like an onion peeled down to its center. As Unamuno describes the introspective process, this is exactly what happens: "As you enter more deeply within yourself and you sink down within yourself, you discover your own inanity, the fact that you are not all that you are, that you are not what you might want to be, in short, that you are nothing but a nonentity" (XVI, 265). In the end, therefore, a skeptical attitude toward self-knowledge begins to emerge.

Unamuno's point of departure in his skeptical journey is the notion that to know oneself is to be gradually disenchanted with one's nature. True, plenitude leads to a concentration of self. But during this state, our qualities and motivations eventually dissolve into nothingness. This is both the result and "the evil of all pent-up sensibility." That is, a state of excessive self-awareness does us harm because its scrutiny undermines our full possession of self. Consequently, the reality of our character is exposed as a mere appearance. The situation is comparable to a chemical analysis, where the researcher "studies a very complicated and unstable compound. When it is acted upon by a reagent it is destroyed, and instead of the substance that one sought to study and know, one is left with the products of its decomposition. So too with psychological analysis" (IV, 494). The analogy is indeed useful in its account of the disintegrating process. It is deceptive, however, insofar as the makeup of the original substance is concerned. Whereas the chemical compound is essentially a synthesis of its component parts, the self is no more than a series of laminations. On analysis, therefore, the self is found to be an emptiness around which the strata of personality are overlaid.

This is why Unamuno is cautious about the results of self-knowledge, despite his approval of its first stages. "Study yourself," he counsels, "whether or not you come to know yourself, and it may very well be better that you do not come to do so." Even though the initial encounter is a psychological accomplishment, a lingering embrace may prove fatal. It is preferable to rub up against the soul during the illusory first stage than to learn subsequently of one's own nothingness. The warning, then, for the spiritual novice is that "the more you study yourself, the more you will expand and go spiritually deeper into yourself, and the more you expand and deepen, the more difficult it will be to know yourself" (IV, 493).

What, then, of the introvert, the person who is accustomed to profound soul-states? In contrast to the novice, "it is very bad" for him "to go digging around in his consciousness, alone and in darkness." But, if this kind of exploration is forbidden to him, what alternative is left? He can attempt to know himself in a more objective light, namely, by coming out of himself. He can avoid solitude and "set [consciousness] before men by the light of day, in the sun and air, so that it grows golden and glows." Thus, cognition may be measured by means of a social perspective instead of a private one. Unamuno diverts attention from the psychological factors within the individual to the field of action around him. The command now becomes, "Study yourself by working, in your work, in what you do, outside of yourself" (IV, 493–94; IX, 902, 967; XVI, 356). And the criterion for this study is externalization. There must be an engagement with society that is set in moral and utilitarian terms. As Unamuno writes, pithily: "To study ourselves is to enclose ourselves within our own sloth. Knowledge is the beginning of egoism, and action the beginning of charity" (VII, 139). The undertones here of social and religious commitment will be discussed later in the book, but we can see even now that the basis of such commitments is psychological.

The implications of this shift from internal to external criteria are profound. We cannot look upon the self as a fixed entity in time, the permanent source of man's standards. Unamuno's emphasis on social and historical conditions, rather than psychological ones, makes that static concept of the self impossible. It is through biography, not autobiography, that human nature is best known. Moreover, the rejection of introspective methods forces us to find a new theory about the knowledge of man. We will never know our complete nature, because we are uncertain of what we can do until we actually do it. Our conduct reveals to us daily some previously unknown aspect of ourselves, with the result that we must constantly revise our notion of who and what we are. Our "completed personality is at the end, and not at the beginning of life." Hence, we are told that it is a mistake to "regulate your action by your thought," and that we must "allow the former, instead, to form, inform, deform and transform the latter." This means we must abandon preconceived notions, recognizing that we are not the same today as we were yesterday, and that tomorrow will find us again different. The advice offered by Unamuno, therefore, is that "as you change, allow change in the ideal of yourself which you are forging. Your life, in the presence of your own consciousness, is the continuous revelation, in time, of your eternalness . . . you keep discovering yourself as you work" (III, 420). The foundation of our self-knowledge thus rests on a temporal base. Our deeds succeed each other in time, and it is the succession of acts which comprises a biography. On the other hand, the less worthy autobiography depends upon inner thoughts that have no dimension.

The idea of defining the self in terms of social behavior leads Unamuno to three major principles. The first is the notion that "no one, in reality, knows himself *a priori*, before he acts." Secondly, "a man knows himself only in the same way that he knows others." And finally, we find our actions "not infrequently strange even to ourselves" (III, 96). All three ideas are behavioristic in outlook. They limit knowledge to observable events and deeds, and eschew prior assumptions about the self and its behavior. The method is pragmatic, a direct and practical observation of men as if they were objective data. Small wonder, then, that their actions frequently seem strange to them. To regard oneself so objectively is indeed to see a stranger. As Unamuno exclaimed, "How often does one not say to oneself, 'I didn't think I was capable of such a thing,' or 'I don't recognize myself, I'm someone else'!" (III, 195). The observer is alienated from himself in a way which will be discussed in detail later, but which can be seen here to dramatize the value of action over contemplation. The social act gains importance before the shrinking area of introspective knowledge.

Unamuno concludes, therefore, that "there is no direct intuition of oneself that has any value. The eye cannot see itself except by means of a mirror, and the mirror of moral man is his works, of which he is the child" (III, 195). We should be careful to note that Unamuno limits himself to the non-subjective aspects of the self. By identifying the social self with the real self, he takes the pragmatic view that only the exterior world is knowable. This assumption, of course, raises several questions, as we will see. And yet from one point of view, it is correct. Normally, it would seem that "each man continually lives with himself, without separating from himself" (III, 96). That is, our feelings seem so closely tied to our acts that both apparently represent the same person. But how can we be sure that this belief is anything more than an intuition? Perhaps the fact is that without realizing it, we infer our character from our acts. It may well be, as Unamuno believes, that we observe ourselves as we do our neighbors, and indeed, "each man is nothing else but his own first neighbor" (III, 195). In other words, each man is first of all a neighbor unto himself. Before anything else, he watches his social acts and learns who he is, just as he watches his neighbor's conduct in order to learn about the latter.

We may conclude, therefore, that Unamuno is optimistic about self-knowledge when it is limited to interpersonal situations. Here, information about the self is as sound as the plenitude which was experienced in the first stage. And yet that information cannot deal with the total self precisely because there are other elements which eventually destroy this plenitude. Unamuno must also consider the elusive and unfathomable part of himself which intrudes upon his consciousness. In view of this factor, which, as we saw, makes visible the hollowness within, Unamuno cannot say that the entire self is knowable. Instead, he must admit that the sum of his biographical acts is quantitatively less than his total self. He thus confesses that "I never thought myself capable of doing 'a' book, 'my' book. . . . I believed myself to be my book, for in all of my books I have put the man that I am, and I don't think I fit into any of them" (VIII, 586). That is to say, the frame which encompasses all of Unamuno's activities—here a literary frame, but by extension a social one—is still too small to hold the entire Unamunian self. To write a book is to perform a social act, but no single performance of this kind reflects an entire personality. Nor does the sum total of our acts reveal a complete self. There are also internal factors which contribute to its wholeness, thus limiting the principle of externality to the social self.

Inevitably, then, Unamuno directed his attention inwardly, sometimes with hope, but more often with skepticism. He grew increasingly aware of the emptiness within, and of how it could cause suffering. But, if the uncertainty of his self-knowledge was a source of pain to him, the contradictory emotions of his introspection were just as painful. It was best, therefore, to probe the disturbed area and root out the undesirable feelings. The difficulty, however, was their vague and undefined nature, as if they were beyond the sector of the conscious self. To the extent that those emotions were conflictive, they caused the self to unconsciously undermine itself. Hence it was "better to sink down in it, to scrutinize it, dig around in its entrails and become fully aware of that hatred of ourselves. It is bad as long as it remains unconscious, but once it is revealed to us for what it is, as self-hatred, as an abhorrence of the self, it is already on the road to becoming something noble, strong, redeeming" (IV, 406). Although Unamuno's point concerned self-hatred, he intended it to represent more generally the idea that any feeling which jeopardizes our inner well-being can also enrich it. But this can only happen if we descend into the self.

Unamuno's suggestion that an undesirable feeling can be turned into "something noble" recalls Freud's notion of sublimation. Actually, these two thinkers have little, on the whole, in common, but we should note that they do coincide in one respect: they agree that another region exists beneath the conscious mind. For Unamuno, this means that "each one of us bears within him many men, but at the least, two: a deep-seated, radical, permanent self, the self that many now call *subliminal*—below the *limen* or level of consciousness—and another self, superficial, pasted on, and fleeting, the *supraliminal* self" (III, 1061). Given these two contrasting levels, our previous distinction between social and inner selves needs to be revised. The existence of a subconscious suddenly alters our concept of an active personality. We must now group together all the units of awareness, social and private, into a single, conscious self. Regardless of what we have called inner awareness, the self is quite external when it is compared to the subliminal area. But this simply means that the supraliminal self is exterior in the sense that it is conscious. Its basic structure remains the same: a social manifestation and a consensus of private feelings, both subject to change. The subconscious remains immutable and isolated, the permanent foundation upon which the waking self is established.

This deep-seated stability as opposed to surface change is one thing, but a total lack of response is quite another. Despite the separation of the subconscious from the conscious world, they do maintain some kind of active, irrational communication. This contact is only vaguely described by Unamuno, but we do know that it takes an intuitional form. The subconscious discloses its existence to the individual by means of occasional insights which reveal its spiritual content. According to this idea, "between the subconscious depths of our spirit and its consciousness there are currents of mutual relationship, of reciprocal actions and reactions, the depths acting on the surface and the latter on the former, and the surface in reality serving as a field in which the commerce between our spirit and the exterior world is effected" (VII, 479). Exactly how these currents behave psychologically is never explained, and Unamuno drifts instead into a sea of religious thought.

The mutual relationship between the subliminal and conscious selves does, however, have an impact on self-knowledge. During the many conflicts arising from the search for selfhood, Unamuno finds his soul to be "no longer just dilated, but rather loosened and falling apart; that is, with its strings and ligatures all undone." And yet beyond this experience, his analysis reveals "another self, the most primitive, the one which is beneath the soul." This basic self is analogous to the subconscious depths mentioned in the preceding paragraph. That is, it is a hidden source of emotional life which we barely perceive. As Unamuno reminds us, "the truth is that ordinarily we have no notion of the profundity of everything that happens to us" (IV, 593). We are scarcely aware that the primal self nourishes the soul from beneath, helping to reknit the undone ligatures. Yet at the same time, it remains essentially passive, being unable to know or to act in the conscious world.

The passive nature of the subconscious can, however, be changed in some areas. This is possible because everyone has within him "spiritual loose ends, corners of the soul, nooks and crannies of consciousness that lie inactive and inert." Normally, these would go undetected while existing just at the surface of the subliminal self. But they can be activated by the spiritual stimulation which comes from communion with a fellow man. There are, in other words, "potential feelings which will only pass from the potential to the active state if someone comes to awaken them in us" (III, 1027, 1032 ff.). This means that the subliminal self ordinarily lies in a state of latency, overlooked by us because we live under more familiar states of awareness. Nevertheless, when a kindred soul enters into communion with us, our dormant self responds by awakening. This is how we usually pass from a natural condition, as Unamuno would phrase it, to a spiritual one. Only during moments of crisis does our perception quicken without the presence of a stimulus. Then alone, "the instinct for perpetuation, the need for survival, can provoke the development of spiritual germs, or, rather, the eruption in the consciousness of an entire subconscious depth, which slumbers there in disuse" (III, 746).

Thus it seems that an instinctual factor exists alongside of spirituality in the subliminal self. This is why the mind occasionally erupts with such emotional force. At work is a subtle process of submergence and repression, by which our conscious experiences are gradually neutralized. They undergo a series of stages where "at each step, a state of consciousness disappears as such in the individual, submerging itself in the rich sediment of the unconscious." This process is more than a forgetting or a storing away. The experiences become part of a primitive region that later can yield them up again under more violent circumstances. And so when the "depths" of the subconscious finally do manifest themselves, they "surge to the consciousness in deep spiritual crises, in genuine psychic cataclysms." During such moments, we recognize "the savage that we carry within us, barely repressed by the crust of culture, opening a crack in the soul like an extinguished volcano that is suddenly rekindled" (VII, 480). All of this is virtually involuntary, not to say infrequent. As such, it occupies a secondary position in Unamuno's overall view of the self. But it does remain, like a hidden vault, an unknown area holding secret facets of Unamuno's own psychic life. And since the idea was stated in 1896, it anticipates the categories of modern psychology which were to be developed subsequently by so many investigators.

# 2 THE SPLITTING
OF THE SELF

[◈][◈][◈][◈][◈][◈][◈][◈][◈][◈][◈][◈][◈][◈][◈][◈][◈][◈][◈][◈][◈][◈][◈][◈][◈][◈][◈]

*What we* have seen of Unamuno's psychology so far has been primarily intuitive and poetic. His idea of the subconscious gets lost in lyricism, and indeed, this happens typically whenever Unamuno tries to describe his anguished attempts to know himself. But, as he turned his back on anguish and narrowed the focus to the conscious self, he became more analytical, and he recognized certain divisions within himself. For example, he saw that he could ignore his feelings, or write about them as if they were someone else's. Sensing that he was many different men at the same time, he delved further into the problem of the split personality. He was intrigued by a process which he called *desdoblamiento,* a splitting of the self in which the self is objectively reproduced and the individual becomes two people at the same time. This process of reduplication can occur physically, within space and time, or within the mind.

As we know, this phenomenon has traditionally been described by the myths of Narcissus and the *Doppelgänger.* But Unamuno was the first to discover its profounder meaning, and, as we shall see, the first to analyze it conceptually. Still, he always returned to the imaginative forms which the problem assumed, falling under the fascination of their uncanniness, as well as being personally disturbed by the experience itself. An interesting example is the fact that he read and wrote about Adelbert von Chamisso's story of

*28*

Peter Schlemihl, the man without a shadow. But instead of express-ing concern over the hero's plight, Unamuno wondered about what had happened to the shadow. He conjectured that if it had gone wandering in search of its body, then the story was really a parable about contemporary man, himself a mere shadow looking for his vital substance. And in turn, the shadow that men cast by daylight is, in reality, a tenuous projection of a self without substance (IX, 305 ff.).

In this vein, Unamuno wrote several pieces of short fiction: *Tulio Montalbán and Julio Macedo,* and the more intriguing *The Man Who Buried Himself.* The protagonist of the latter story is a man ridden with the fear of death, who one day sees his double enter the room and sit down opposite him. The hero dies at that very moment, but his consciousness passes over to the double, who then regards the dead man, and subsequently tells Unamuno what happened. He can even produce the corpse as proof (IX, 194 ff.). The allegorical meaning of this tale is quite basic to the entire question of the split self. Its point is that when an individual ob-serves himself, he takes a step back and looks at himself as if he were another man. And yet the fact is that he *is* the man who stands before him. What, then, has happened? The original person has duplicated himself by engaging in self-contemplation. But, by doing so, he dies. That is, he ceases to exist in any vital way, and becomes nothing more than a contemplator of the real man. He is a pure consciousness, and the objective form which he now observes is the real self.

These moments of fictional speculation were part of Unamuno's never-ending wonder at man's capacity for self-objectification. Once he imagined a primeval scene in which "primitive man, seeing and watching himself in the mirror of a still pool of water, arrived at the splitting of the self." Man could for the first time "know himself outside of himself." Since he was able to think about him-self as he might think of another object, he could then "believe in his soul" (X, 111). In other words, the mirror gave material proof that man existed in the world as integrally as any other visible object. Prior to seeing himself, man could not really believe in his soul—in the fact of his own existence—with the same conviction that he had regarding the existence of the objects around him. But after the discovery of his self, after watching himself as one more object in the world, he knew that he was not merely a contemplator of the phenomenal world but an actual part of it.

Beyond this elementary stage in the development of human awareness, Unamuno was also fascinated by a number of modern techniques for objectifying the self. But instead of stirring him to admiration, they made him fearful, even while giving him much to meditate on. He thought, for example of the many devices which might induce *desdoblamiento*, and felt that the supreme test would be to recite poetry before a recording device and then listen to it play back at the same time that he watched himself in the mirror. "It must be terrible," he said, "to see oneself completely reduplicated, in figure and voice, to contemplate one's face as a stranger's and hear one's own voice as a stranger's. For this reason, our best mirror is each of our neighbors" rather than the mirror of self-contemplation, which beguiles us into "sinking down into our consciousness" (XI, 746, 747). It was the terror, as well as the truth, of introspection that bothered Unamuno. This was why, as we saw in the preceding section, he preferred a social mirror to a private one. And yet he was drawn to the latter, as the quotation shows. Like an unnamed friend described elsewhere, Unamuno had a "solid head and warm heart," but felt a "frightful shiver" on hearing his own voice while regarding his mirror image. That individual reported how he had received the impression of having "an interview with my dead body" (IX, 898). Thus, the episode repeats the situation in *The Man Who Buried Himself*, except for the question of which double becomes the survivor.

The phonograph-mirror combination so intrigued Unamuno that he tried a similar experiment on himself, and spoke of the result as a "sensation that can reach a frightening point." His technique was to remain alone for a while, watching himself in a mirror: "I ended by seeing myself as another person, as a stranger, and saying to myself: 'Aha, so it's you!' and even calling to myself in a low voice" (X, 241). If we make an effort to picture this mentally, we cannot help but feel that the scene borders on madness. By means of his steady gaze into the mirror, Unamuno managed to drive himself into a state of near-hypnosis. He stared at the face in the mirror so intently that he began to lose his sense of reality, and was no longer able to recognize the face as his own. The whisperings to the mirror, the calls to himself, and the listening to these calls, are all deliberate techniques designed to induce the feeling of dissociation. And the result was in fact a failure to identify with the face that looked back at him. Anyone who has experienced a similar moment of strangeness will understand why Unamuno called it "frightening." He was not mad, of course, by any means, even though his willful experiment may seem odd to us. The situation probably occurred to him under normal circumstances as well. The point is that Unamuno lived the problems that he wrote about even in this twilight zone, and fulfilled his condition as an existentialist philosopher in the deepest sense possible.

Here, then, is Unamuno converted into a "spectator of my own person." This means, in more philosophical language, that his condition demonstrates the principle of self-objectification. In other words, the observer takes an objective stance toward himself and regards himself as an object instead of as a feeling subject. The mirror image—what we can call the self-in-the-world—is so completely objectified that he can scarcely identify it as his own. This is what is so terrifying about the situation: Unamuno is emotionally unable to accept the fact that he exists in the world as one more object. Indeed, there are other remarks by Unamuno which confirm his failure to grasp this fact. He talked about how his style does not "sound" like him when read out loud, and he wondered, "Isn't it perhaps from another self? Even if I hear myself, do I always recognize myself?" (XI, 840). And again, on seeing his name in print he felt that he had found "another self," and that this "doubling of my personality" in the midst of literary activity was "as if in the thickest of the fight I were pursued by a mirror" (VI, 615). Indeed, had Unamuno become dissociated from the self which acts in the world, he would have had to "look for the person that I once was" and seize him by the shoulder (X, 242). Thus, he grew afraid of the discovery that he was a "thing" in the world instead of a knowing subject. And he feared the splitting of the self all the more because he knew how easily—even accidentally—he could slip into dissociation.

If we compare Unamuno's many expressions of interest in the purely personal experience of reduplication (*desdoblamiento*), it becomes fairly clear that his concern was obsessive. Occasionally he disguised this preoccupation by referring to an unidentified third person instead of to himself, but the result was the same: "A singularly disturbing effect was produced in him when he read himself as he would a stranger, reading his writings as if they were someone else's. This reduplication of his person reminded him of another scene of passing self-reduplication, which he could never remember without a shiver. That was when, watching his own glance in a mirror, he came to see himself as if he were an other. He contemplated himself like an immaterial shadow, like an impalpable phantom, and he was so frightened by all this, that he called to himself by name in a low voice. And his voice sounded like the voice of another person, a voice coming to him out of space, out of the invisible, from the impenetrable reaches of mystery" (III, 703–4).

Unamuno's obsession was due to his need to understand the complex nature of his perceptions. For him, the act of knowing was comprised of a detailed series of events in the human awareness. When he regarded his image in the mirror, therefore, he perceived that it seemed "unconscious" to him. That is, it simply stood there like an inert object which submitted to his consciousness, but which apparently was not conscious itself. Here, then, was Unamuno, feeling himself inwardly to be aware, and yet unable to see this aware self. And out there, on the other hand, was a reflection which he could see but could not feel, a replica which was a mere "shadow" of himself. At the same moment that Unamuno was experiencing certain inner sensations, he contemplated a ghostly image of himself that appeared devoid of those sensations. Even worse, Unamuno had no way of getting inside that image in order to learn whether it had feelings. This is why he felt impelled to call out and ascertain its nature. He whispered to it, trying not to disturb the image by producing facial movements, and when he heard the disembodied voice he became frightened, because it sounded like the voice of another man.

The result of this solitary experiment is to complete the process of dissociation. The material Unamuno is projected into a visible image which stands before an Unamuno who has retained nothing more than his feelings and cognitive faculties. In this situation, the problem of authenticity becomes a critical issue. It is clear that Unamuno had no objective way of confirming the reality of his self. Being alone, there was no impartial witness. Moreover, he grew uneasy and afraid because he had "become an other." As he tells it, he began to "doubt my own existence and imagine, seeing myself as another self, that I am a dream, a fictional entity" (II, 926). His confusion in this case has two sources. First is the fact that Unamuno could feel a self that he could not see, and see a self that could not be felt. This discrepancy forced a doubt in his mind as to which of these was the authentic self. The second source of confusion is metaphysical in its implications. Since solitude is not a condition which provides for objective criteria, Unamuno could never be sure that his image self was not a fantasy of his own creation, or indeed, that he himself was not dreaming or participating in a larger dream. Consequently, he succumbed to a new kind of anguish, this time metaphysical, which compounded the immediate psychological anxieties that he had suffered during the initial encounter.

This metaphysical anguish has many ramifications that will be discussed at other points in the book. Its focal point is centered on the question of authenticity, and it is here that we may link it to the mirror theme. In one of his anecdotes, Unamuno refers to a photograph of himself as a variation of that theme. He relates how once, during a visit to an insane asylum, a patient asked him whether he were the true Unamuno or the one whose picture appeared in the newspapers. Struck by the profundity of the question, Unamuno wondered subsequently why he had answered so affirmatively that he was indeed the authentic Unamuno: "Was I myself certain of it? Couldn't the authentic one be the other, the one whose picture occasionally appears in the papers? A photograph is a translation; but, even I, don't I translate myself? My Unamuno, mine own, is he the authentic one?" (X, 696–97). What we saw in previous examples to be mirror images of Unamuno is now the same reproduction done in photographic form. The picture reproduces him in the same way that he himself did while looking into the mirror. And once again he is plagued by doubts, for he cannot be certain that the photograph represents the same man whose feelings he knows so intimately. To phrase this in more analytical terms, he compared a projected image of himself with his psychological state, and found that the nature of his true self escaped cognition.

Unamuno's anguish was not merely aroused by face-to-face meetings with his reflection. It was also sharpened by the instrument which helped to analyze those meetings: his self-consciousness. Like the mirror reflecting his face, his inner awareness caused him pain by crystallizing a mental image of himself. At one point, he complained that the "oppressiveness of the consciousness upon itself is life's greatest sorrow" (III, 815). This suffering was a cumulative process, and it continued to build up until he was prompted to examine more rationally the reasons for its tenacity. Once this was done, Unamuno was able to see the existential value of pain, and the way in which it corresponded to nature's basic laws.

What were the methods involved in this rational examination? There were, of course, projections of Unamuno's enigmatic self which could be studied: his articles, academic lectures, photographs, and mirror images. But the basic technique consisted of exploring his consciousness, an activity which added to the burden of pain already upon him. And yet the anguish was less important than the steps comprising that analysis. Unamuno described it metaphorically by referring to nature's scenic landscape. He said that "water is, in effect, the consciousness of landscape," where trees and rocks "reduplicate themselves, acquire self-reflectiveness" (I, 580). By drawing this analogy with the inner mirror of awareness, Unamuno came to see in man the same beauty of that "living, moving consciousness" which he found in nature. It was beautiful insofar as it was instrumental. By the same token, people who lived without it were lacking in any true sense of their own reality. They lived as "natural" men, "with their life's pace as slow as the growth of a tree reflecting its immobile self in waters that are never the same for more than a moment, yet that seem nevertheless to be a dead mirror" (II, 156).

What these unconscious people needed was a step-by-step acquisition of nature's "living, moving consciousness." In human terms this would mean gaining a psychological awareness of themselves which was so intense that it would border on the physical. Unamuno called this palpable self-awareness "spiritual kinesthesia." As with many of his terms, Unamuno borrowed this one from the sciences, and he explained it with an allusion to physiology. Ordinarily, kinesthesia refers to a "general sensation of the body which is different from the special sensations of the senses." In a similar way, "what we call consciousness has a certain feature which corresponds in the spiritual realm to what in the physiological and even in the psychical realm is known as kinesthesia" (III, 754–55). This tangible sensation of one's own spirit begins with an intuitive *feeling* of one's psychic self, and then transcends it in two ways. In the first stage it leads to a more specific knowledge of the self, an understanding of motives and sentiments. In the second, this knowledge sharpens feeling into a more precise sense of pain or anguish, as it was described before. Thus, "consciousness, *conscientia*, is a shared knowledge, co-sentiment, and to con-sent is to feel co(m)-passion" ("es con-sentimiento, y con-sentir es compadecer" [XVI, 267]). This idea, in the present context, represents much more than just a religious or moral value. The shared feeling and knowledge also refer to how the individual regards himself after observing the splitting of the self.

This is when the concept of pain acquires an even more subtle function. Besides being the product of awareness, "suffering is the road to consciousness" in a deeper sense than ordinary self-analysis. Along that tortured route, we gain consciousness of ourselves as individuals. Pain replaces the physical distinctions that separate one human being from another, and substitutes psychological ones in their place. It makes each of us know more intuitively that our personal feelings differ from what other people are experiencing at a given moment. The dawn of self-awareness, therefore, arrives with the recognition that suffering is private and differentiating. At the same time, this knowledge of separateness goes beyond the discovery of how independent each self is. It also reveals the possession of a personality. The *something* of which we are conscious is our set of psychological reactions which we designate as private, unique, and characteristic. "To have consciousness of oneself," therefore, "to have personality, is to know and to feel oneself different from other beings, and one only comes to feel this distinction by means of a shock, by a rather intense suffering" (XVI, 268).

Paradoxically, this knowledge can be either substantial or insubstantial. That is, we are aware of the something that we are, but we are also conscious of where our substantiality ends, of what we are not. For this reason, the "sensation of one's own limit" comes from plenitude, but it also leads to the edge of nothingness. And again paradoxically, our meeting with nothingness reaffirms the substantiality of the self. In other words, "I feel myself on feeling that I am not other people. To know and to feel the point up to which I am, is to know where I stop being, where I am not." Self-consciousness, we should note, has a peculiar function here. It becomes a dialectical gauge that slides along the axis of spiritual affliction. It enters the sphere of the self at one pole and probes down deeply, but it draws away from the self at the other end as it emerges. The deeper the descent into the sphere, the more remote the possibility of apprehending the self, and so "submergence into the self is the road to alienation" (IX, 837). In this way, a final paradox is created, by which introspection results in the eventual loss of self. And yet it is also true that by means of pain we keep in contact with our self even while we are alienated. While our awareness focuses on the limits of the self instead of on its substantiality, we are conscious of our suffering. Thus it is that we retain our sense of selfhood kinesthetically, even though we lose it cognitively.

We could ask, at this point, why pain is the guarantor of retaining the self, rather than some pleasurable sensation. The answer is that no true kinesthesia is possible in the experience of, let us say, joy, because this type of feeling leads to another form of alienation. Unamuno asks the same question in *The Tragic Sense of Life:* "How can one know that one is existing, if not by suffering in some form? How can one turn upon oneself, achieve a reflective consciousness, if not by means of pain? When a man feels pleasure, he forgets himself and the fact that he exists. He shifts to another self, to what is alien to him: he alienates himself. And when he submerges into himself, he returns to himself, to being him, in pain" (XVI, 268).

What Unamuno is saying is that pleasure is a refractory phenomenon. Its effect is to carry us out of ourselves by allowing us to concentrate on the sensation of delight rather than on ourselves as recipients of this delight. In other words, the sensation of pain is unpleasant, and causes us to focus on ourselves as the objects of a discomfort we wish to be rid of. In contrast, the sensation of pleasure receives our full attention, and we become oblivious of ourselves, ceasing to be the objects of our awareness. There is a transference of consciousness to an entity outside the self, even though that entity (or phenomenon) exerts an impact on the self. This transference is what Unamuno regarded as another form of alienation.

Thus far, we have talked about consciousness in terms of the different irrational means by which we apprehend the self. But there is also a rational approach, which is contained in the formal problem of the contemplating self, the *cogito*. This involves Descartes's proof of the existence of the self. For Descartes, the very fact that he can think is evidence that he exists. The famous statement *cogito ergo sum*, means "*I think*, therefore *I am*." The *cogito* in this statement is the self that says "I think"; and this same thinking self also says *sum*, "I am." In other words, the proof that my self exists ("I am") rests on the fact that the *cogito*, the self that thinks, thinks that I am and says so. This, in turn, assumes that there is a real identity between the self that is thought to exist and the self that says "I think." In short, Descartes assumes that the *cogito* and the *sum* are identical.

Unamuno refutes this proof by demonstrating that part of the Cartesian self, the cogito, cannot be an existential reality. He states that "the *ego* implicit in the enthymeme *ego cogito, ergo ego sum*, is an *ego*, an unreal or ideal self, and its *sum*, its existence, is also something unreal" (XVI, 162). That is, the cogito is no more than a thinking entity that is aware of itself thinking. It exists, therefore, not in the world of phenomena but in the conceptual or ideal world of the mind. Consequently, the supposedly existing self (*ego sum*) which is derived from the cogito is just as unreal and abstract. The "I am" in the statement "I think, therefore I am," is merely a self that is present in the consciousness of the thinker. It does not exist in reality. Descartes's error, according to Unamuno, was to not realize that " 'I think, therefore I am,' cannot mean anything except 'I think, therefore I am a thinking being.' " This fact does display one faculty of the existential self, namely, that it can think. But it does not prove the existence of that self. In truth, "the being of the 'I am,' which is derived from the 'I think,' is nothing more than an act of knowing. This being is knowledge but not life" (XVI, 162). That is to say, the self is real, whereas the *notion* entertained about that self is an abstraction, once removed from the existential condition alluded to by Unamuno: "What is most elementary is not that I think, but that I live, because those who do not think also live." Consciousness, therefore, along with its intellectual faculties, makes up one category of the entity called the existential self.

Unamuno believed, consequently, that the reality of the self eludes our efforts to know it through self-consciousness or contemplation. He pointed out that the basic self is a pre-reflective phenomenon which exists in the real world before it knows that it is there. This *pre-cogito* is capable of knowing itself, but the cognitive act is not an existential proof of the self's reality. On the contrary, the cognitive act is only possible because the pre-reflective self—the pre-cogito—does exist prior to undergoing the process of *desdoblamiento*. In other words, the self learns that it is in the world by becoming reflective and perceiving itself in an objective way during reduplication. But this perception merely represents the phenomenon of the self-in-the-world. By nature, the perception is little more than an idea of the self-as-phenomenon, an idea which is received by a faculty of this very self: its consciousness. Thus, the reflective self, or cogito, is the real self only to the extent that it resides in the self-as-phenomenon. So much less real, then, is the idea of the self which is entertained by the cogito. Not only is this self a representation and not a reality, but it represents the self in the process of contemplation rather than in a pre-reflective, vital state. The Cartesian use of awareness, therefore, does not satisfy Unamuno as an epistemological argument. On the other hand, since he is interested in an ontological proof, he stresses awareness as a function of being and personality: "The truth is that *sum, ergo cogito*, I am, therefore I think, although not everything that is thinks. The consciousness of thinking, can it not be, above all, the consciousness of being? Will it perhaps be possible to have pure thought, without consciousness of itself, without personality? Can there be pure knowledge without sentiment, without that kind of materiality which sentiment bestows? Does one not perhaps feel a thought, and feel himself at the same time that he knows and loves himself?" (XVI, 163).

These rhetorical questions are intended to explore the relationship between consciousness and personality. As Unamuno suggests, there is no such thing as pure consciousness. That is, it is impossible for a knowing self to contemplate its own act of knowing. Such a possibility would be equivalent to the ability of an eye to see itself directly. In both cases, a mirror is needed to reflect the image. Therefore, when Unamuno talks about the "consciousness of thinking," he does not mean that the cogito is aware of itself as a knower. He is saying, rather, that we sense the cogito's activity and feel it to be part of the total self. In this way, consciousness forms the mold for personality.

The exact nature of personality will be discussed in detail later. For the moment, it is enough to note that consciousness is a precondition for the self's possession of a personality. We apprehend our personality in several stages, and we first are conscious of perceiving the self. In other words, we are aware of being conscious of the self. This is why Unamuno stresses the fact that we cannot be aware of awareness itself. We must feel or intuit something material, and pure thought is immaterial. What we do feel is the substantiality of the self, not some hypothetical purity of consciousness. And this intuition is felt by means of an emotion. Thus, we have two modes of self-awareness, one irrational and the other intellectual. We may derive our sense of being either from an act of knowing or an experience of pain. But both instances involve a certain amount of feeling that is associated with the perception. This is extremely important, because without that emotion the cogito would be utterly divorced from the self. Normally, therefore, the cogito is rationally dissociated from the self, but it is tied to the self by means of an emotion.

In spite of the emotional tie binding the cogito to the self, the very fact of a splitting of the self creates a grave threat to the latter's health and harmony. When the cogito differentiates itself from the pre-cogito, it comes to understand a disturbing truth. It realizes that it is part of a self which is entirely knowable except for the one fragment that is doing the actual contemplation. As I hinted a moment earlier, the cogito can know everything except its own nature. This is a terrible realization for Unamuno, because it weakens his confidence in whatever knowledge he has of himself, and raises doubts about his self-reflection. For example, if his cogito cannot know itself, how reliable can its information be about other parts of the self? And if the cogito remains unknown, who can say what tendencies, for good or for evil, are potentially within its range? And so a period of intense scrutiny begins, with Unamuno submitting the various fragments of his ego to the doubt and distrust of the conscious self.

The result of this uncertainty is that the cogito develops into a divisive agent, turning the fragments of the self against each other. For instance, when a man is aware that only part of him is a social self, and that another part of him is watching it perform, he begins to question, in turn, the legitimacy of both fragments. He examines, let us say, the exterior or social fragment from the standpoint of the contemplative self, then reverses the procedure, and ends by vacillating between them both. The center of activity for these doubts is always the cogito, and it is this faculty which occupies the role of disrupter of the ego's harmony.

At this point, Unamuno begins to refer to the presence of a "satanic self." Up to now, his impulse to doubt had its source in an overactive awareness. But when the cogito is trying to choose sides, it is plagued by doubts of a different sort. Its decision-making is egged on by insidious hints and gleeful slanders against each fragment it focuses on. This is the *satánico yo*, the active cogito demoralizing its own efforts to confer legitimacy on a particular self, and alienating each fragment in turn. Whenever it decides to recognize a fragment as a self with special feelings and role, a new insinuation bedevils its resolution. However, once the choice is finally made, the mechanism of self-awareness is localized to the perspective associated with a specific fragment. In other words, when the cogito finally accepts a fragment, it adopts the latter's viewpoint and transfers its contemplating mechanism there. The cogito can then say "I am," and thus identify itself as a faculty residing in a particular self. This localization is possible for many perspectives or selves. And so, once settled, the cogito renews its doubts and begins the conflict all over again. Indeed, the satanic self often exacerbates consciousness to the point of "rejoicing in that contemplation," an act which places the entire ego structure in peril.

Here, then, is the cogito instigating the man against the components of his self, and undermining the security which each element enjoyed just before being subjected to self-conscious analysis. But at the same time, the cogito falls victim to its own questioning. Even though it is unknowable, it can be aware of, and make statements about itself. It reflects back upon itself and wonders why it is detached from the rest of the self. Moreover, it wonders whether this cleavage invalidates its participation in the self's structure. Thus, it comes to understand how destructive its role is. And so Unamuno speaks about "my friendly self and my enemy self," dividing the two into separate camps according to his conflicts (X, 86). To the extent that his consciousness can alienate the contemplative and active components of his self, he is his own enemy. Or, more precisely, he can develop a hostile *yo enemigo*.

This, consequently, is Unamuno's notion of the satanic self. The reflective faculty has the ability to say "I," but knows that by doing so it destroys the authenticity of the other parts of the self. These other selves cannot say "I" at the same time that they are being objectified. Thus, having lost their capacity for self-identification, the fragments are contemplated as disconnected objects instead of as the components of an integrated self. The satanic self works as an interstitial corrosive in this ego disintegration, and must be considered an evil force. This, at least, is how Unamuno regards it: "They say that the enemies of the soul are three: the world, the devil, and the flesh. But a fourth and worse enemy must be added: the soul itself. Unless this enemy, which other people call the satanic self, is included in the devil. The satanic self is harmful as long as we hold it enclosed within, contemplating itself and rejoicing in that contemplation" (III, 818). Unamuno calls this influence "satanic" because it questions the individual's motivation in every respect. As soon as an action or an emotion is objectified, a certain psychological detachment takes place. We begin to feel the action or emotion less intensely, because we are watching ourselves. This places the sincerity of the action in doubt, and we attach an ambiguous or even morally adverse judgment to it.

Ambiguity of this kind can be said to characterize any social act in which we watch our own performance. But to Unamuno, the insincerity is nowhere more apparent than in the practice of virtue, and in this regard he found that even saints act out their parts: "saintliness never reaches beyond the stage setting." The saint exalts his virtuous role as if it truly belonged to his personality, suppressing any awareness of the fact that he is only playing a part. That is, he does not allow the kind of self-contemplation which produces a disruptive cogito. In Unamuno's words, "the stifling of the satanic self is the supreme affirmation of personality," because it censors criticism of the latter. Without suppression, the thought that the saint is only a performer would come as an ugly intrusion upon his personal sense of having a virtuous character (V, 1193–94). Thus, Unamuno terms this disturbing thought diabolical.

But is it so diabolical? asks Unamuno in the next breath. Upon reflection, his answer is that while the satanic self is indeed harmful and divisive, it cannot be judged to be evil. The fact is, rather, that all ethical values arising from the splitting of the self are suspect. Whether they represent the "good" side of an individual or his so-called "evil" inclination, the very occurrence of these values in a psychologically divided state of mind is sufficient reason to doubt the authenticity of them all. And in any case, the psychological process which produces them is much more fundamental to our nature than the values themselves. Traditional moral judgments are valid only to the degree that they are not subjected to the phenomenon of self-awareness. When these values are examined during the "inner battle with the evil enemy," the values become inverted.

For example, in the novel *Peace in War*, the uncle practices abstinence on a certain day, "thinking he had undertaken the fast in order to mortify himself. And observing that he found intimate, spiritual pleasure in this mortification, he began to think that the real way to mortify himself would be by not fasting, thus depriving himself of solace" (II, 354). We have, in this situation, a value which is rejected by the very mind that is exercising it. The condition of this mind is such that, at the very moment that it upholds the value, it questions its own motives. Such a state of intense self-contemplation negates the worth of the value. Yet the negation occurs not by attacking the value's intrinsic quality, but by structuring a psychological attitude that prevents it from working. As soon as this structure hardens, the value's inherent weakness becomes visible, because it can only operate effectively when the faculty of consciousness is relatively quiescent. This is why Unamuno remarks that "definitive spirits are usually unconscious." That is, the normally self-confident man who advocates a position has not, in all likelihood, engaged in the kind of divisive depth-probing described here. How judicious, therefore, can his position be? How valid, in fact, is any position if it may be constantly jeopardized by "opposing" ego fragments? In both cases, the soundness of the values is dubious. Unamuno gives it less importance, therefore, than the depth of one's self-knowledge, even though the latter can only be achieved by the kind of reflective consciousness that permits a satanic self to emerge.

Thus, the satanic self is not judged to be pernicious by moral standards, but because it deprives us of the consolation of a dependable, unchanging value system. By casting doubt on an attitude and on the self that embraces it, the *yo enemigo* does more than just overthrow the ruling set of values. It also appears to establish itself as an immoral agent, the adversary of conventional ethical positions. Furthermore, it suppresses the hope that reliable standards of behavior can be found and adhered to. And above all, it betrays the individual for what he is: an actor, an impostor, and a hypocrite. Nevertheless, what is most important is to admit the condition, "to realize what the state of one's own soul is, whatever it may be. For I doubt the sincerity of dogmatic men. Or rather, the man who makes affirmations is usually one who does not see within himself clearly. Definitive spirits are usually unconscious. And I would rather be quiet or vacillate with full consciousness than be agitated and resolve something without it" (IX, 762; cf. II, 474, *et passim*).

Unamuno stresses the importance of our reflective faculty because it has the power to enrich our experience of the self, this in spite of its possible corruption of our faith in traditional values. Such an advantage—which results in plenitude—is achieved by discovering the range of our psychological dimensions. We are required to project each aspect of the self upon an inner screen and watch it. Whatever facet is objectified will be viewed by a contemplator, the cogito, which may often seem to be antagonistic because of its critical position. The self thus objectified may, then, eventually be vilified, and its "good" qualities, so obvious before being introduced into the field of consciousness, will now seem insincere. But this insincerity is a judgment arrived at by accusation. It did not exist prior to the appearance of the satanic self, and it is labeled insincerity from the latter's standpoint only. As a result, the divisiveness that arises within the self is comparable to a struggle between two separate people with opposing perspectives and impulses.

With this idea in mind, Unamuno created the self-devouring character of Artemio A. Silva, who bore within him, "like every child of man and woman, at least two selves, perhaps more . . . his good angel and his bad angel." Given the situation, Unamuno wondered what would happen when Artemio's reflective mechanism split the self into ethically dichotomous entities. And so he asked, "Isn't it possible that a man come to envy himself, or a part of himself; that one of his selves [envy] another of his parts, his other self?" (IX, 284). The question makes an important assumption. It affirms the existence of two autonomous selves, each capable of independent attitudes toward the other, and both sustained by their ability to stand apart and regard the other objectively. As a result, the faculty of self-awareness is transferable to either entity.

The problem of Artemio's envy, which is the emotion dominant here, does not in itself matter. It is important only insofar as it represents our ability to develop emotional attitudes while we contemplate ourselves. These feelings can only appear alternately, one at a time, depending upon where the reflective mechanism, the cogito, happens to be operating. In Artemio's case, one of his two selves, "the more external or public one, the more cynical one, was a self without scruples." This self is endowed with consciousness but does not use it, being instead impelled to act without concern for evaluating the action. In contrast, Artemio has an "other self, which we would call more internal, a private self, a hypocritical self, filled with scruples and moral concern" (IX, 285). This second, highly contemplative self observes its opposite and considers the latter's conduct from a moral standpoint. And so Artemio "called that self his conscience, as if the other were not one also." And this, of course, is the point. The so-called immoral self is also a conscience, which from its own ethical viewpoint condemns the immorality of the scrupulous self. To the latter self Unamuno attributed a greater degree of awareness, which is why at first glance it seems more obviously a conscience. On the other hand, the unscrupulous self appears to have more spontaneity of behavior. It was cast, for this reason, in the role of a social self, while the scrupulous self assumes the function of a moral accuser.

Nevertheless, the contemplative self is regarded as hypocritical precisely because it is aware of itself as a conscience. That is, it can recognize the discrepancy between its own scruples and the opposing impulses of the social self, even though they are both part of the same individual. This kind of hypocrisy confers equal status upon the social self by bringing the moral self to the same level. In fact,

Unamuno indicates that the social self also has a conscience with which to judge itself right and its adversary wrong. Hence Unamuno speaks of the mutual envy that the moral and the social selves have for each other. Each wishes to be like the other, so that the individual might be able to act with integrity: either without scruples or with moral deliberation. However, the result is that the two selves neutralize each other. They are situated in a single body, and not in two separate ones. And they appear in a field of awareness that allows the reflective mechanism to shift from one self to the other. Thus, Artemio grows to hate himself as he sees that "neither of his two selves, neither his good angel nor his demon, had conquered, and that, in truth, both were defeated, each by the other" (IX, 285–86).

It is no accident that Unamuno entitled his story *Artemio, Heautontimoroumenos*, calling his protagonist a self-eater. Whether this form of destruction consists of envy, hatred, or ridicule, the working principle is the same. The structure of the ego disintegrates by means of a conscious act of self-objectification. Within this posture, it is possible to assume, at the same time, an attitude of irony. Self-mockery thus becomes another form of self-corrosion. But, since only one part of the individual eats away at the other, the individual himself remains sufficiently intact to watch the drama of his own self-destruction. Given the equation "to devour oneself, to make fun of oneself," Unamuno suggests: "Devour yourself, and since the pleasure of devouring yourself will be confused with and neutralize the pain of being devoured, you will reach a perfect equanimity of spirit, ataraxia. You will be nothing more than a mere spectacle for yourself" (II, 968–69).

Here Unamuno reaches the logical conclusion in his treatment of the splitting of the self. He decides that *desdoblamiento* is not a tragic condition for which he will suffer unduly. His argument is that since we possess many selves, and since none of them dominates for any length of time, it is pointless to take the struggle seriously. On the contrary, there is a certain diversion in observing the constant shifts in awareness as one self comes into the ascendency over another. By renouncing the hope that we can have a consistent personality with stable attributes, we gain a healthy equilibrium in the face of our conflicts. In fact, the condition can be turned to our advantage by viewing it ironically, or as a source of distraction. Thus, what was originally a cause for anguish is now converted into a spectacle, and the sense of play implicit in seeing ourselves in so many roles may create a well-being that, in turn, will ensure a fulfillment of the self.

Needless to say, Unamuno was unable to practice this attitude consistently. At times he suffered anguish, at other moments he strutted theatrically, and for every instance where he openly mocked himself there is another where he concealed this mockery with an anguished pose. At all moments, he was sincere in what he did, in that he genuinely felt or believed in what he was doing. Similarly, he was hypocritical at every moment, in the sense that he watched himself in the act. This is why his writings are so contradictory and, indeed, irreconcilable in the final analysis. He was capable of everything from the tragic to the burlesque during these moments of self-contemplation.

There is one final attitude which Unamuno adopted during his ironic self-awareness, and this was to surrender his sober perception of the self. From optimistic self-irony he went to a pessimistic outlook on perception. To phrase the problem in general terms, he suggested that we may begin to doubt that any of our selves is real, either to us or to the people around us. The question "Who am I?" then, now loses its private frame of reference and is stated instead as a problem of perception. As the hero of *Mist* described it, he felt many times that "I am not I, and I walked down the street imagining that other people did not see me. And at other times I fancied that they did not see me as I see myself, and that while I believed myself to be walking soberly, with full composure, I was playing the clown without knowing it, and that the others were laughing and making fun of me" (II, 836).

Thus, what began as a psychological problem—anguish or irony—ends as a purely realistic one. There is not only doubt concerning the authenticity of each self in the individual's own mind, but there is even uncertainty about the way a given self can be perceived. This is no longer a problem related to that of the three Juans, discussed by Unamuno in the prolog to *Three Exemplary Novels*. Rather, the issue is whether the social Juan that Juan sees himself projecting is indeed the social Juan seen by others. The social self objectified during *desdoblamiento* is an image which Juan accepts seriously as being accurate. And yet now there is a complication, for this social self may be seen by others in an entirely different light. Nevertheless, the possibility represents an extreme position for Unamuno, who brings it forth in order to initiate a metaphysical discussion of reality.

# 3  SOLITUDE

[decorative border]

*Having explored* some of the labyrinthine features of self-contemplation, we can understand why Unamuno rejected excessive introspection. In the last analysis, he urged men to act in the social world and to avoid the abyss of soul-searching loneliness. Of course, his rejection of the introspective life was never decisive, nor even characteristic of his own habits. But it was the result of a long, alternating process in which a desperate private self threw itself back into the world in order to find meaning in action. Unamuno's despair was the product of a self-scrutiny which is only possible in solitude. Indeed, to submerge himself so deeply could only have been possible in circumstances of extreme psychological isolation. But, by the same token, this very isolation gave him the opportunity to weigh his various courses of action and, ultimately, to decide on returning to the external world. It is clear, then, that the condition of solitude was a critical one for Unamuno, and one that requires our close attention.

When we think about solitude as a concept or a way of life, we usually call forth associations of a romantic nature: a certain poetic quality, nostalgia, sadness. For Unamuno, however, solitude meant much more, and in a less subjective way. Despite his strife-ridden exterior, he looked upon solitude as a method rather than a mood. He adopted a rationalistic attitude toward loneliness, and saw in it an opportunity for rest and respite after the strain of social engagement. This idea of solitude as a technique was best expressed in his statement that "it is good to withdraw oneself, but [only] after having spilled oneself out, and in order to spill oneself out" (IX, 654). By the image of the self spilling over, Unamuno meant to convey—and emphasize—the notion of dedicating oneself to the fulfillment of social responsibilities. Because of his skepticism concerning self-knowledge, he came to value the self less in isolation and more when it was involved in its environment. But at the same time, he recognized the importance of solitude as a provider of restorative powers. And it was by this dualistic attitude that Unamuno sought to reconcile the opposing positions. He approved of the self becoming exhausted by its social activity, for it would withdraw and be replenished. Then, after a period of meditation in solitude, it would again be ready to commit its energies to the social world.

In addition to its powers of restoration, solitude was looked upon by Unamuno as a technique for self-discovery. In fact, it is here that we must begin our examination, since the decision to re-enter the social world is made after a surfeit of solitude. Obviously enough, loneliness offers the best opportunity for introspection, for it acts as a screen against external distractions. As the process of self-contemplation begins, the individual initiates a submergence within the self (*ensimismamiento*). This enables his consciousness to bring about a splitting of the self in the manner described earlier. As we saw, this condition leads to an eventual loss of self, an alienation caused by excessive self-awareness. Thus, solitude is no better in altering the course of self-alienation than is extreme sociability, where a similar estrangement takes place. For this reason, Unamuno cannot decide "which is worse, alienation or submergence within the self. Even while opposites, they lead to the same thing" (IX, 654).

This similarity of effect is but one paradox. There is also a paradox in function, with solitude and sociability exchanging roles. What happens is that companionship gives rise to loneliness, while loneliness provides the occasion for company. For example, if a man who is acutely self-conscious finds himself in a group, he may easily feel as withdrawn and as psychologically isolated from that group as he would be if he were actually alone. He would echo the words of Unamuno, who spoke of "the solitude that encircles and invades and presses me as soon as I find myself in the company of others." And conversely, the condition of solitude acts to create a social situation. If, for example, a man is alone reading a book, the communication he establishes between himself and the subject matter is eventually extended to a communication with himself. He becomes one person, then another, and he contemplates these various selves as if they were people. Thus it is that solitude frames a social situation and usurps the function of group communication. This is the meaning of Unamuno's claim, "I isolate myself for the sake of sociability" (X, 433). The condition of solitude enables the self to differentiate into two or more parts, which in turn create a social situation. Between them, they construct a dialog with separate points of view, although the setting is the common psychological arena of consciousness.

Solitude, consequently, is above all a method, and not an end in itself. Without it, felt Unamuno, we could not acquire self-knowledge. We have to be alone if we are to see the difference between our private and social selves, and especially if we want to identify the context of each. Without solitude, the self would be defined wholly within a social context, and we would fail to recognize how independent the reflective self is from its active counterpart. We would either not see their separate existences, or we would consider consciousness a function of the social self. Such was Unamuno's fear when he lamented: "Unfortunate is the man who cannot dispense with the noise and the bustle of his fellow men, for he has not found himself and does not even know how to look. Nor does he see himself except as reflected in other people" (II, 629). Only through the medium of solitude and its tranquility can we sharpen the contours of the private, as well as the public, self. Otherwise, the failure to withdraw will oblige us to regard the self entirely in relation to other people, a reflected image instead of the reflective, private entity that it partly is.

The reason that Unamuno never made solitude an end in itself is clear enough. As a condition, it would lead to alienation, and thus make introspection useless, not to say unnecessary. The real need for meditation, he believed, stems from the turmoil of social engagement, not inner conflict. It is the social situation which precipitates our withdrawal, just as it is the required context in which to begin our self-discovery. That is, our first act of recognition is to see our self—the social self—in action. When we become aware of being different from the other selves in a group, we have taken the initial step in the direction of true introspection. Only then do we withdraw into solitude.

Let us trace this process by beginning with its initial stage. According to Unamuno, "no one knows himself if he does not know the other person. Only through others does one know oneself. For the act of folding over and over oneself, like a recluse in solitude, and of living in a perpetual examination of conscience, is the means of forgetting oneself, of emptying oneself out, of becoming detached from one's own being" (IX, 1017). Thus, our first step is to separate our self from other selves, and we accomplish this by recognizing who the others are and what they feel. The deeper this understanding, the more complete the separation, since we widen our basis for distinguishing personal and alien traits. It would seem, therefore, that we now are ready to take the second step into solitude. However, if we withdraw, there will be no further justification for self-awareness. Unamuno's reasoning is as follows. In a state of solitude, the social self disappears as a reality, and the contemplating self is left with virtually nothing. All it has is its consciousness, or at best, the task of learning the nature of self-reflection. Hence, the real problem of identity slips away. To be left alone with just a reflective mechanism is, indeed, "the way to forget oneself." In this condition, we preserve the empty vessel that once contained the self which was projected into the world ("emptying oneself out"). Meanwhile, the social self is psychologically cut off, "detached from one's own being," and is no longer a meaningful reality to the isolated contemplator.

Solitude, therefore, ultimately defeats its own purpose by helping to reduce the self to nothingness. This is why Unamuno is doubtful about the absolute value of withdrawal. Thus his concept of solitude involves a structure made up of levels and phases which lead to the center of consciousness and back into the world again. The life of a "spiritual" man pulsates with an alternating rhythm of solitude and sociability, with the second beat having the stronger thrust. His being is defined from a psychological standpoint as the realization of the self in a committed interpersonal framework. This state can be characterized by an "unconscious" social self engaged actively in the world. Or, there can be two protagonists, one acting and the other watching. In either case, the importance attributed by Unamuno to sociability is clear.

Consequently, the only solution to "our supreme yearning" for self-knowledge is to have a head-on meeting of individuals. Men should meet in a direct confrontation, each pushed up against the other and made to see what, among their differing qualities, is personal to each man. To Unamuno it seemed "almost impossible that someone who shuts himself off in the desert to spend the days contemplating himself, should come to know himself . . . . The best way to know oneself is to bump, gut against gut, which is to say rock against rock, right into one's fellow man" (I, 538). This statement represents the beat of sociability in the existential rhythm mentioned a moment earlier. After his taxing effort, Unamuno is forced to rest, and so he shifts to the alternate beat, telling later how he "retired to the country to bathe my sick spirit in its sedative stillness." It was there, in solitude, that he meditated "with my whole body and with my entire soul, not just with my brain, the seat of what you call personality" (II, 749–50).

It is interesting to note how earthy and yet how vague Unamuno's vocabulary can be on this point. In part, this reflects the way in which he thought with his entire being, which in turn reflects his desire to retain the whole of his divided self. He wanted to hold on to the intellectualizing self-contemplator, which was in danger of falling into a solitary void of pure consciousness. He also wanted to keep the social self that had fatigued him into seeking this solitude in the first place. What he did not want was to define personality as a mere self-conscious ego fragment. Thus, he tried to preserve his social condition even while he was isolated. As a result, Unamuno had to renounce "that fictitious and abstract self which sank me into the solitude of my own emptiness." By this he meant that the contemplative self tends to move toward abstraction when it is cut off from the external world. The self advances toward pure consciousness when it contemplates itself in isolation. In the process, it creates a concept of itself, an abstract self. This *yo abstracto* is a creation of Unamuno's mind, and is not a reality. Consequently, it is also a fiction, a *yo ficticio*. Unamuno rejected this mode of existence because it implied that solitude can be an end in itself. Instead, he reverted to the original situation of the "whole" self, even when he was alone: "I have returned to myself, to the poor mortal who suffers and hopes, who enjoys and believes" (II, 750).

In this condition, he tried to be as concretely aware as possible of all aspects of his being.

It is difficult to judge the depth of Unamuno's convictions with regard to this introspection. He repeatedly returned to the idea that the contemplating self, when alone, reflects back upon itself more and more, until all sense of self is lost when the state of pure consciousness is reached. He tells us that "introspection is quite deceptive, and when carried to an extreme produces a genuine emptiness of consciousness. . . . A state of awareness which consisted purely and simply of the consciousness contemplating itself would not be a state of consciousness at all, owing to a lack of content" (III, 617). Yet he also said that the problem is to "obtain the maximum of one's own personality with a minimum of other company. Less company, or a less complex company, would diminish our personality, and it would also be diminished by more company, or a seemingly more complex company" (I, 540).

Part of the foregoing contradiction is inherent in the nature of submergence into the self and alienation. Both of these conditions lead to the loss of self. How, then, do we acquire a maximum of personality? By avoiding excessive introspection, especially in the last stage where the self dissolves into its own consciousness. Unamuno warned that even if one wishes "to drown out one's own self, the streets of a large city are better than barren mountains" (I, 541). He meant, among other things, that we may lose our self just as nicely in a crowd as when we are alone. Why, we may ask, is it preferable to lose it in the crowded city? Because loss of self means being rid of the contemplating self, which leads to nothingness. If this happens in solitude, we really fall into a void of pure consciousness. On the other hand, the loss of self among people would result in our becoming "another person," an alienated social self. This second alternative, at least, offers some kind of fulfillment, no matter how little. Even so, there is still another question. Is it not true that solitude, as we saw, enables the self to develop a many-faceted personality? This is, of course, quite so. But in this case Unamuno is interested in pointing out the limitations of solitude in contrast to sociability. That is, he is concerned with the realistic, non-psychological aspects of existence, and not with personality. Admittedly, he is obliged to point out that one may acquire "the maximum of one's own personality with a minimum of other company." But the converse proposition is also true, namely, that personality "would also be diminished by more company." It is diminished by total immersion in society and by excessive self-consciousness to the same degree. Nevertheless, the city streets are better for drowning out consciousness than mountain peaks, because we cannot be pushed from the street into the abyss of pure contemplation. The demands of sociability always force another self upon us, and we become useful.

At this point, several important questions arise concerning the nature of personality, but since they lead away from the concept of solitude, I will discuss them later. Let me say for the time being that Unamuno considered "self" to be the larger entity within which "personality," among other fragments, is contained. It should also be clear to us that from a psychological viewpoint, solitude represents a more complex condition than sociability. In other words, a social situation does not bring the entire personality structure into focus, whereas solitude does. With this in mind, we may follow Unamuno still deeper into the lonely region of the self.

As he looked within himself, the solitary Unamuno found an inbuilt form of society already contained there. His very act of introspection created a social structure within the self which is identical to what we normally call society. On the basis of this experience, he concluded that when the individual is isolated, he reflects his social state in miniature. Then, upon rejoining the group, this same individual contributes to the latter by drawing upon his private personality: "You yourself, in yourself, are society, and likewise for each man. And because of this, what we call society emerges, since no one gives what he does not have" (III, 424).

Exactly what happens in the private social structure of man? Its focal point is the communication system that allows the differentiated self to have some kind of spiritual intercourse with its fragments. Thus, each self may converse, so to speak, with the others. The result is to place the individual in a kind of social situation where, equipped with an inner listening apparatus, he can hear himself communicate with his self. In structural terms, this means several things. First of all, he is aware that his ego fragments are engaged in conversation as if they were other people holding a dialog. He is also conscious that at least part of him is now another person, and perhaps more than one. Thus, the situation constitutes a form of alienation: the overall effect is that the self is no longer his own, but an "other" whose voice he overhears.

When Unamuno tried to give a literary form to this type of inner sociability, he wrote what he termed a monodialog. He could not call it a dialog because physically he was only one person, and yet it was obviously not a monolog because there was more than one voice involved. And so he hit upon the word "monodialog," which meant that it looked like a dialog in form except for the fact that neither speaker was clearly identified. This fact has an important effect on the reader, who finds it confusing and difficult to link a given argument or line of thought with a single voice. After reading a page or two of a nameless exchange of speeches, we can no longer be sure that the same voice is consistently supporting one point of view. Unamuno deliberately provoked this confusion in his readers in order to make them familiar with the many-sided conversations which he was hearing with his inner ear. Indeed, one monodialog talks about an "inner audience" which listens to an interior conversation among "many" other people within the self (IV, 559).

This notion of a dialog in solitude shows how cleverly Unamuno set up a psychological bridge between self and society by means of internal socialization. If we inspect this bridge more closely, we can see how its different segments were put together. As we noted, every dialog must have at least two participants, each distinct and independent of the other. When the dialog takes place in the mind of one man, it develops only after a process of differentiation and objectification. The self divides into two separate selves, one of which is objectified as an "other" person. The situation is also a form of alienation, with a psychic distance forming between the interlocutors. Thus, each fragmentary self can discourse with the other as if they were fellow men, and gain insight into each other with remarkable lucidity and sincerity. The bridge is built, therefore, on a platform of solitude, and this is the only true way to reach the outer world. There is "no other genuine dialog than the dialog that you undertake with yourself, and this you can only undertake by being alone. In solitude, and only in solitude, can you know yourself as your neighbor, and as long as you do not know yourself as a neighbor, you will be unable to see other selves in your neighbors" (III, 883).

At first glance, it would seem that any knowledge of our fellow man must be less than profound. Let us remember, however, that the value of seeing ourselves as another person lies precisely in the objectivity which a less intimate relationship provides. In this respect, Unamuno's sensitivity as a psychologist is most apparent. He believed that our range of emotions in society corresponds to our private emotional spectrum. In the world, we begin with indifference and extend our interest toward a neighbor as we become more familiar with him. So too does our individual band of feelings toward ourselves start with unconsciousness, and extend to a higher frequency of introspection. This is why the only genuine dialogs are interior ones: we have all the advantages of the social dialog without the social strain. Moreover, as these inner conversations are prolonged, our emotions become more ambiguous and complex. The monodialog manifests feelings that ordinarily occur only in social situations. However, there is no insincerity to obstruct the clear vision of the fragmented self and its sentiments. As the contemplating self learns to treat the other selves as strangers, our "inner audience" develops emotional attitudes usually reserved for other people. Inner sociability then becomes more than a mere structural objectification of ego fragments. Instead, it grows into a complex interrelationship of selves. But these selves are so emotionally detached from each other that their mutual communication is as objective as our daily social intercourse is with our neighbors.

The fruits of inner sociability are many. Not the least important is the way it helps social intercourse. As we noted, social dialog is never completely transparent; there is always an unspoken element, a possibility of uncertainty, a trace of insincerity, all due to the fact that neither of the participants fully knows the other's thoughts. What makes the inner dialog sincere is the constant fluctuation of consciousness. The locus of consciousness shifts back and forth, allowing us to know at all times the attitudes of our various selves. In other words, "our inner conversation no longer is a dialog between two, but among many. Society imposes upon us silence and fictitious conversation. True conversation is the one which we sustain inwardly. After you and I separate, we will continue conversing with each other, and I will tell myself what I should be telling you now and don't, and I will answer myself with what you should be telling me and do not" (IV, 557–58).

Thus, solitude is a positive value because it serves as a bond between men, and as a method for individual self-knowledge. The barriers that exist in the social situation are eliminated in solitude, and although this might not be of immediate practical help, it can lead to mutual understanding. We will never know what our interlocutor might have said, but we can determine what he *should* have said, and with this in mind it is easier to forgive or to understand the actual words spoken. This kind of dialog is different from the "monodialog" of conflicting selves, in that the former reproduces a normal social conversation inwardly. However, the principle of sociability remains the same. In both situations the ideal is to achieve an honest confrontation, one that will remove the veil of insincerity from men's hearts, and dispel the mist of consciousness from each man's self. If we can learn to meet our many selves with understanding, we will be able, when alone, to recreate our external, social circumstance with equal judgment. In this way, we will bring to the world the insights gained from observing our solitary self-alienation. Thus it is that "only solitude can melt from us the thick layer of shyness which isolates each of us from the rest. Only in solitude do we find ourselves, and on finding ourselves, we find within us all of our brothers-in-solitude" (III, 882).

# 4 INDIVIDUALITY AND PERSONALITY

*Now that* we have talked about solitude, and about what mechanisms work to divide the total self into solitary and social selves, we are faced with some important questions. What exactly are these selves, and what is their nature? How is our individuality affected by them? Just where does personality fit in, and what is its relationship to the self? Which self? How do we define personality? These are the problems which Unamuno struggled to resolve, and they were made clear only after his analysis of solitude. Once he realized that the self would be most valuable as a social entity, he began to seek more precise definitions of the roles and conditions in which the self was placed.

The first task was to separate the psychological categories of a man's being: his self, his individuality, and his personality. The self was the most general of the three, consisting of the capacity to say "I" to a given response, feeling, or idea. It became a problem to define when it split into other selves, and there is little more that we can say about it here since our entire discussion in Part One is dedicated to its many ramifications. More pertinent are the concepts of individuality and personality, and Unamuno always took pains to distinguish between these two categories. He made qualified statements that pointed out this difference, as, for example, "The great cities de-individualize us, or rather, depersonalize us" (I, 535). The exactness of his phrasing betrays a concern over the possible confusion of these two terms. Unamuno wanted the reader to think out the transition from one term to the other by himself, and so he made the correction in this way. The main point, for Unamuno, was that the difference was a matter of quality and essence. He spoke of "the antinomy which I establish between personality and individuality," thus suggesting a duality or opposition (VII, 699). However, he also saw the two in a complementary relationship. That is, he looked upon individuality as a fact or phenomenon, within which the quality or essence, personality, was found.

What exactly is personality for Unamuno, and how does it differ from individuality? Personality is only one aspect of the self, but it is a part of the self's integral structure. It is an attribute which combines with other characteristics to help in defining the self's essential quality. Individuality, on the other hand, is a condition rather than a quality. It refers to the self as a state of being, and not in qualitative terms. By having individuality, an entity can exist in the world of events even though it has no special qualities that distinguish it from other objects, entities, and events. An individual may be separate in physical or emotional terms without necessarily having unique personal traits. We can see this fact readily in a group of animals belonging to the same species: the animals project no recognizable personality and yet they maintain their individual features ("animality, or, individuality" [V, 1193]). This is also true for human beings. Unamuno finds that "there are people who, with an extremely marked individuality, lack almost completely their own personality" (VII, 699). They exist in the world as separate and cipherable entities, but they lack the essential qualities that would mark them as personalities.

According to Unamuno's definition, individuality is a phenomenological condition and little else, a mere existing in the world. Within this condition, essential traits pertaining to personality can be manifested. As Unamuno developed the concept, its existentialist implications grew clearer. He said, "I call individuality what we might say to be the container, and personality the spiritual content. There are men who are very strongly separate from the rest, who live as if enclosed in a shell, crust, or thick husk, while being empty inside" (VII, 699). The physical container is the unmistakable frame and figure of a particular individual. But at the same time that it belongs to him, it takes part in the world of phenomena around him. It delineates his spatial and temporal separateness from other entities that display their own individualities. In short, the container is limited to an existence without substance or spiritual peculiarity.

On the other hand, the receptacle contains something that is not bound to the conditions of the existence just described. It contains spirituality, which bears the uniqueness of primary and inimitable essence. But in itself, individuality has none of this. It is a kind of cipher, the mark of the degree to which we keep ourselves separate from other men. Moreover, it is another form of social disengagement, since its spiritual emptiness works against a meaningful expression of selfhood. This is why Unamuno's imagery of hermetic isolation—"shell, crust, or thick husk"—is so significant. He believed that extreme individuality was synonymous with impenetrability against the pressure of the outside world. And he felt that it was necessary to break this human shell in order for spirituality to "personalize" the individual. And spirit, of course, could develop only by the interaction of the social and private realms of being.

Here, then, is the point of departure for a definition of personality, at least as far as it is distinguished from individuality. Individuality alone is a brute state, unsocial and uncommitted. Personality is the humanizing quality that knits the individual into a social and cultural fabric, and causes him to act as a person. The nature of "acting" and the "person" is a problem which I will treat later in detail. The issue at this juncture is that the individual can be knit into a social fabric. What Unamuno calls "public, civil, or historical life," that is, social life, is the "only one in which the personality acts—for in private, it is only animality or individuality which acts" (V, 1193). The question is how that public life can be developed. Since the unengaged individual leads a crustacean existence, the best method is to shatter it. We must break through his shell and stimulate the socializing capacity of the self, which Unamuno called personality. This sector of the self is, although hidden and underdeveloped, a basic area. It becomes the means for propelling man into his most human interpersonal situation. As we will discover, personality is a mask which identifies the empty individuality with the role it performs in society. To perform this role without personality is to go through life without a fully humanized self. As Unamuno puts it, "each person wears his mask. And if it is taken away from him, what remains is the animal, and nothing more than the animal, the individual" (V, 1195).

We see, therefore, that true personality is always revealed by some veneer or mask of sociability, an exterior which covers the idiosyncrasies of the unengaged individual. Moreover, true personality involves a higher level of human communication than does individuality. The latter, on the other hand, remains immersed in the primitive isolation of brute privacy. The distinction bears emphasizing, for "it is best that we not confuse person with individual. Individuality is an animal thing. The pure idiot—if he exists outside of the pathological—is an individual but not a person" (XI, 797–98). The lack of distinctiveness common to this animal individuality begins with a state of detachment, a state which prohibits the growth of an exterior social self. If a man in this condition enters a social situation, he does little more than allow his raw individuality to grow polished by rubbing it against other individualities, although never hard enough to break into the primitive uniformity underneath them all.

Each of these shell-like lives is "an empty individuality, poor in personality. It is a thick and hard container, like an earthen jar with a very heavy casing, but which contains nothing but the same water as the other jars" (V, 380). Living in unawareness of his own motives, the individual remains oblivious of the feelings of his fellow man. His life consists of a grazing of surfaces. As an individual, his separateness is totally "absorbent," with his consciousness suspended in the oblivion of his empty spirit. He does not seem aware of what it is within him that makes him different from other individuals. And indeed, being unreflective, there is "nothing but the same water as the other jars." However, even the first stirrings of an attempt at self-knowledge would start the growth of a personality. The man would gather the diluted contents of his "shell" and project them into a social situation. In other words, by concentrating the scattered experiences of his self-awareness, he could have the seed of a spiritual substance. Otherwise, he would have to continue the hermetic existence of his peculiar individuality.

Unamuno's image of the earthen jar aptly confirms the dualism of his thinking. He views matter as the receptacle of spirit. But even though such containers show physical variations, these are trifles when compared to spirit itself. As we saw, spirit can become the substance of personality if the individual enters a social or interpersonal situation. But this is only possible after a splitting of the self has been completed by means of self-consciousness. As a result, "the same water as the other jars" becomes recognizably different—personal—from the rest. This is why self-awareness is so important. Without it, man is pure individuality, "like a fakir who falls asleep contemplating his navel" (V, 380). His life is a vacuum that can neither hold his attention nor permit him any intellectual or emotional life. In contrast, consciousness allows the social self to emerge, first introspectively when the self undergoes its split, and later as a personality. Those who remain at the lowest level of insociability leave their potential personality buried within them, while they turn their shell of individuality against the world, like the crustaceans. In an age so filled with talk about depersonalization, we have come to lose our sensitivity to this phenomenon, and even to the terminology describing it. However, the situation was a vivid reality to Unamuno, and he kept the concept alive by his analogy with shellfish. Individuals, he wrote, "with a thick and hard introspective individuality . . . are to spirit what crabs are to the body: dermoskeletal, having their bones on the outside and their flesh within" (V, 380). Unamuno would have had this anatomical structure reversed. He felt that men should display their humanity, the soft part, on the outside. But they could only do this by discovering their inner selves, and developing a personality to dress the skeleton of individuality.

What we have said so far serves to isolate the concept of personality. Let us now discuss its existential role. Unamuno was obviously dissatisfied with the material condition of simply being in the world. For him, a purely phenomenological existence—individuality—was incomplete and without spirit. For this reason, he urged the development of personality, which was achieved by the technique of self-consciousness. It was this method which lifted man above the level of phenomenon and placed him in the realm of spirit. As a mere object in the world, he is unable to assume a transcendental role as doer or agent. However, as a self-aware man, he is conscious of his status and of the activity attached to it. That is, he is once removed from his participation in the world, and he is able to see it as a role instead of as a blind event.

This ability to see himself in a transcendent role is the essence of a spiritually substantial life. And the role itself is his *persona*, his personality, as he sees it acting in the world and as he experiences it in his awareness. It is, in other words, his existential personality. We have, therefore, a basic psychological distinction. Man as phenomenon—individuality—is a question of his physical occurrence in the everyday world, whereas man as personality is a question of substance in the arena of his consciousness. However, this arena encompasses the external world, which is where the everyday social self is active. Thus, the terms personality and persona are synonymous in this particular area. They both refer to that aspect of existence where man acts self-consciously in the world.

Hence Unamuno's interest in the philological development of the word *persona*. He found that with each change in its usage down through history, the term had progressively lost the literal quality of its meaning. The persona, he said, referred originally to a mechanical device used by actors, whereas it had later come to mean the role we play in the world and in our own minds. In other words, the persona has transcended its phenomenological status and assumed a nonmaterial application. By denoting a personality instead of an object, its new usage reflects the psychological distance which the existential self puts between man and the world. And yet the term preserves the connotation of theatricality, because it refers to the role which the social self performs in the world. Even more, the persona is scrutinized by its self-conscious master, who watches it perform on the inner stage of his awareness.

Thus, it is useful to note the many transitions which the word *persona* has undergone throughout the centuries. As Unamuno remarked, we can find "many lessons in the process of its acquiring meaning, from its designation as a resonating box for the voice, then as what was attached to the masks used by the Roman actors, and then as the mask itself; later, as the personage represented in the drama, after that as the role which we portray on the stage of human society, and finally as [our role] in the stage setting of our own consciousness" (III, 319). These successive phases provide us with a miniature history of existential psychology. At first, the persona was simply a device manipulated by a human being. This relationship was a classic example of the duality between the subject and the object, where both elements retained their full autonomy. Later, the resonating apparatus was inserted into the mask, thus preparing the way for the subjective and objective realms to merge. Still later, when the persona was identified with the mask itself, it ceased to be a mere device and became an anthropological symbol. Man was no longer using an independent object; he was incorporating it into the motivations of his subjective world. The concrete object was symbolically transfigured, and made to represent a human purpose or pose.

This symbolic representation was much more apparent when the persona later changed from a mask to a personage. The word *persona* then came to be valued more highly than the object itself, because the word symbolized an abstraction: the principle of human activity. The term became less literal in meaning with each change in its usage down through history, until now it has come to designate the role we play in the world and in our own minds. By denoting a personality instead of an object, its current usage reflects the psychological distance between the material world and the self. And yet it never surrenders its underlying connotation of theatricality. We watch the performance of our role in society, and then, in self-contemplation, we watch it performed on the private stage of the mind.

In an important sense, therefore, the word *persona* bears witness to the triumph of a spiritual condition over the material world. Out of the substance of our inner life, we create a role, and a character to play it. We then send this player and his part into the world and use them to bridge the two realms of subjective and objective reality. Thus, while the word *persona* was once linked etymologically to the origins of play-acting, it is now the cultural emblem of our psycho-social activity.

This is why Unamuno so carefully enumerated the last three degrees in the historical development of the persona: the personage in a play, the role in society, and the role on the stage of our awareness. Let us note how each of these phases calls forth reality in an increasingly sophisticated way. In the play, we have a fiction instead of a reality. Conversely, we have in society a reality instead of a fiction. And finally, in the theater of consciousness, we have a fiction created by a self in contemplation of itself in society. The point may seem too subtle, but this is how Unamuno conceived it. For him, the most perfect fiction was not the dramatic play presented on the stage. It was, rather, the sum of illusions which our imagination fosters about ourselves. Since we project this fiction into the social world, the nature of social reality must necessarily alter. A bit of play-acting is injected into a world heretofore considered devoid of fictitious elements. Reality will, then, have to be regarded—as Unamuno indeed did regard it—in a less objective way than we first anticipated. Social situations are charged with the subjectivity that descends upon them from a self-conscious projection. Thus, the social self performs in an arena tinged with the fictitiousness of a creative subjectivism.

The existential implications of this situation now come into focus. Reality in itself is an inadequate concept. We must speak of significant reality, which is the common area that remains after the dividing line between subjectivity and objectivity disappears. Simple reality is a meaningless field which is invaded by a personality that begins to act upon it. This personality transforms the field into an existentially meaningful reality, one which is, of necessity, partially subjective. This is possible because the personality itself gains easy access to the objective world of phenomena, and in turn becomes transformed. How does Unamuno explain the nature of a personality which is so effective? Basically, it is the invention of a self-conscious man who wants to affirm his existence in the world through a creative act. However, this act is really a performance, with the actor being held in the power of an omniscient awareness. Therefore, his personality becomes a kind of property, a "person" in the juristic sense of being entitled to certain rights without necessarily being autonomous. In this respect, "the present psychological meaning of the word *persona* is derived from its juridical meaning. A person is the subject of the law, and this juridical meaning was taken from the histrionic one" (X, 241).

Yet it is precisely this condition which is an existential one. The histrionic quality of the persona is instrumental in fulfilling our existence. Without it, we would be back in the void of our shell-like individuality. But our freedom to elect that fulfillment rests with the subjective self. The persona is the instrument of its will to fulfillment. In this sense, therefore, personality is a possession of human will. It acquires a will of its own later on, after it enters the social world. But it always remains the possession of a superior will that first brought it into being.

We may say, therefore, that persona and personality are synonymous when the self deliberately creates a social role for itself. However, the creative act is deceptively simple, and can easily be replaced by false roles that are mistaken for true ones. The difference lies in the manner by which the persona shifts from solitude to sociability. As we know, sociability is possible only when two genuine personalities interact with each other. Having emerged from solitude as true social masks, properties of the self, they are able to communicate with each other. On the other hand, if a man fails to make his social mask a complete possession, he falls back upon the emptiness of solitude. This loneliness, however, is the hollow silence that separates two individuals who have not developed real personalities. What they have instead are ill-fitting masks which stifle the communication that usually occurs between well-integrated social personalities. Their problem is that "there is no true sociability . . . because individuals instead of persons associate and penetrate into each other. And instead of personality . . . men have a mask, the fiction of a personality. And this mask is all too frequently wont to be the mask which others impose upon us, a mask which does not stem from our own face" (VII, 701). We have, then, more than one mask, even though we may only have one true personality. Let us pause to examine what Unamuno meant by this statement.

As we have seen, genuine personality is a mask, but one which grows naturally out of the will to be socially active. Our own face gives rise to the mask, and in this narrow sense it may be said that if the social self is fictitious, this is only insofar as it is a creation of its owner. There is however, a truly "false" and ill-fitting mask which can be imposed from the outside. Instead of being shaped by the self, its contours are fashioned by the imagination of other people. Living by social pressure, by the image others have of him, or by what he thinks people expect him to do, the owner of such a mask is never the true proprietor of his own property. This is what Unamuno called the "fiction of a personality," a mask twice removed from the individual. As long as people confront each other with these false masks, they can never enjoy "true sociability," where "persons associate and penetrate into each other." Instead of communicating, they mouth empty words that bear no relation to their true being. They are not in possession of their personality because their social mask, being imposed by others, is not really their own. Consequently, they fall back into the worst form of solitude: the one that occurs in a social setting.

In contrast, the authentic social self asserts itself without regard to opinion or pressure from the outside. It moves in the legitimate theater of true sociability. However, the success of its actions in this external area is due to factors which lie beyond the immediate scene. If the personality is distracted by internal interferences arising from excessive self-contemplation, an inauthentic situation arises. It is here that the problem of true and false masks comes up. A false mask develops when we respond too self-consciously to the environment and the people there. When we wear the true social mask, we tax our psychic energies so much that our contemplating self has no time for such inner divisiveness. Instead of watching, doubting, and acting for the benefit of ourselves and others, we are wholly plunged into the social self. Moreover, the seat of consciousness has been transferred to that self, and only the mask can say "I." Meanwhile, the other ego fragments stifle their needs in deference to the demands of the social self. More accurately, these fragments are not visible, since there is no divisive self-contemplation to evoke them. The inner self has ceased to exist except as an awareness of the social self, which consumes our entire psychological life. In other words, self-consciousness is entirely taken up with our external role. In turn, this makes the distinction between interior and exterior worlds unimportant. We have instead a meaningful existence, which is the result of interiorizing the external social condition.

In addition to the true and false masks, we have a third possibility. We may live our existence in reverse: by having an authentic inner life and a false exterior one. In fact, Unamuno might be suspected of having done just that, as we shall see in Part Two on Nietzsche. However, let us disregard this idea now, because the issue of personality involves social validity. What remains, therefore, is the final possibility of having a false exterior life and no inner life at all. In this case, the individual fails to do any of the things necessary for existential plenitude. He neither creates his own role, nor does he contemplate his performance inwardly with a sense of spiritual fulfillment.

Instead, such a man portrays a character that he is unwilling to become in fact. He never finds the "spiritual underground" through which he might meaningfully "penetrate" other people (IX, 842). He is troubled by a vague uneasiness, for he senses the hollowness within, and knows it can be filled only by an unreserved commitment to his role. This is what Unamuno refers to as the difference between playing a part and becoming a person. Only the latter involves living genuinely in psychological and social terms: "Doesn't that uneasiness . . . depend in great measure on one's yearning to escape from oneself, on the terror of facing one's own emptiness? Most of the uneasiness is due to a lack of what we call inner life. And above all, [it is] due to not knowing how to turn exterior life into inner life, not knowing how to appropriate and submerge history into oneself. How few people live, what is called living, a public life! How few live the role which they are called upon to fill there! At most, some desperate ones" (IX, 1017).

We see, then, that the concept of an inner life involves no more than the psychological transformation of a social experience. It can be much more in a religious sense, but in terms of personality it means only this interiorization. The socially formed self turns inward and is embraced by consciousness. This is directly opposed to the notion that we can project an inwardly formed personality upon the social scene. Such a projection, if we think about it, is not possible in any real sense. It is true, of course, that in the splitting of the self the various ego fragments separate to the point where the contemplating self can alienate the social self by objectifying it. But this is no true projection of the social self into the external environment. What does occur, true enough, is a kind of image projection, in which the social self is observed in the outer world. But this is simply an operation of the reflective mechanism. It remains, therefore, for the social self to evolve on its own in the material world. It can then be absorbed into man's psychological world as the undisputed guarantor of his authenticity.

On the surface, it is difficult to accept the idea that a person is no more than the mask he wears. It seems as if Unamuno is judging a superficial effect to be an essential quality ("Tell me what mask you wear and I'll tell you who you are" [V, 929]). However, if we resist this notion, it is because of the pejorative connotation of the word "mask," which Unamuno never intended to imply. This is why he stressed the etymology of the word *persona*, with its eventual synecdochical shift in meaning from object to the entire person. In fact, he even hoped that the concept of a mask might be accepted as a positive value, and he praised "the festival of the mask, the *persona* of the Latins, noble ancestry and heritage of our overburdened personality."

Unamuno's interest in the mask parallels the use made of this theme by modern art. Just as the latter has dramatized the idea that facelessness means absurdity, so too did Unamuno conceive of the mask as a cover for a face without features and a life without meaning. He believed that man restores sense to his existence by becoming a player within a comedy or tragedy, and that he measures his own value according to the value of the play. The play, then, is extremely important, especially because it takes place in an otherwise meaningless universe. Indeed, it is well to ask with Unamuno: "In the final analysis, are we really worth more than the role we play in the mummery of the world? I *am* my mask . . ." (V, 929). Thus, the comedy would ring false if there were no integrity between the mask and its bearer, if the mask, when removed, did not lay bare a faceless mannikin's head.

However, the play would also be invalid if the mask were inauthentic, simply a disguise for the real mask that we ordinarily call "face." Actually, Unamuno establishes three distinct categories. First, there is the man without personality, who is faceless. Then, we have the man who has acquired a personality and whose face is the mask he wears. This is the authentic condition that we have been describing. And finally, there is the man who conceals his personality by wearing a false mask over the real one. Clearly, some masks are damnable and others not. In fact, we may even speak of a natural mask, and Unamuno does just that. What he means is that as we grow more proficient in the role that we are genuinely willing to live, the gestures involved in this role become integral to our nature. Instead of remaining just habitual motions, they are assimilated into a life style. Thus, our mask is successfully grafted on like some vital tissue to an incomplete area of the body. And, "when the fleeting expressions are solidified into permanent features, we receive our physiognomy, our natural mask" (V, 929).

Thus, the natural mask is not a paradox when understood in this organic sense. Personality is the psychological analog to the body's physiology, and it is an aftergrowth in our total development. In one sense, it is a cover that masks our emptiness, but more profoundly, it is a natural growth which completes the human being who was but partially formed prior to acquiring a personality.

Unamuno also explained the difference between having and not having a personality-mask by a somewhat humorous reference to folklore. He spoke of the custom of wearing masks in southern Europe, and the fact that this custom is infrequent in the north. In northern countries, he said, people's expressions are blank, and they do not need an additional cover for their feelings; the "impassive face of the northerner is already, in itself, a mask." But Unamuno felt that as southerners, "we must somehow conceal the mobility of our revealing expressions," and that masks came into use in response to that need. On a symbolic level, we may consider these masks to be the social disguises which man employs to conceal his real personality. If there is a discrepancy between the role he plays and his inner self; if, in other words, his consciousness has alienated the social self by judging it to be inauthentic, then his mask is no more than a detachable convenience which hides a more fundamental self.

What, then, can be said about the individual who shows no such discrepancy? The man who has developed an organically integrated personality within himself has, in Unamuno's phrase, a "private and congenital mask." However, most people have not accomplished this, or if they have, they cover it up with a social mask. So effective is the concealment that Unamuno remarked ironically that "in order for an individual to go unrecognized, there is nothing better than to disguise himself as himself." Regardless of what the real self is, the false social role that conceals it becomes so habitual that it is generally accepted as being genuine. Thus, if a man wishes to hide his real feelings, his best recourse is to expose his real self, which will appear so out of character that it will be unrecognized and dismissed. As Unamuno summarized the problem, "I have my *persona*, my private and congenital mask. But in addition, I possess a good selection of false faces and disguises, faked and compromised *personas*" (V, 929).

The preceding statement also poses another problem: Who owns the genuine mask of personality? Our personality is not simply "there," as a bodily member. It must be possessed by a consciousness, from which it is separated reflectively. And this separation obscures the legitimacy of the social self because another self is clearly at work within us, making a similar claim to authenticity. We have already seen one aspect of this problem in reference to the splitting of the self. Now, however, the issue concerns sincerity. If we are aware of acting a part, how can we avoid the accusation of hypocrisy? The answer is, by recognizing that "hypocrisy" is a morally loaded word, and therefore out of place in any discussion about psychology. Admitting this point, Unamuno takes the principle of self-consciousness, isolates it from all moral considerations, and treats it solely as a psychological event. In other words, he bars the use of value judgments in the analysis of personality structure. Thus, he reminds us that "in the beginning, hypocrite meant actor or comedian. Hypocrite is the person who plays a role, except that today we call him this only when he plays it without feeling it" (V, 1191). Why, then, bring in a moral issue? If we are concerned with the mechanisms of role-playing, then we must be attentive to the man's emotional involvement in the role, to whether he "feels" it or not. Inevitably, this means noting the extent to which he is either self-conscious in that role—and therefore detached from it—or swept up in the role—and therefore committed to it. If we evaluate these mental conditions by using the moral terms "hypocrisy" and "sincerity," we exchange psychology for ethics.

This interpretation of social behavior is a drastic innovation. It revolutionizes the idea of social commitment by ignoring the traditional standard of sincerity. For the truth is that "there are hypocrites who profoundly feel the role that they are acting, and who would like to be what they pretend they are." Unamuno is here speaking about himself and about his alter ego Saint Emmanuel the Good, Martyr, in the novel of that name. His purpose is to advance the idea that hypocrisy can be an authentic mode of existence. A man may actually become what he starts out by pretending to be, provided that his social self masters the other fragments that normally divide the self-conscious mind. To do this is to learn that "hypocrisy and personality are twin sisters, if not one and the same thing" (V, 1191). They are, in fact, identical because the persona is the personage played, and this personage is affirmed by the self to be the true personality. In other words, the mechanism of self-consciousness does not exert a divisive influence against the personality. If the actor were self-conscious in his role, he would stand outside the drama proper, pointing, in moral awareness, an accusing finger at his own act. When actor and man are integrated, when his hypocrisy and his personality are "one and the same thing," this does not happen. For then, his moral awareness is eliminated, and all that is left are the personality and its act, which are both located within the dramatic context of the performance.

The elimination of self-consciousness is an important requirement here, and we must see how this comes about. The central event involves a situation in which the individual is so fully committed to his role that his reflective mechanism is not distracted by roles pulling in other directions. For the genuine hypocrite or actor, the field of awareness becomes identical to the field of action. The harmony between consciousness and role-playing occurs both in his own life and as part of the world's total drama. If all the world is a stage, then the "moral" hypocrite is the actor who is not only dedicated to his role, but who has forgotten altogether that it is a role. He knows he must "continue acting until he forgets his part out of sheer knowledge of it" (V, 1193). And his lapse of memory is due to the disappearance of his self-contemplation. His reflective self is no longer absorbed either with itself, with the mechanism of consciousness, or with its own estrangement from other ego fragments. It has turned into a total awareness of the social self, a fact proven by the lack of guilt feelings.

There is much more to be said about the actor and his sincerity, as we will see later on. The point to make now is that role-playing is a prime force in shaping the existential personality. Since "human society is nothing more than a dramatic company—sometimes in verse, sometimes in prose, at times for operetta, at others opera," the differences among social roles are quite varied. But, despite the many kinds of participation in life that people take, all must be classified under the single formula: "the social being is no more than a hypocritical being" (V, 1193). Life must be defined as activity, and the psychological being which undertakes life ("the social being") is called a personality ("a hypocritical being"). The nature of being is, in itself, a larger question, for if Unamuno qualifies it here as "social," he thereby implies other aspects of being which are not active in this way. This is certainly true in the general focus of Unamuno's ontology, but within his theory of personality, there is no being outside of the social self. Only a social field of action will nurture the growth of the genuine psychological being that we call existential man. The realization of the self does not occur in the insubstantial world of an awareness turned inward upon itself. This can only happen "in public, civil, or historical life, the only kind in which personality is active—for in private life only animality or individuality is active" (V, 1193).

We may consider this position to be an orthodox tenet of Unamuno's existentialism as it concerns personality structure, and the way the latter stands in the world. Basically, it means that Unamuno eradicated the distinction between the essential person and the role played before other men. He believed that "personality, what one is, is nothing more than acting. One is simply what others represent him as being" (V, 1192). Since social action is a group participation in which each man plays a role, the role of each is affected and determined by the roles of the others. Even though each man selects the part he wishes to play in his theater group, this part is in large measure already represented for him, because it belongs to the structure of the dramatic production. But once a man accepts his role and plays it authentically, his entire socio-psychological world is fully reintegrated. The phenomenological substance called personality masters the domain of self-awareness. That is, the other selves which originally demanded autonomy in the area of consciousness remain unconcretized fragments, or are reduced to unobtrusive mechanisms. Personality fills the entire experience of the individual. Moreover, its reality underscores the difference between mere existence and being a self. An individual can simply be, but "to be (ser) is not the same as to be oneself (serse). An animal, even a human one, is; a person is himself. To be oneself is essential to the idea of personality" (V, 1192).

The point that Unamuno is trying to make is that human existence does not rise above the animal level unless it has a psychological experience rooted in the drama of social engagement. Consequently, being (ser), in itself, is an attribute of any object as it appears phenomenally in the world. But, being oneself in a meaningful human condition (serse), supposes a psychological state in which the phenomenon of personality is not only in itself but for itself, and for others as well. Man has both a private consciousness and a public mask. But he transcends his private being by a reflective act in which he watches himself project a personality into a social drama. And then he becomes reintegrated by directing his awareness entirely toward that social self, so that he is living for it alone. Yet he is also living for others, since his act is only possible in the presence of other people.

Thus it is said that "to be oneself is to be for oneself, and to be for oneself is to be for others. He who is not for others and who is not [composed of] others within him, he who is lacking in theatricality (*representación*), is not himself and is not for himself, and thus lacks personality" (V, 1192). This idea of "to be for" refers to the individual's emergence from himself in order to become a personality. Furthermore, since this being *for* himself is by definition a social act, it is of necessity a living for others too. Unamuno repeats the point by saying that "the animal that one is does not go beyond being; the *persona* that one is, is himself." And this person is dimensional and concrete, "he is the historic man, the one who acts his part on his stage, in his little world, the one who plays the actor, the hypocrite" (V, 1192).

It is clear, then, that the social personality unifies human experience, and is equivalent to the existential self. But the existential awareness of self that plagues man is the very obstacle preventing the psychological wholeness of that personality. Despite his desire to be fully the character he plays, his other fragmentary selves eventually assert their importance. And so the question "Who is one's self?" has the answer, "He who acts, he who is for others." This means that the perspective from which a personality must be defined requires objectivity. A spectator's point of view would be best, but there are two different kinds of spectators. The first is the man who watches his own act, and the second is his neighbor, who also watches it. However, since the act is social and not private, the more valid judgment of it is made by the second observer, who is already in the social context. The reason for this is the fact that a man acts in order to be socially effective. Therefore, his performance is directed toward others and is best evaluated from their standpoint. This evaluation could be made if the various impressions of a personality held by a number of spectators were fused into one. If that were possible, the "compound and collective representation, with its nimbus of contradictions, would be the self that I am much more so than is the self that I think I am. It would be my historic self, my extrinsic personality, the role that I play in our little world" (V, 1193).

The question of truth does not enter here. The issue is not whether "my extrinsic personality" is more accurately known by myself than by others, but rather that I cannot ever see what others see. They perceive "the self that I am," whereas I see "the self that I think I am." This difference stems from my subjective awareness of myself, which separates me from the reality of phenomena and thus fosters my psychological disintegration. Unamuno states this idea quite plainly, and yet he refuses to accept it without reservation. He is troubled by the fact that his social self is best framed in the perspective of other men. As a result, he claims that even if they have their social "truth," he still retains his subjective "reality." What does it matter that their view "should give rise to the legend about me fashioned by other people? Do I not have my own legend about myself, my *autoleyenda*?" (V, 1193). This statement, in effect, nullifies the absolute value of the social self, and the importance of a unified, single-purposed self. While not a complete turnabout, it is a contradictory position for Unamuno. He was a man torn by his own internal strife, and for this reason preferred the integrated, socially oriented self that we have described. But he also recognized the inevitability of his self-contemplation, and its divisive psychological mechanism. Therefore, he adjusted his notion of personality by judging it according to a relative standard of validity.

It is impossible, then, to establish which self is the real one, or to aspire to any fulfillment of self. The equivocal entity called personality exists as a phenomenon, is interpreted by others and forged into a legend about us, and is contemplated by us as we ourselves make our *autoleyenda*. These three aspects are the main threads in the subtle web of contradictions left by Unamuno in his writings. The first, serving as a reminder that the self is an objective reality, is a constant source of distress as we realize that no one can ever know who he is. The second, legendary self contains two facets. One is a voluntaristic impulse toward the future, in which we elaborate beforehand the performance of the person that we wish to be. The other facet is the mental image of our social projection now, in which the person that we think we are adopts an illusory form. That is, we view our social self in the arena of our own awareness, and we form a private interpretation of the drama enacted by this social self. It is illusory in that we can only imagine it to correspond with what other people see.

But there is a third feature to personality in addition to being a phenomenon and a legendary self. There is also the legend that others have built up around us, and this too is determined by several factors. As spectators, those people offer a perception of our present performance, the expression of which is nothing more than a chronicle of current history. But at the same time, they have an idealization of what our personality is, of how they expect us to behave on the basis of their past knowledge of our actions. This idealization they try to make concrete by means of social coercion. Thus, they obligate us to conform to the image that we have created of ourselves in their minds, an image inspired by the characteristic pattern of our historical actions. There is, in short, "the self that one thinks he is, and the one he wishes to be. But there is [also] the one that others think he is, and the one that they wish him to be. And the latter is his role, which is imposed upon him. Our roles are distributed to us by others. And the duty of each man is to act as well as possible the role given to him in the casting" (V, 1193).

And so we find Unamuno caught in the same existential dilemma which Sartre was later to find so critical. Circumstances force upon him a role which he is free to reject, but which he accepts and considers to be of his own choosing. And yet once he elects to act in the world, he discovers that there can be no knowledge of objective reality, even as far as his own nature is concerned. In that reality there exists a war of wills. On one side are the subjective yearnings of a man who wants to create his own character. Opposing them stands the collective desire of society, which pressures him to aspire to its own ideal. Thus we learn that the drama of personality has a dual authorship. Consequently, we have a series of double standards that have precipitated the modern notion of absurdity.

Existence is absurd because it has fallen under a divided directorship that converts its protagonist into a living contradiction. On the one hand, reality is confused with myth. This happens when we accept the burden imposed by our social role while continuing to nourish the psychological image of ourselves in this role. And on the other hand, history is confused with legend. We fulfill the responsibility of our social self while being unsure of how we interpret the latter, and while remaining just as uncertain of society's view of how our part should be played. Thus, the disintegration of the self is assured not only by *desdoblamiento*, but by incompatible creative tendencies in the private and public domains. In their ultimate effect, they accomplish nothing but the eventual destruction of the personality they set out to create.

In the light of all that Unamuno wrote on this subject, we must regard with sadness, and even with a light cynicism that Unamuno did not intend, the implications inherent in his statement about man's social role. For if it is true, as he argued, that only an integrated self fulfills us as human beings, and that such a self evolves out of the complete psychological and ethical experience of our social role, then it is disturbing to learn that we receive our roles from others. For then, freedom is limited to choice without creativity, and the alienation of our social self from our subjective awareness is a foregone conclusion. This is precisely what happened to Unamuno, who accepted the image which the public yoked him with, and who observed himself living up to, and indeed, living, that role. As a result, he suffered, because his creative will to personality (*autoleyenda*) no longer corresponded to the legend that was being recorded by society.

# 5 SINCERITY AND THE ACTOR

*In discussing* the evolution of the term *persona*, we saw that two separate concepts converged gradually until they fused into one. Theatricality and sociability were each found to be role-playing situations that required the creation of a personality. We saw further that the word hypocrisy referred to the condition of acting out a part by means of this personality, and did not imply a moral judgment of it. Finally, we saw that personality flourished best when there was no psychological division in the consciousness. Nevertheless, Unamuno was, like many other men, incapable of preventing the recurrence of his habitual self-contemplation. He had to face the fact that his personality, his social self, was often nothing more than an actor performing on the stage of his awareness. As a result, the relationship between the social self and the world was no longer more important than the interaction between the social self and consciousness. Quite the contrary, it was necessary to examine the entire question of the actor and his sincerity.

Unamuno's feelings on the matter of hypocrisy are undeniably clear. He rejected social and moral standards for judging the sincerity of an act, and he took instead a psychological measurement. His view was that hypocrisy posed a semantic problem, not a moral one: "I know that hypocrite means actor. Hypocrite? No! My role is my truth and I must live my truth, which is my life" (X, 884). Once we accepted the idea that theatricality is genuine in life, there would be no difficulty in understanding the term "hypocrisy." Although this is a correct assumption to make, it neglects to include other factors. The Unamuno who penned those words was himself an actor playing the role of philosopher. Thus, as we read his statement, we have no assurance of how he felt as he wrote it. In other words, there is no testimony that can speak for his consciousness. His living the role was independent of his writing about it, just as his living it was independent of his contemplative experience of it. Therefore, by revising the term "hypocrisy," Unamuno did more than exclude its customary ethical connotations. He also laid bare the existence of the very part of him that his words ignore: the self that never participated in his life as an actor. In effect, Unamuno's awareness of himself acting was per se a life abstracted from that act. Thus, the phrase "to live my life" means more than just to live "my role [which] is my truth." As seen from our own perspective, which views the entire phenomenon of man and writer, Unamuno misrepresented himself when he declared the actor to be his entire self.

This is the basic fallacy of Unamuno's analysis. However, once it is understood as a technical necessity—that some sort of intelligence must stand apart in the writer in order for his thoughts to be articulated—the revised definition of hypocrisy becomes acceptable. If we think, then, about the motives of a man whose only truth is the role he acts, we may well agree that "the actor can be sincere and full of feeling. . . . for he who acts out a sentiment does so to enliven and maintain it . . . every truly conscious man is playing the part of himself on the stage of his own consciousness" (IX, 1046). This is the proper context in which to discuss the problem. Sincerity is a matter of the player's own awareness, and has nothing to do with us as readers or observers, who see his movements but not his motives. In fact, the entire concept of the actor is removed from the social realm and relocated in a psychological field.

What happens in this relocation is significant. It is the actor who, as an individual, watches himself perform, rather than an individual who watches the actor in him. As a result, the problem of the split self is minimized, if not eliminated. Ordinarily, if the contemplative self were watching the actor, the separation of selves would raise doubts about the authenticity of each. But, when the individual allows the social self to be expressed fully, without the interference of a second, contemplating self, its legitimacy remains unchallenged. In such a case, alienation is not possible, because the social self is the seat of consciousness. It is the actor, then, who is aware of himself as a performer. Furthermore, without self-alienation there can be no accuser and hence no danger of inner moral recriminations. Sincerity becomes a matter of how well the actor can fend off the appearance of an alienated contemplator in his consciousness.

In another sense, sincere acting may be viewed as a state of unconsciousness. Actors are really "unconscious hypocrites. Their whole life is a theater." Just as "the good actor is the one who moves and explains himself in life as he does onstage," so too does the sincere hypocrite place the spectator's gallery right on the platform, abolishing the separation between play-acting and "real" or "sincere" living. What can be said of actors also applies to hypocrites. That is, "they continually live on the stage. And since they know nothing else, it becomes natural to them" (X, 265). But "natural" is not the best term for Unamuno to have used, since it does little to play up his psychological insight. "Sincere" would have been more exact, and for good reasons.

Naturalness is a matter of being faithful to the external world of sense data. For example, a facsimile or reproduction seems natural because its spatial and sensory qualities have no air of make-believe about them. By the same token, we call human behavior "natural" when all traces of artificiality are removed, just as we call theatrical scenes "natural" when the actors' gestures are true-to-life. But, naturalness in man is a purely external matter when compared to its psychological counterpart. The inner form of naturalness is the lack of self-consciousness. That is, a man may appear socially poised and still not be at ease with himself inwardly because he does not feel "natural." Yet this feeling has nothing to do with the natural-ness or precision of his performance, which will convince us any-way. His discomfort arises from the awareness of his condition as an actor instead of as a whole self. He is not conscious of himself as an integrated man but only as an actor. Therefore, he is insincere. There is no correspondence between his inner psychological state and the outer surface. And so, having produced a natural exterior, he fails to experience a sincere inner rapport with it. This is why sincerity cannot be a social or a moral value. The public may be deceived by a perfect simulation of real emotions and even real people. But only the individual knows whether he is authentic or not. Only when he is unaware of acting may he be characterized as being sincere. In such a case, he is an "unconscious hypocrite," as Unamuno phrased it, referring to the fact that there was no self-conscious splitting of the self.

It is interesting to see how ironically Unamuno viewed this psychological dilemma. He described "an actor who received loud applause each time he committed suicide hypocritically on the stage, and the first, only, and last time that he did it theatrically, but truthfully, that is . . . he really killed himself . . . he was jeered" (X, 896–97). Of course, Unamuno was referring to an actor, not to a man's social personality. But the same lessons apply to the latter as well. One thing for us to learn is that spectators are people who are least able to judge either a man's sincerity of purpose or the truthfulness of his acts. And the second lesson is that a man's private or contemplative self cannot intrude upon his social or acting self and be successful in the latter's domain. Thus, the anecdote demonstrates that as long as a man is a complete actor and nothing more, his audience will accept the role because it is enacted for their benefit. But as soon as he dramatizes his private self, they will reject it as unsuitable for public performance. In that event, his error would be to have experienced an inner life different from his social role, and to have transplanted the one to the domain of the other. In the process, he would have disrupted the psychological harmony which, as an actor, he had been presenting to the public.

Unamuno placed the entire question of the actor and his sincerity within the framework of existentialist thought when he declared that "the main source of the most personal of men's misfortunes lies in the contradiction between character and profession" (XI, 320). He tells another story about an actor who is annoyed because the audience applauds him and not the personage that he portrays. The actor explains that he "should like to go unnoticed, so that they don't know that it is me." With each act he tries "to erase myself, to disappear among the characters that I portray, so that no one can see me, or look at me instead of them" (IX, 291). The actor goes so far as to prefer being nameless and without civil status, in order to keep the public from knowing who is playing the role. This curious attitude reflects, by way of parable, the mentality of a man who has not fully submerged himself into his social self.

He senses a discrepancy between his personality and what he professes to be—his profession—and he fails to authenticate either. The situation can apply to any activity, although here the actor's case is an extreme one. The point is that it reminds us of something we usually fail to remember: that at some point everyone withdraws psychologically from his role, and thereby ceases to be committed to it. In Unamuno's terminology, this means that no one is a completely integrated personality, for each of us is capable of the actor's detachment.

But the question remains as to why this actor, named Octavio Robleda, should worry that his audience might see him lurking behind the personage that he is playing on the stage. Why does he confess that "I take so much care in becoming a character in order that my own personality be erased" (IX, 290)? The answer is that he does not want his hidden self, so different from the social one, to be known to others. As long as people know only the exterior personality, they will accept its authenticity. If they suspect, however, that another, concealed self exists, they will begin to doubt the actor's sincerity. So too with men acting in the theater of the world. They are suspect because the private self has always differed from the social personality, and always will. Its position as an observer bars any psychological identification, let alone integration, between the two.

The difficulty for this situation, of course, stems from the reflective mechanism. Many of Unamuno's psychological themes—the Cain myth, the self-devourer, self-envy—are analytical variants of this central problem. Moreover, they often structure the problem according to the pattern of the Octavio Robleda story: namely, an audience trying to discern the man behind the actor. Just as Unamuno had scrutinized the public figure for a self-conscious ego fragment, so too does the audience grow aware of another person disguised behind the actor's role. It grows uneasy in the presence of a disparity which it senses but does not understand. And at the same time, the man behind the actor thinks he must obliterate his private self because it detracts from the public image. However, such an attempt would be futile. Even if he succeeded in projecting a totally successful personality, he would develop a second private self after a state of self-awareness, and the situation would be repeated. As we know, self-conscious man is his own best audience.

Unamuno knew this also, and he reported the fact during his conversation with Robleda: "Now I understand what happens to the audience in your case, and why you arouse in it that undefinable sense of uneasiness and disconcertion. Underneath the tragedy that you are acting we feel that other tragedy . . ." (IX, 290). To which Robleda makes the sad and fatal confession, "Which I also act out," acknowledging that even his private self is playing a role. He thus indicates how much of an obstacle consciousness is when the formation of an integrated personality is at stake. It all amounts to the admission that psychological wholeness is virtually impossible. Every man is an actor in part, not for the pleasure of mimetic accomplishment, but for the alleviation of a solemn burden. If he is totally committed to a role, his responsibility is so serious that it cannot allow detachment. Psychological fragmentation is a cardinal sin in the devotional commitment of existentialism. And yet, man grows weary of unrelieved dedication, and his light-hearted impulses take an escapist form through a partial abdication of his role.

However, this partial withdrawal is in no sense a renunciation or betrayal, at least not for Unamuno. Man's abdication is really an awareness that his role *is* a role, and so by observing the fact of his commitment he dissociates himself from it. He adopts an ironic attitude toward himself, a stranger's point of view. As he enjoys the spectacle of his personality at a distance, he eases the strain of a role which he may very well believe in, but which offers him no relief. The actor's bent, therefore, gives him an escape route by converting his life from a serious activity into a dramatic diversion. Let it be noted, however, that the distraction is intended for the private benefit of someone who is already conscious of himself in the world, and in no way detracts from the sobriety of the social self and its role. As such, the spectacle assumes either of two forms. It can be a public exhibition, which is taken seriously by everyone except the contemplating self. Or it can be a personal enactment witnessed in withdrawal, where the contemplating self takes the social self seriously, but remains ironically detached.

The ironic stance and method was summed up by Unamuno when he wrote that "each one of us bears the comedian within him, and woe unto him who must stifle it for want of an audience and a stage! But in any case, he will act for his own benefit. Haven't you ever surprised yourself when alone, doing a comedy for yourself, pretending to be what you are not and would like to be, even if only for a moment, and reciting your role to yourself?" (X, 240). In other words, who is the man without his own technique of diversion, by which he can be aware of himself as an actor and thus lessen the weight of his role? We need not deny that this role is genuine, for it has a valid and active place in real life. But the man himself need not always take it seriously because there are other people who are present to do so while he merely looks on. Or, if he is alone with his comedy, he confers legitimacy upon it by regarding it seriously even while recognizing its theatricality.

We may admit, then, that an ironic pose is a useful means by which to relieve the burden of the authentic social self. How different this stance is from the professional actor's situation can be imagined easily. The latter is completely oblivious of himself as he portrays, or "lives" the part he is acting. The success of his social self hinges upon the total absence of any self-contemplating consciousness. If he wishes to have a perfect stage performance, he must suppress his awareness of himself as an actor. But even though he fails in this suppression, he does not run the same risk of anguish as does the self-conscious man. Indeed, the difference between the two men was wide enough for Unamuno to muse, "How would comedians and actors act if they were to see themselves reflected in a mirror while they were acting? And nevertheless, how many times does one not act to himself!" (IV, 633). The inference is that the actor knows his own identity and forgets about it when immersed in his part. Therefore, if he were confronted with his own mirror image, he would confidently maintain the discrepancy between his private and his public selves. Not so for the man who rehearses his life to himself in the mirror. In such an individual, the unity of his personality has broken down, for he has ceased to be the self that he is watching, in order to become its spectator.

What continued to hold Unamuno's interest, consequently, was this inner enactment, and for more insight into the problem he turned to the psychology of memoir writing. Here, he conceded the possibility that the self-prober might be sincere in the analysis of feelings, despite the fact that *desdoblamiento* would make this unlikely. Even so, reasoned Unamuno, the need to record those feelings in written form would destroy their intimacy. That is, the author's inner sincerity would turn into a public confession, because in order to communicate his unspoken experiences he would have to objectify them. This would mean, of course, that the "feeling" man would become the observer, the writer in search of the right words, the man who, instead of being conscious of his feelings, is increasingly aware of being their chronicler. Thus, the depth of his emotional life would concern him less than the excellence of his autobiographical talents. His immediate psychological involvement would be with the memoir writer's problems, and not with the man who was going to be chronicled.

For these reasons, Unamuno wrote quite pointedly that "personal diaries are the enemies of genuine intimacy. They kill it. Many a person who has taken to keeping a diary began by noting in it what he felt, and ended by feeling in order to note it down. He would awaken each morning worried about what he would note down in his diary at night. And he did and said nothing that was not for the sake of the diary and in view of it" (IV, 494). The "genuine intimacy" that Unamuno was referring to concerns the authenticity of a self-sufficient awareness. This means that the private self has no need to share its experiences with the outer world. Quite the contrary, for if the self were not self-sufficient, its experiences would arrange themselves into a social profile. In other words, to adopt a critical detachment toward these sentiments, or to exteriorize them, would be to initiate the kind of psychological division mentioned a moment ago, namely, that of the person who rehearses his own life to himself and becomes thereby a spectator to it. This is what the memoir writer does, for he lacks genuine intimacy. Thus, he creates for his readers a patently inauthentic image, since the self depicted in his pages leads an emotional life that is designed with an eye toward the audience. Even if his feelings were, at first, genuinely experienced, they are converted into a performance by the diary keeper, whose critical and detached position while writing anticipates a similar attitude by his public.

But there was another factor in the memoir writer's condition that caused Unamuno to suspect his truthfulness. Even if the self-prober were sincere in his feelings, he might fear that the audience would doubt him, or misunderstand his intentions. Supposing he contradicted himself, or showed himself to be inconsistent or unpredictable, would they not be suspicious of his motivation? And wouldn't the writer try to correct this? Therefore, reasoned Unamuno, he must convince the readers of his sincerity, and he would do this by being consistent. On this account, his truthfulness is suspect. As a man, the writer wants to communicate the sensibility of his entire personality. But as a writer, he knows that his contemplating self is not experiencing the feelings within that sensibility. And yet in the diary, he conceals this inner contradiction for the sake of external consistency. The diary always reveals the man, seldom the writer, and never the confessed contemplator admitting to his detachment.

For this reason, Unamuno always distrusted diaries and their apparent consistency. The writer cannot be consistent and self-conscious at the same time. Awareness of the self implies self-contradiction. Indeed, the splitting of the self due to self-contemplation is nothing more than a state of contradictory psychological positions. Thus, if the writer communicates a sense of consistency, he is not being sincere, because he gives no indication of his inner division. On the other hand, if he were to expose the contradiction, he would invite misunderstanding, since he would be admitting to having sentiments and being detached from them at the same time. As a result, he would be forced to renounce those feelings as inauthentic, because they belong to an objectified, hence alienated, self. In turn, this would defeat the whole purpose of the diary, which was to describe the very feelings now unfelt. This is obviously an absurd situation for the man, who wants to convey his true sentiments, and for the author, who wants to write about them. And so they disguise his self-conscious feelings in such a way—deliberately or without realizing it—that the diary sounds sincere.

As a result of this reasoning, Unamuno knew that there was no way of learning the degree to which the writer had manipulated the description of his sentiments. To this issue he addressed the following remarks: "[It is] the duty of sincerity which orders us to watch over and conceal the viscera of our souls. For if we were to lay them bare, the other people would see them as they are not, and we would thus be liars. He who says 'yes,' knowing that he will be understood as saying 'no,' is lying, even though the 'yes' is the truth. One must, it is true, keep one's soul bare; but this does not mean having it torn in shreds from top to bottom. The more sincere a soul is, the more zealously it guards and shelters the mysteries of its life" (III, 1031). If we could know the man's feelings prior to the splitting of the self, there would be no problem. Indeed, if we could know both these feelings and those of the self-contemplator as well, there would still be no problem. But the diary keeper changes feelings into scenarios. How can he confess this publicly and still claim validity for his diary? Would we not discredit its confessions as theatricality? And yet for *him,* those feelings were once very genuine. The best thing for him to do, therefore, is to avoid mentioning the reflective mechanism altogether. It is better to "conceal the viscera" of his soul than to expose it and know that it will be misunderstood. This is a greater "duty of sincerity" than it would be to reveal everything and invite certain misunderstanding. He may bare his soul, but he is not required to expose it to vivisection. Thus, by concealing the theatrical activities of his soul—"the mysteries of its life"—he lives an inner insincerity, but guarantees a very sincere communication between the man whose emotions he is trying to convey and the public who is reading the diary. By "lying," he keeps his original sincerity, and this, after all, was the purpose of his writing the memoirs in the first place.

It is clear from Unamuno's second-guessing and inferring the unspoken feeling from the spoken word, that public sincerity was of no psychological use to him. He had to have the entire man before him: the public self and the contemplator; the performer and the hidden spectator; the personage in the diary and the writer. Memoirs were useless in this respect because they kept half of the man hidden, albeit for his self-protection. And this was one more reason for Unamuno to detest them. They placed the diary keeper under a social pressure which was treacherous to both his personality and the inner sincerity of his being. In writing with the public in mind, he had to present himself in what he believed to be a comprehensible manner, while hiding his reflective self. Unamuno regarded this as a submission to intimidation from the outside. It did violence to the man by denying his contradictions and self-alienation. And it did violence to his personality—his social self—by exerting the influence of public opinion upon the actor within the man. As a result, the entire process stunted the growth of the man as an existential whole, because it obliged him to ignore an essential aspect of his psychic structure.

This failure in our ability to communicate our intimate selves even by means of a diary led Unamuno to despair on several occasions. It seemed impossible to perform any act sincerely without being aware of oneself at the same time. If this were really so, he thought, then nothing that we might do or say could be taken seriously. Indeed, Unamuno was so impressed with the theatrical nature of life that he was prompted to say at one point that "the only thing that we all do seriously is to be born." This statement is a grim judgment on the fact that we are unable to be serious except when we are unconscious. The implication is that an action acquires an ironic tinge when it is seen as a spectacle. As our capacity for self-consciousness grows larger, the game element increases with it, until we find that there is no conscious deed which we do not commit hypocritically. Thus, it is reasonable to affirm, as Unamuno did, that "birth is the only serious thing in the life of all men" (IV, 633).

This theory of sincerity, in its most pessimistic terms, holds that "insofar as man speaks, he lies, and insofar as he speaks to himself, that is, insofar as he thinks, knowing that he thinks, he lies to himself" (II, 901). It therefore follows that all thoughts are conceived fraudulently, because whereas their purpose is to speak truthfully, in fact they are insincere utterances. By this logic, any human endeavor involving psychological participation misrepresents what existence is seriously meant to be. Indeed, "there is no truth other than physiological life." Existence is serious when it is sincere, when it is not viewed as a game, and when the ironic perspective is absent. But these conditions can only be met by suppressing the reflective process. This involves the elimination of language, as well as every form of awareness that requires an image or a representation. In short, it means to live in a purely reflex-acting and unconscious state of being. Everything else is a distortion of existence, both in word and in act. "The word was made to exaggerate all our sensations and impressions." Because of this truth, we are "all *personas*, all masks, all comedians. No one suffers or enjoys what he says and expresses. . . . At bottom we are so calm. Just as I am now, acting out my comedy here alone, made up of actor and spectator at the same time" (II, 901).

Unamuno's extreme negativism bespeaks the futility of our attempt to be both sincere and aware at the same time. Grief and joy are sincere only when they are not articulated by consciousness. To contemplate these emotions is to turn them into spectacles and hence to falsify them. This is why the memoir writer cannot be serious when he represents his sorrow by words; his pain was only real up to the threshold of conscious articulation. Everything else is theatrical and insincere, for it will be staged in a psychological setting abstracted from the truth of the original condition. "Physical pain does not kill. The only truth is the physiological man, he who does not speak, who does not lie" (II, 901).

Bearing this in mind, it is evident that the real tragedy of life lies in the impossibility of our sincerely articulating the fact of our existence. And the reason we cannot is that our criterion for sincerity requires us to reduce the definition of genuine life to the barest minimum. But, if this is true, what are we to do with our self-consciousness? Is the most profound and most human aspect of life to be discarded? When faced with the question of his spiritual survival, Unamuno was forced to retreat from his extreme position. Consequently, he looked for a principle by which he could elevate life's conscious phase to a level of significant value. And he found it in the irrevocable fact of human consciousness. Thus, he converted the insincere forms of existence—self-awareness, acting—into justifications and confirmations of life's meaning. The irony is, of course, that this represents a complete reversal in Unamuno's analysis of existence. He began by saying that only the unconscious and physiological situations are the "true" ones, whereas representations of the latter are "false." But he ends by pronouncing these conscious states to be valid as well. In other words, hypocrisy ceases to have any moral weight in evaluating existence. Instead, the fictional quality of our conscious activities is recognized as an inherent part of the human condition, and it is this which validates our behavior. For Unamuno, the only moral precept that binds us in this area is the one that exhorts us to live consciously. Thus, we make our lives meaningful, and therefore "true," by the cultivation of their "false" elements. As Unamuno says, "I am a myth that I am making for myself day by day. . . . And my work is myth-making, to make and become myself in terms of myth" (X, 512). Since man is basically a conscious being, sincerity may not count as a value when judging life. On the contrary, what is peculiarly human is just this consciousness. If the latter produces fictional situations, then the resulting existential level is high enough in value to justify the new moral imperative.

Here, then, we have the concept of "making" the self through the creative process of myth and legend. The result, paradoxically enough, is a real or "true" self. It does not matter whether the myth of personality exists as a fictional creation in the minds of others or in our own minds. In either case it is the product of conscious activity which accepts the premise that personality is concretized by a course of action and purpose. The injunction, "Know your work and carry it to completion" is the key to self-realization, because "to know one's own work is to know oneself" (XI, 330). Our work is the making of our myth, and our myth is our personality.

The best illustration of this idea can be seen in the public figure. His myth is made in society, and his "work" consists of developing his social self fully, the creation of which is in fact a myth. But the source of his creativity is his own consciousness, and if he draws nothing from this, his myth will be inauthentic. Thus, he must strive to heed the counsel, "Learn to become what you are." The nature of the "what you are" is not a preformed personality, but the substance of creativity in his own consciousness. A man's tragedy, therefore, is "to become what one is not, to act the part for which one has not been born, to produce oneself from the emptiness of self" (X, 579). In other words, such a man fails to allow his self-awareness to determine the direction of his myth-making. Instead, he goes to a source outside of himself, and, due to his spiritual vacuum, creates from nothing a personality that is inauthentic. To be sure, we may call the "true" self fictional, and therefore no better. But at least it is a product of the psychological labor which we plan on the stage of our own awareness, and which unfolds constantly throughout the years.

# 6 THE STRUCTURE
# OF THE SELF

## The Other

Up to now, our definition of the self has been implicit rather than formally stated. I have used the term to designate the entire complex of conditions, roles, and mechanisms belonging to the psychological life of man. This includes his sense of identity, his personality, and the way he uses his consciousness in order to say "I." A tacit or working definition of this kind was best suited for our discussion of Unamuno's thought because it is neither doctrinaire nor vague. On the other hand, it has led us in one direction only: toward an analysis of psychological processes and the values associated with these processes. Such an analysis is indispensable for understanding Unamuno's philosophy, but it does leave certain areas unexplored. Our task now, therefore, is to turn back to the fragments of the self as they emerge from the process of self-contemplation, and to see how each one develops. All of them have psychic experiences of such a nature that Unamuno chose to call them "selves" (*yos*) even though they are manifested in one and the same man. For this reason, I will speak of a structure of the self, in which various ego fragments distinguish themselves and sometimes claim autonomy. But these fragmentary selves belong to the same psychic entity that we normally call "self" in ordinary parlance.

Perhaps the best way to begin is by considering the self in relation to what it is not: to non-self. This involves the concept of the Other, which occupies a dualistic position in Unamuno's psychology. It can be described by moral categories or by psychological ones, and it functions in part by antithesis. The Other has its origin in the process of alienation, which, let us recall, takes place during the last phase of the splitting of the self. As the individual contemplates himself, he grows detached, and begins to regard the self as if it were an Other. Furthermore, he extends this awareness to the realm of moral qualities. Then he spans the gap between his own self, seen as an object, and another object—the self of his neighbor. Thus, his awareness is not only psychological but ethical as well, since it includes the relationship between himself and a different Other, namely, his neighbor. Consequently, the Other illustrates both Unamuno's psychological approach to ethics, and his theory of personality structure too (III, 883).

As we saw earlier, an act may be judged to be insincere if our self-consciousness turns us into detached spectators. This state of detachment, in turn, causes our "selfness" to be reduced. In other words, the man who remains unaware of himself and of others can never be alienated, and will thus preserve his full self. And again, the man most fully himself is the one who has no reflective mechanism. However, this condition keeps the individual sealed within his shell, unable to escape his subjectivity. His absorption within himself is so complete that there is no way for him to lose part of himself by self-contemplation. "The man with absorbent individuality hardly notices anyone else, and he who does not notice others does not notice himself either." This is what Unamuno called fullness-of-self, a situation in which the individual is so "filled with himself" that no part of that self can be displaced (V, 379–80). Since it is not a contemplative state, there is no subject-object structuring within it. On the other hand, as soon as consciousness begins to operate reflexively, the loss of self is immediate. Part of the self is objectified, and this fragment is either alienated or estranged from the rest of the ego. The objectified fragment is now called an Other, and, furthermore, becomes a *possession* of the self. It loses its subjective relationship to the self and is now an object.

Unamuno's purpose in describing this alienation is to show how inevitable the presence of the Other must be. As soon as a man

exteriorizes himself socially or in self-contemplation, he becomes a
possession of himself. Whether he "has to use his body or other
bodies, he remains bound to their rigid laws. He is a slave." He is
tied to the conditions and qualities of these objects, including the
Other, which is one more object. Thus, even when they are his
possessions they are never fully his, in the sense of being integrated
into his plenitude of self. " 'My acts'—he thinks—'are never exclusively mine . . .' And he adds: 'In fact, even I, am I my own
self?' " (III, 705). We would normally expect, of course, that if we
entered into a subject-object relationship we would possess the
object and yet acknowledge that it had its own independence as an
object. But by the same token, we cannot imagine that a self can be
objectified, achieve an independent state, and still belong to us.
This is why Unamuno asks, "Am I my own self?" The alienated
self is still in fact his own, but not in the old subjective way. It has
lost its identity with the subject, Unamuno, who in turn does not
recognize it as a former ego fragment. He can no longer feel his
consciousness through it, as he does by means of his subjective self.
In short, the alienated self is unidentifiable with the self's subjectivity. Therefore, since selfness means subjectiveness, this other self
must indeed be an Other.

Thus, the Other emerges from the initial fact that "each man is
nothing else [to himself] but his own [immediate and] first neighbor" (III, 195). But the effect is to make the man feel depersonalized. Part of his identity is transformed into something which is
perceived by, but no longer partakes of, his consciousness. If we
pause to think about it for a moment, this is a pathetic situation.
The man's private efforts to know himself, and his public acts in
society, cause him to objectify part of the self, but in doing so he is
forced to surrender it. Unamuno saw this situation in terms of a
"tragic battle" between himself and the external world: he struggling to personalize it, and to avoid being depersonalized by it in
turn. In psychological terms, this means that he is trying to preserve
the unity of his consciousness while acting in the world, and at the
same time not be affected by the objective nature of that world.
This, of course, is impossible, unless he wants to avoid all action
and awareness completely. What happens, therefore, is that "whatever I say, write and do, I must do by means of the world. And so
it immediately depersonalizes these things and makes them its own,

and I appear as another person which I am not" (III, 706). Hence, the Other is two things: a psychological product of alienation, and the social alter ego which the individual uses in order to participate in the world. But since activity is an external form, the Other loses its identity with the originally integrated self. And since Unamuno cannot be conscious within this objective self, it must appear to him to be an Other.

Unamuno's concept of the Other is linked to existential awareness, and his intuited experience of the Other is anguish. He feared depersonalization because it meant ceasing to be what he had been in order to become someone else. This loss of self was conceived as an ontological loss, since his being would be nullified and supplanted by another being. In other words, to change is tantamount to losing one's being altogether, because one ceases to be what he is. For Unamuno, "to become an Other, breaking the unity and continuity of my life, is to stop being what I am. That is, it is simply to stop being. And this, never" (XVI, 137; cf. II, 1090).

The problem is expressed dramatically in the novel *Abel Sánchez*, where Joaquín reveals a strange psychic fragmentation. In him are found all the ramifications of the alienation theme, including the fact that it is an involuntary condition. His remarks are also helpful to us in forming clearer definitions. The Other is that ego fragment which, free of volitional stricture, is the least likely to be viewed as originating in the self. It appears in the last phase of depersonalization, where an intimate segment of the ego is lost through the inability or the unwillingness of the individual to recognize its source. The Other represents an alternative personality, either a different self for which the individual strives, or the result of an ego transformation. Joaquín refers to both types in a conversation with his daughter: " 'Does it please you to hear me say that I will be someone else?' . . . 'Yes, papa, it pleases me.' 'That is, the other, the other, the one that I am, seems bad to you?' " (II, 1095). The "other" person, "the one that I am," is Joaquín the hater, a man whom Joaquín does not recognize as his true self because his moral (i.e., conscious) self resists the idea. His plan to "be someone else" nevertheless confirms his acceptance of "the other, the one that I am" as a reality, although not his original self. The change he proposes ("I will be someone else") is not a conversion to non-hater, but a reversion to what he believes was an original, non-hating Joaquín.

But our hero compounds the significance of the Other with extra-personal associations. The companion to his anguish is "the constant presence of the other, of Abel, in his spirit," a presence inseparable from "the sick, sad awareness which came to him" (II, 1068). The interdependence of Abel "the other" and Joaquín's awareness of him turns into an ambiguous identity of the two. The Other becomes an irrational replacement for the anguished, conscious self: ". . . in solitude, he never succeeded in being alone, for the other one was always there. The other one! He began to surprise himself in dialog with him, inventing what the other said to him . . . in those solitary dialogs, in those monologs in dialog form" (II, 1068–69). With the ambiguity of the Other comes a confusion in its perception: Does Joaquín hold a mental dialog with another person or a monodialog with himself? The question is futile, since Joaquín incorporates Abel into his own awareness, fusing Abel "the other" with the self as Other. In fact, the use of the Cain-Abel myth reinforces the ambiguity, because in Unamuno's own mind the brothers' roles are reversible. And each of us reveals the characteristics of both men in equal proportion.

The resolution of Joaquín's personality dilemma is precipitated by his identification with Abel, which follows his wish to be envied by the latter: "He said to himself later, 'But doesn't this mean that I hate myself, that I envy myself? . . . O Lord, Lord, you said to me, Love thy neighbor as thyself. And I don't love my neighbor, I can't love him, because I don't love myself, I don't know how to love myself, I cannot love myself.' Later, he picked up the Bible and opened it to where it says: 'And Jehovah said to Cain: Where is Abel your brother?' Slowly he closed the book whispering, 'And where am I?'" (II, 1069). Joaquín's discovery that he hates not Abel but himself parallels his replacement of Abel "the other" with the self as Other. This ambiguous identity is also developed in *Tulio Montalbán and Julio Macedo*, although for different effects. There, the theme of fraternal enmity and mistaken selves is illustrated by the myth of Jacob and Esau struggling in their mother's womb (IX, 398 ff.). Unamuno used this Biblical story, as well as the Cain myth, to establish a psychological identity between the hostile brothers. By doing so, he illustrated that we all have traits which we would not easily admit to possessing, but which we would have to acknowledge were we to assume an objective posture before ourselves. This is what happens in Joaquín's case, but since he scarcely recognizes himself with such characteristics, he thinks of them as belonging to another self or person.

Thus, moral and psychological principles become analogs in the analysis of human behavior. The exhortation to love one's neighbor as oneself continues to be a central principle, but it supposes two things: that one knows the neighbor who is to be loved, and that one loves oneself. But the fact is that "since, in spite of the inevitable egoism, we do not love ourselves, neither do we love others" (IV, 403). The burden rests with the individual's own psychic energy, because he must begin with himself before he can deal with the other person. But his relationship to himself has to be characterized by the same kind of intercourse that would take place if he were engaged with his neighbor. He must treat himself as if he were another person, and try to know the "other" self that reveals qualities not previously understood or noticed.

The result of this introspection is an alienated self, an Other which makes it possible for the subject to have an ethical relationship with his neighbor. Thus, the Other has two roles. It is the objective self which we come to know and, hopefully, to love, and it also becomes identified with our neighbor as the Other, by virtue of common moral traits. Consequently, it enables us to fulfill the precept "Love thy neighbor as thyself," a dictum which really has several implications. It suggests, "on the one hand, that one is to love oneself, and precisely in the way that he is to love his neighbor. And on the other hand it implies a 'know thy neighbor as thou knowest thyself,' since without knowledge there can be no love. And how am I to know my neighbor if I do not know myself?" (IX, 839-40).

It is important to remember that the ambiguity of the Other, and especially the identification of the self as Other with the neighbor as Other, is only found in complete form in the Cain-Abel, Jacob-Esau myths. Unamuno used these extremes to explain our own less severe circumstances, where we would normally communicate with each other more readily if we could first communicate with ourselves. Alienation, therefore, may be a final psychic state, but it is also a means for achieving ethical goals ("Therefore, submerge into yourself, in order to be alienated from yourself" [IX, 842]). The dual nature of the Other, consequently, may not apply to most people, but its mythical form serves Unamuno metaphorically to illustrate in its most perfect state the primeval identity of all men with each other.

The idea that all men are brothers and share a common origin proposes an ethical value, but Unamuno corroborated it psychologically. He explained that "when by submerging you enter into yourself, and advance along the dark inner galleries of your soul, you never know when you have left your own spiritual underground and have entered your neighbor's" (IX, 842). By this he meant that the most fundamental human emotions occur with equal frequency in all men ("spiritual underground"), as do the basic psychological mechanisms. The analysis of feelings through the use of these mechanisms ("dark inner galleries") does not vary much from person to person, so that it is an easy transition from our own Other to the Other who is our neighbor. Indeed, in theory, the deeper into the subliminal areas we penetrate, the closer to identity the two Others approach. This explains the confusion in the perception of the Other, which Unamuno described metaphorically by means of the Biblical twin brothers. Passions such as envy, hate, and love are too primitive to be differentiated by personality, and they are precisely the emotions involved in the appearance of the Other.

In contrast to these fundamentals stand our unique characteristics, which may be more exclusive, but which are also more superficial. We are, as Unamuno put it, "somewhat like castles rising, isolated from each other, in the middle of the desert, with paths from some of them to others. . . . But under the earth there are also . . . subterranean galleries through which we can each communicate with the other. And it is easier to enter the most intimate part of the neighboring castle through one of those underpasses than by means of the path" (IX, 839). What Unamuno left unexplained is the reason for wanting to penetrate the personality of our neighbors. One answer, as we learn from his religious works, is the value of Christian love. However, there is always the possibility that man, upon "knowing" himself, will discover the evil within him, and consequently be unable to love himself. How, then, will he be able to love his neighbor? For the fact is that despite Unamuno's statements about love, the myths of fraternal intercourse that he uses for the theme of the Other are torn with strife and evil. The answer is, then, that man is terrified of encountering the Other: both his own, because he cannot face the ugliness of his personality, and the Other who is his neighbor, because the evil he finds there reminds him of his own nature.

Unamuno understood this subtlety very well, and spoke of it in his defense of writers who publicly expose their inner selves. Why, he asked, are these writers accused of being egoists, and why do people protest against them, demanding objectivity? "It is certainly not because these people are bothered by another person's self. What bothers them is their own selves. What happens is that egoists place before us, in the light of our consciousness, not their selves but our own selves, and it is the latter which we do not wish to see. . . . [We] fear our 'selfness and sameness' [*mismidad*]" (IX, 837–38). In other words, if men were only isolated castles and nothing more, the decay of one would not disturb the condition of the other. But the reality is that all the castles share a common foundation, and to see the weakness in one area is to suspect a similar defect closer to home. The appearance of the Other, therefore, is a reminder of our own *mismidad*, the basic emotional substructure which does not change from person to person. The Other tempts us to adopt a reflective position toward ourselves, to alienate ourselves and discover our own Other. But this is too unpleasant in many cases—perhaps not when the capacity to love is present, but certainly when the Cain-Abel, Jacob-Esau condition exists. Consequently, the perception of the Other becomes not only a fact of personality fragmentation, but a symptom of moral evasion and the stimulus for existential anguish as well.

## The Psychochronic Self

Unamuno's analysis of the self does not offer a fixed structure of human personality, although we are trying to delineate its general outlines here. The reason is that his theory describes dynamic traits, rather than a rigid classification of parts or areas of the self. The fact that man is a paradox suffices to make a definition impossible, but, aside from this, man is constantly discovering that his self is never complete until the day he dies. His existence is a process of "becoming," and in the course of living, the self unfolds continually, thereby revealing itself in different phases at progressive moments in time. Thus, Unamuno's structure is more like a set of categories that show the reasons behind the evolving nature of the self. Moreover, Unamuno never really believed in a real and constant self, of the kind that was always there objectively if one could only see it without circumstances getting in the way. Despite his frequent references to "the three Juans," there is no clear description anywhere of "the real Juan, known only to his Maker" (IX, 416). The latter might be the "true" Juan, but he is not the "real" Juan who is seen and felt by others and by himself. In fact, Unamuno renounced the "fictitious and abstract self that sank me into the solitude of my own emptiness" (II, 750). He thought it futile to search for a non-dimensional concept when personality is embodied in a concrete reality bounded by space and time.

This dimension of time by which the self is measured makes temporality the prime factor in tracing and defining personality. Time is the medium through which consciousness functions when we organize two or more perceptions about ourselves. A single perception of self, taking place at a given moment, does not require the measure of time. However, a number of such experiences about the self and its conditions must be charted along temporal co-ordinates. Otherwise, we could not make sense or order out of them. And although the self is only one entity in a variety of conditions, and although self-consciousness is the mechanism used to perceive the self, time is the only vehicle which co-ordinates the self of one condition with the self of another. In other words, temporality provides the self with its continuity. By means of time, we are assured that we are the same now as we were earlier, and as we will be later in other situations.

It is clear, then, that phases of personality will change from moment to moment, and selves will exchange roles from condition to condition. And yet we point confidently to ourselves at every stage, anticipating the future or recalling the past, and we say "I." The question for us, then, is what self can this be that is constantly with us in the midst of change and development? As Unamuno expressed it, "the feeling of personality in the individual man depends before and above anything else on continuity. I feel myself to be I, and not someone else, because I feel myself to be the same one who thirty-nine years ago was a witness to the bombing of his native city, a recollection that serves as the foundation of almost all my later experiences" (VIII, 479). But what does the phrase "I feel myself to be the same one" really mean? Since we do in fact change with the passage of time, our sameness must be our identity. We can identify ourselves by identifying our self. Our self of one moment equals our self of another, not in qualities, but in sameness. Hence, the term *mismidad* has a double meaning: selfness and sameness. The sense of self (identity) is the feeling that we have always been the same person, and this sameness can only be perceived through the sense of continuity which time gives us.

But time is not only the medium used by our consciousness to unite all the temporal selves into a single identity. Time also marks the existential boundary that sets off the real self from all of its possible but unrealized forms. As long as we remain in the atemporal world of potentiality, our nature will consist of a multiplicity of selves. But, by bringing the self into existence, we submit to the rule of time, which demands that we surrender all our possible selves and limit our existential self to a single manifestation. This is what makes Unamuno's position an existentialist one. He was not interested in our *possibility* for self-realization, even though this would define us as essentially multipersonal men. Rather, he stressed the self that we are, and the self that we choose to become. This means that as the future merges into the present, we constantly abandon one self to become another. And yet throughout the duration of life we have a clear sense of our identity, a psychochronic sense, so to speak, which preserves the continuity of self amid all the choices and stages in time.

The psychochronic self is the unity and continuity of our identity in time. If we wish, we can use our memory to go back in search of the other selves which were left behind "at the intersections of the highway of life. For, at each of the crossroads that life presents us with, when we have to choose between one resolution and another affecting our entire future, we renounce one self in order to become another. Each of us bears within him a number of possible men, a multiplicity of destinies, and as we accomplish something, we lose possibilities" (I, 618). Thus, the psychochronic aspect of personality is in one sense reductive. Although it belongs to our psychic nature, it forces us to reduce our possibilities by making us choose from many alternatives. And by this choice, we cut away our nominal selves in order to fulfill a single phenomenological self.

Thus, in the complete temporal framework of existence, what we call identity is the aggregate number of selves which reveal themselves at different moments in our lives. These individual selves may bear little resemblance to one another, but the unifying element shared by all is their link in time to a single consciousness. This identity in time, established by a unifying consciousness, is what I have called the psychochronic self. It is quite different, therefore, from the many selves that arise under different circumstances and in different periods in the life of one individual. The temporal self, or identity, is the seat of our consciousness and is responsible for our psychological continuity. The feelings of sadness or anguish experienced at the sense of loss of the self, or in observing the changes in oneself over the years, are reactions that occur in the psychochronic self. It is this most fundamental "I" which persists in time and makes an identification between the same man and all the vicissitudes suffered by him throughout the years.

In view of this, "to live is to be dying and to be born again. The person that I am today, my self today, buries my self of yesterday, just as my self of tomorrow will bury today's self. The soul is a cemetery wherein lie all our selves that desisted, all those that we were. But we are left with the consolation of dreaming that when our final self arrives, the one in death, all those that we were, angels of our infancy and youth, will hasten to come round our bed to console us in our last solitude" (VII, 827). Existence, in other words, is an acquisition and expenditure of selves. But the loss of a self is not the loss of awareness, nor less the demise of the corporeal entity. On the contrary, the existential self appears to be a vigorous and pervading continuity that survives these lesser births and deaths. There will always be a "self of tomorrow," and even the graveyard of selves is located in some mnemonic region of the soul. The implication is that Unamuno distinguished between the present fact of a self wherever it occurs in time, and, on the other hand, all past selves which are successively replaced by the present self. The assurance that there will always be a "self of tomorrow" is not a guarantee against death, of course, but rather the knowledge that the individual will always retain his identity in the midst of change. His "final self, the one in death" is the final present self in all of its aspects, one which can remember past selves, but which cannot itself be replaced. Man's death, consequently, means the disappearance of the consciousness that resides in his present self.

## The Concrete Self and the Cerebral Self

By looking at the extension of self in time, we were able to understand some things about how consciousness is centered around a unified identity. We also learned how the development of self brings with it a wealth of experiences that keep the self in a state of perpetual transition. Summing this up succinctly, we may say in our best jargon that the psychochronic self tells us much about the homocentricity of consciousness and the heterogeneity of becoming. But it says little about which self is the real one. This question, let us quickly add, is partly a matter of semantic difficulty, and in good measure involves metaphysics as well, an issue which does not concern us here. But by and large, the problem of the "real" or the "true" or the "genuine" self can be approached in several ways. We have already used one of these approaches while considering the question of authenticity. Another approach is to discuss the self as a phenomenon in the general problem of reality, which, quite clearly, will lead us into an ontological corner. Although this might indirectly apply to personality because of certain psychological categories, it would present us with more metaphysical problems than are appropriate for this book. Our best method, therefore, is to assume the reality of the self in the metaphysical sense, and concentrate on the "real" self in the sense of how truly it represents our basic nature.

If we ask how accurately the self is represented, we are assuming that some kind of concrete self exists which can have another representative form. In this light, the basic duality of the self may be seen, for it can be observed either as an entity in itself or as a phenomenon in relation to other people. Unamuno had this distinction in mind when he described Pedro Antonio of *Peace in War* in those terms: "He lost himself in shadow, passed unnoticed, enjoying within his pellicle, like a fish in water, the intimate intensity of a life of work, dark and silent, in the reality of himself and not in the appearance of others" (II, 78). This suggests that the reality of the self is constant, hardly affected by the changing currents around us. The nature of the "others" will vary, along with our relationship to them, but when we are alone we do not alter greatly. Thus, the real self is set apart from the many images that it presents to different people, while our nucleus of permanent qualities remains the same whenever we are alone.

When we become aware of this difference, we try to pinpoint and anchor the self which we consider to be real. Thus, Unamuno exclaims, "My name! Why should I sacrifice my soul to my name? To prolong it in the uproar of fame? No! What I want is to set down my soul in the silence of eternity" (II, 748). Aside from the theological meaning in this statement, there is also the distinction drawn between the real self and the apparent self. Unamuno felt that we all look for a way to demonstrate the self's uniqueness, and to make it stand out in the world. For this purpose, we use names, which serve to separate entities and identify them. But Unamuno regarded names as mere appendages that add nothing to the characteristics of the hard personal core ("my soul"). The self which is known by its name is an apparent self, manifested in time and space, and prolonged in the "uproar of fame." The real self, on the other hand, is the same, unfailing self that we find in solitude and recognize without calling it by name. It is the reality that we wish to preserve eternally.

We discover, then, that names merely identify appearances. Unamuno equates "soul" with reality and "name" with the shadow of reality. This means that a name represents the exterior form of the self which the latter adopts when it appears in the world. The external self is the mortal reflection of the hard personal core, and Unamuno did not want it to overcome his inner substance. Thus, he wrote: ". . . many sacrifice the soul to the name, reality to shadow. No, I do not want my personality, what literary men call personality, to stifle my person." This does not mean that we must question Unamuno's earnestness regarding the importance he attached to the social self. As we saw earlier, personality and authenticity were key values in bringing about a life of fulfillment. But Unamuno then was speaking about the harmony of exterior and interior selves, and the criterion he upheld was that of social validity. Now, however, he is talking about the real self, the self to be perpetuated throughout eternity. Obviously, this cannot mean personality. The issue here is the persistence of consciousness, and the criterion used is immutability.

We may, if we wish, call this one of Unamuno's contradictions. I do not believe that it is, however, because he usually used different standards at different times to talk about the same issue. In this case, the issue is personality against person, or, as I have restated it, apparent self against real self. When the criterion was social meaning and the integration of outer and inner selves, then Unamuno did in fact affirm the value of personality. But now he has shifted his perspective and is concerned with immortality for the self. The criteria are independent. Thus, it would have been inappropriate to speak of a "real" inner self in the context of valid social action. And similarly, we cannot now refer to a "real" social self in the context of eternity unless we want to discuss metaphysics or theology instead of psychology. In psychological terms, there can be no "real" social self—at least not for Unamuno—due to the law of becoming. This law states, as we have seen, that man evolves through a series of present selves, each different from the one preceding it. These selves are, of course, bound to time, and are *authentic* as long as they are functionally valid within their time span. But we can never refer to the *reality* of these social selves without entering into a metaphysical discussion. When Unamuno's criterion is the reality of a self, he is thinking about permanence. If the criterion is the authenticity of a self, he is thinking about becoming. The one involves fixed time, the other involves transitoriness. Consequently, there is no comparison possible between a social self, or a temporal manifestation, and the real self to be immortalized.

If this is so, what is the psychological problem involved in the reality of the "real" self as opposed to its manifestation? The question involves the way in which they are perceived; in other words, the self-conscious basis of perception. Unamuno's idea is that the real self is the "concrete self that breathes, suffers, rejoices, lives," which is to say, not the self which other people can see and touch, but the self which the man himself can feel (II, 748). This is the "untransmittable self," as Unamuno termed it, a self that is neither transferred nor transformed. Above all, it is a self incommunicado from everyone except the subject. The reality of this *yo intrasmisible* is borne out by the fact that it cannot be converted into an image in the awareness of others. It can never be an appearance either, because it is known and perceived by the individual alone. Its reality is subjective, to be sure, but for psychological reasons, not metaphysical ones. And yet the substantiality of this self is a certainty, for it is confirmed by the warmth of the soul in its own embrace. The subject actually feels himself, whereas he cannot feel his apparent self, knowing only that it exists as an image in the minds of others.

From this first opposition of reality and appearance we have a second set of opposites: the "concrete self" and the "cerebral self." The *yo concreto* is real in that it exists in the world, as distinct from the opinion or legend that people form about it. This does not mean, however, that its reality consists of mere corporeality. It is real because it is the hard core of fundamental qualities which we have had all our lives. The concrete self embodies "our intimate being, the one that stems from our deepest bowels, the one which entones the song of purity of our distant boyhood" (II, 748). This "song of purity," although unspecified, implies the innate traits and tendencies that make up the basic stratum of personality before adult roles and awareness are superimposed on it. With this as the hard core, the concrete self takes its place in the world and develops.

Nevertheless, when the concrete self acts in society, it is subject to the interpretations of the people around it, and to our own minds as well. We think of ourselves as being a certain way, and our neighbors imagine us to be something else. Normally, the discrepancy is slight, but it was the principle involved that interested Unamuno, not the degree of variance. Thus, he fought against losing the concrete self: "I don't want to sacrifice it to the idea that I have of myself, myself converted into an abstract ideal, that cerebral self which enslaves us" (II, 748). The enslavement that troubled Unamuno is due to the tendency to impose an abstraction upon the concrete self and transform it. Being conscious of it, our neighbors react by abstracting it from reality and transfixing it into a rigid idealization. This, in turn, exerts a tyrannical influence upon us. Moreover, we ourselves can become our own tyrants. That is, either we try to live up to the image others have of us, or we conform to the ideal image of ourselves that we have made in our own minds. Both decisions are detrimental to the real self, which goes undeveloped.

This need for self-development was just one reason why Unamuno resisted the conceptualization of the self. There was also the factor of the stubbornness of human energy in the face of external pressure. In order to understand this idea, let us take the example of a hypothetical Juan. The notion that I have of Juan's personality will take a specific form, depending on the pattern of behavior that I observe in him. But this notion of Juan tends to regularize the contours of his personality. If he is sensitive to me—and by extension, to public opinion—then he will feel dictated to with regard to conforming with his public image. At least, this is what Unamuno believed. Thus, Juan either acts in order to anticipate what I think of him, or he feels restricted in his own mind by the knowledge that I hold a fixed image of him. If he is like Unamuno in temperament, he will rebel against the restriction which my concept of him represents. Otherwise, he must be denied the absolute freedom of growth which he possesses as an autonomous individual. Not wanting to allow this to happen, he breaks the rigid limitations of an idea with the expansive vitality of his self.

This feeling of surpassing the established limits of the self is one aspect of Unamuno's vitalism which illustrates his strong sense of reality. He conceived of man as more than the definition made about him. Whatever this supplementary element is, however, does not suddenly materialize after the self has been defined. It is there all the time, but becomes visible now because the self is beginning to exceed its definition. After all, an idea about the self can only take into account what the self is up to the moment of the idea's formulation. And yet the self continues to expand beyond that moment, thus destroying the definition. Moreover, the concrete self vibrates with an energy that stirs the individual, whereas the image of this vitality is simply "the reflection of ourselves which the world gives back to us, surrounding us with its thousand mirrors." Reality, therefore, is expansive and without demarcation, but the reflection thereof fixes it at a given moment, without indicating what will develop subsequently. However, development of any kind is endangered by the abstract self, which can paralyze the future growth of the concrete self by confining it to the limits established by the definition. For this reason, Unamuno described the abstract self as a "foreign and superimposed being, nothing more than the idea of us which the others form, an idea which is imposed upon us and finally stifles us" (II, 748). The danger, therefore, is that we might lose contact with reality by conforming to an unreal self, and misdirect our vital powers in the process.

The pernicious influence of the abstract self was not the only source of danger that Unamuno saw. He was also moved to assert that he was "convinced that the external Unamuno will end by suffocating the genuine self" (VII, 553). This is a confusing statement, because it is not clear at first glance what selves he was referring to. The "genuine self," of course, is the real or concrete self whose development has been urged all along. This real self has, as we have seen, an abstract representation that usually misrepresents, a cerebral self in the mind of both the subject and his neighbors. But, at the same time, the real self has several equally real social manifestations. That is, the real or concrete self, which is permanent and constantly evolving, takes many forms in the world as time passes. These social selves are real and authentic, but they are temporary, like individual manifestations in time of a basic, lasting self.

The question remains, however, as to why "the external Unamuno" will stifle the genuine or real self. There is no clear answer, but quite likely the reason is that since this external self will disappear, its particular form ought not to have as much significance as the permanent self. And yet this is exactly what happens, since it is actively engaged in the world, overshadowing the reality within. Be this as it may, the temporary social self is just as genuine or real as the permanent one. Moreover, when compared to the self that appears in the minds of other people, this public self is very real indeed. That is, the self "that is for others and serves them, is not exactly . . . the one that these others forge and set up before us" (IX, 899). And precisely because they are distinct, a new threat appears to the real self, although this time to the temporary one. As Unamuno put it, "that other self, the one that the rest of the people forge for us, is our murderer; it is the murderer of our genuine self. And our genuine public self, not the private one" (IX, 899).

This last observation presents us with still other problems. Unamuno has suggested that the concrete self has two components: the public and the private self. Furthermore, he referred to them as being genuine or true. This must mean that it is possible for untrue selves to exist as well. And in fact, Unamuno believed just that: there is a true and a false public self, and a corresponding true and false private self. All four of these selves exist; they are all perceived by somebody at some time. And they are all offshoots of the original and basic real self. The true public self is the socially instrumental one, prompting other men to react to it. But since it stirs their imaginations as well as their judgment, it moves them to create subjective and hence erroneous images and even legends about its public condition. On the other hand, the true private self is also the victim of an imagination: that of the subject himself. Consequently, the individual has not only a public legend, but a private one as well, both untrue to the original self, both idealizing and distorting it at the same time.

There is little doubt that Unamuno was excessively complicated in devising all of these variants of the concrete and abstract selves. He did, however, simplify matters in one essay when he stated that man "bears as many ideal types as there are neighbors who know him. But it usually happens that they end by fusing into one. . . . The various ideas held about me by Tom, Dick, and Harry . . . consolidate into a single one which is my legend. Aside from the legend which I myself forge of me" (XI, 329–30). From this explanation, we may trace two separate areas of conflict. Each man must deal with other social beings through the offices of his real social self. And yet these people do not, in turn, deal with his real social self, but with their own interpretations of it. And so the man must sometimes compromise by accepting their legend as true, even though this does violence to his true public self. Something similar happens with the man's own image of himself. He has a legend that he wishes to communicate to the world, and his plans of action are bound to this image. Thus, he not only lives a public legend, but tries to live up to the private legend which he has created for himself. Eventually, these two areas enter into conflict, to the detriment of the original basic self.

Here, then, is Unamuno's concept of ego captivity. It states that "Juan just as he is, the primitive and radical Juan, probably lives a captive of the Juan that he thinks he is, but he lives much more a captive of the Juan that the others have forged of him. The many concepts which are forged about each of us by our fellow men who deal with us, fall upon our spirit and end by enveloping it in a kind of shield, in a hard, spiritual dermoskeleton" (III, 1049). This is the famous theory of the three Juans and the three Tomases: the real one known only by God, the one each thinks himself to be, and the ideal one each imagines the other to be (XI, 329; X, 376; IX, 416; VII, 698). This means, in psychological terms, that man's sense of ego-identity is severely weakened by his fiction-creating activity. His own willful legend-making envelops him once, from within, and the legend made by others repeats the process. In effect, the "spiritual dermoskeleton" that shields him thickens as his sense of self becomes uprooted. As he contemplates himself, therefore, he is pulled in different directions, according to the force of the four poles of his character: the true and false private and public selves.

The theory of the three Juans is often mentioned by critics even though Unamuno never analyzed the issue in detail. The problem that it poses is epistemological rather than psychological, but it is the latter which is the more interesting. Briefly stated, the question involved the way that Juan sees himself and how he relates his self-image to the world. Unamuno's terminology is frankly poetic in this respect, yet for all his imprecision he is generally lucid in his thinking about personality. Part of his difficulty is the fact that he must talk about integrating certain transcendental aspects of the self with his total experience. For example, he has to consider first that man transcends himself by means of self-consciousness. Then too, he must remember that the man's legends and social manifestations are also external to his real self. That is, they are products which have transcended the radical self even though they are related to it. These factors are all important in determining the relationship between man and his world. The surface components—legend and social self—maintain contact between the primitive or radical self, which nourishes them, and the real world, which activates them. The problem of co-ordinating all of these elements is what makes up the existentialist dilemma, and the achievement of this co-ordination results in spiritual health.

Thus, while the immediate issue is psychological, the larger question for Unamuno was how to relate personality to spirit. This presented little difficulty because he believed in only one reality, and therefore he could place the concrete self within the realm of spirit. This he did, speaking of "the permanent nucleus of our spirit, what we can properly call our 'self,' what in truth belongs to us and constitutes us." By this remark Unamuno suggested the existence of a basic self and, by inference, a larger nimbus that surrounds it. This more amorphous entity is "a kind of atmosphere that engulfs it, protecting it, and at the same time setting it in relationship with the outer world," which has its own atmosphere. Ordinarily, the self is buffered from the world by the atmosphere that surrounds it. The self's interaction with the world usually does not get more intimate than the contact of these two outer atmospheric surfaces, which, of course, correspond to the mutual action of the public self and its social environment. Nevertheless, there are "holy moments in which the two atmospheres, co-penetrating each other, come to form a single one, that carries in its bosom our permanent 'self' and the world's permanent core with such contact, and which gives us eternal and vivifying truth, the truth of good health" (VII, 479).

I repeat, there is a large measure of poetry in these remarks, and yet the significance of the imagery is for the most part psychological, not religious. The two categories do not always exclude each other in Unamuno, and in this case, in fact, they are probably complementary. We may conclude, therefore, that personality becomes the instrument of spirit in the final state of psychic integration. This means that man has harmonized all the elements of his personality, and then embarks upon more profound spiritual experiences. From here on, Unamuno's discussion enters into ontology and metaphysics, and we need not follow its path. Let us simply note that he had to resolve the personality issue before he could proceed further. Without controlling the marginal components of the self—the legends, the social self—there could be no communication between the outer world and the real permanent self. And since those components transcended both realms, they permitted experiences beyond the immediate situation.

## The Primitive and Radical Self

Now that we have seen the many external and inner forms which the self normally adopts, we may well ask ourselves whether there is any truly fundamental core deep within the self. Unamuno never asked the question in just this way, and consequently we have no statement that we can point to for direct evidence. However, it is not inaccurate or unfair to say that he did suggest the existence of a basic self. In effect, each man has a minimal number of innate and unique qualities which Unamuno called the "primitive and radical self" (III, 1049). This self includes the mechanisms of introspection, plus the basic emotional patterns by which the individual reacts to them. For example, the radical Unamuno consists of his psychochronic awareness, the personal way in which he undergoes the splitting of the self, and his capacity to experience and produce irony and anguish. This self is mainly concerned with acting upon the world, a reality from which it is completely independent. Thus, it develops a self-consciousness, a legend about itself, a social self with which to enact the legend, a legend about this social self, and another social self to live up to this legend.

In this way, the external environment stimulates the growth of personality, causing the resources of the basic self to respond in kind. What it does is to thrust the other fragmentary selves into their various roles, thus transforming both the selves and their actions. Unamuno called this transformation the process of naturalization and spiritualization. That is, "the external environment forms the internal one, by means of a kind of organic condensation. And from the world of external phenomena, consciousness is formed, which reacts upon that world and is expanded therein. There is a constant flux and reflux diffusing between my consciousness and the nature that surrounds me, which is mine too, my nature. In the measure that my spirit is naturalized by saturating itself with external reality, so too do I spiritualize nature by saturating it with inner ideality" (III, 472).

In other words, man and the world exchange qualities with each other as they interact, each affecting the other with his own nature. This transmutation is important because it is not based on a meaningless subject-object relationship. Instead, there is an interlocking series of subjects and objects that shift position according to their roles. And it is this shifting which allows for the intermingling of external reality and inner ideality. For example, the social self is an object with regard to the contemplative self, but it is a subject with regard to the world. By existing as both subject and object at the same time, it provides a link to the general duality of man and nature. Moreover, man is able to identify himself by his awareness of the fact that his various selves—mythical and real, concrete and abstract—are participating in the world while existing independently of it. They are his, and yet they are naturalized by the world; and the world is not his, but it is spiritualized by him.

Let us look more closely at the way in which man confirms his identity in this situation. He first realizes that his fragmentary selves are like objects to him. But then he sees the subjectivity of the relationship between these selves and the world: they are the subjects and the world is an object to them. However, the reverse is also true, namely, that the self is a function of the world, and is transformed by it. Consequently, there is a dynamic interconnection between them. To use Unamuno's direct phrase, "I and the world make each other mutually." This means that the self is more than just the sum of its component ego fragments. The self includes the activity of these fragments *plus* "the flux and reflux diffusing between my consciousness and nature." On the other hand, the objective stance of consciousness makes fragments and nature alike independent objects that stand apart from man. It is here that the primitive and radical self is visible as the primary self. The other objects belong to man, are *his*, and the self they belong to is the radical one.

However, the primitive self is made up of nothing more than consciousness and a set of peculiar responses to the world. Otherwise, there is no self, certainly not an essential self. The fragmentary selves that exist as objects are first simply possessions of the individual: "what is *mine* precedes the *self*. The latter is developed in its own right as a possessor, then as a producer, and finally as a genuine *self*" (III, 472). Man must have this sense of possession before he can develop a sense of identity. He perceives the fact that it is *his* self which is in the world, and then he acquires the feeling of identity with this self. Here, then, is the process by which a self is acquired. We begin with consciousness, then naturalization and possession, and finally, identification.

The existentialist implications of this idea will sound familiar. The contemplative self first achieves a personal sense of itself by recognizing that the selves in the world are possessions. From the "play of mutual actions and reactions stems the consciousness within me of my self, *my self* before it becomes pure and simple I, pure self" (III, 472–73). Without this discovery of a self or selves engaged actively in the environment, the process of personalization fails. In such cases, we are left with a subject-object duality. From the point of view of the contemplating self, the fragmentary selves are in the world. From the latter's standpoint, they belong to us. It is this gap between the private world and the exterior world that must be bridged, and we do so by integrating the selves of both realms into a whole self ("pure self"). This is the meaning of personalization. We recognize a possessive relationship between the contemplative self and the world, including the selves in it. Along with this, there is also a "flux and reflux" that diffuses between consciousness and the environment. We then establish an identification between the self as a subject and the objective selves. Thus it is that "the consciousness of myself is the nucleus of the reciprocal play between my external world and my inner world. The personal emerges from the possessive" (III, 473).

It is, of course, also possible to fail to achieve an integrated self-identification. If the objective selves are alienated for some reason, then a protracted subject-object relationship would occur. The result would be a kind of nominalistic alienation. For example, just as a child first calls himself by his name rather than by the pronoun "I," so too can the adult be separated from himself by naming the self instead of possessing it. He can give it an independent being by calling it by name. Unamuno explains this situation very clearly by reminding us of our own childhood: "Before saying *I*, 'I want to go into the garden,' you probably said, 'Johnny wants to go into the garden,' and in solemn moments you say to yourself, 'Look, John, don't do that, for if you do you are lost.' Some time, when you are alone in front of a mirror, at night and in silence, utter your own name softly to yourself, and it is likely that you will witness the phenomenon of the splitting of the self, which is so frightening and which plunges us into a profound nominalism" (III, 670).

Alienation of the self can be overcome by means of an emotional bond that will somehow include the objective fragments within the subjectivity of the subject. An affective mode must be established, first between subject and object, and then between possessor and the fragmentary self possessed. Unamuno believed that suffering was the most appropriate means for achieving this, since the cry of pain is the best indication of possession: ". . . that cry meant, *my* finger, ouch! *my* finger. And there is just one step from the *my* to the *I*, one step from the possessive to the personal, a step which is accomplished through pain" (II, 465). This attitude of valuing pain is one that we have already met before, and is, of course, part of the pervading sense of anguish that Unamuno saw at the center of human experience.

## The Self-Willed Impulse

In the midst of all these selves and awarenesses, Unamuno singled out one faculty within the radical self that would extricate man from the dilemma of personality: the will. In addition to the three Juans already mentioned, he indicated a fourth: "the one that he wants to be." This concept makes man more than what he is in the world and in his own eyes, and rescues him from the fixed dimension of existence. "The man who is most real, *realis*, most *res*, most a thing, that is, most a cause—only he who acts exists—is the one who wants to be or who wants not to be: the creator" (IX, 418). Life transcends the inert state of things by human causality, by means of an agent who wishes to make events happen. This will to action can also take a personal form, an act of self-creation, or a transformation that we want in spite of reality. Insofar as we are desirous of surpassing our present condition, we may apply creativity to the self. Consequently, "the greatest and the most intimate of the many selves that each of us bears within is the self that each one wants to be, the self of our ambition" (XI, 330).

It is quite apparent that this "greatest" of selves is also the most fictitious and least real, since it is a goal and not a fact. And yet the self-willed impulse, or the wish-fulfilling impulse (*impulso querencioso*), gravitates on life's most basic principle. That is, what is mortal, grows decadent, and existence must be vital and active, rather than inert. Thus, in answer to Don Quixote's claim that "I know who I am," Unamuno admonished, "What you are should matter little to you; uppermost for you is what you want to be. The being that you are is nothing but a decaying and fleeting being . . . the one that you want to be is your idea in God, the Consciousness of the Universe. It is the divine idea of which you are a manifestation in time and space" (IV, 111–12). With this statement, Unamuno overruled everything that he had inferred about personality and psychological mechanisms. Not only did they seem unimportant next to the imperative to "become," but it now appeared useless to have speculated about the nature of the self at all. Nevertheless, we ourselves need not be troubled, for our own analysis has not been invalidated. On the contrary, the self that is willed must also be governed by Unamuno's laws of psychology. In fact, once that self is realized, it will be as useless as any other present self that the will is impelled to transcend.

It is this paradox which contains the heart of Unamuno's philosophy. Man is to be himself and yet he is to keep on becoming. He ought not to allow others to pin him down, and yet he must will himself to be. And by means of his self-willed impulse, he transcends his present condition and links himself to the infinite, and even to the divine. This may sound to some like exalted egoism, but Unamuno was careful to explain that he was an egotist, not an egoist, and he distinguished these terms with subtlety: "The egoist is the one who defends and exalts his interests, his things . . . and the egotist is the one who defends and exalts himself, the self which he is" (IX, 840). We need not be convinced by this, but we should at least note how cleverly Unamuno protected himself at all times. For, in affirming "the self which he is," he guaranteed that every expression of self at every moment would be uniquely his, and his right to affirm. And thereby lies another paradox.

The "self which he is" is more than just the psychological structure that we have been analyzing all along. It also includes the impulse to will another self, and this means change, possibility, and hence contradiction. For Unamuno, the right to behave inconsistently is the most fundamental prerogative. And now that we understand his notion of fragmentary selves, we can see that contradiction is merely the expression of a self whose presence we did not suspect. Indeed, we must add that given the conflicting fragments that constitute a whole self, the only way to restore harmony among them is by paradox. Unless, of course, we wish to stifle our varied impulses. Therefore, paradoxes become cohesive forces that assemble disharmonious elements into one identifiable human condition. They are the things "which defend me. They are the ones which prevent me from ceasing to be myself. And I want to be me" (IX, 708). We can never know the true and real self, since we are always becoming. In fact, as Unamuno asked, "Who will dare tell me that the idea that another person has of me is more exact than the one that I have of myself? The fact is that we are many, various selves, and the ideal self lives on and develops from the actions and reactions among them, the idea which I form of myself influencing the idea that others form of me, and vice versa" (XI, 330).

This may well be begging the issue, but, at the same time, a laminated image of personality is the clearest kind to be expected from a philosopher at war with himself. We must remember how spontaneously Unamuno followed his own advice to "allow them to seek you but not to find you, because the day they find you, you will no longer be you. Always be a hope; in other words, always be an enlightenment (*desengaño*); on the day that you are a memory, you will be a deception. . . . Thus you will be master over others, and thus the others will be masters over you. You owe yourself to them, of course; but you are theirs the most when they least believe it" (IX, 732–33). And thus Unamuno's existential psychology is in the finest tradition of humanism. All the aspects of self have been sharply but singly placed into focus. But the magnitude of personality cannot be drawn into a single frame. The fragmentation theory as an abstract encasement enables all the parts to fit in snugly, but it is shattered as soon as reality inserts the additional element of human freedom.

# PART TWO

# Nietzschean Categories

# 7 UNAMUNO CONTRA NIETZSCHE

[decorative border]

*Unamuno's random* observations on the Nietzschean presence in Spain provide us with an informative mosaic of what the cultural scene was like from 1895 to 1910. It will be much worth our while if we pause to take a careful look at this mosaic, because we will find embedded in it attitudes that can help us to understand what relevance Nietzsche had for Unamuno and his epoch. Moreover, we will have a good opportunity to see how times have and have not changed. French intellectual domination of Spain is said to have waned as the Generation of 1898's Germanophilia grew, but this is a debatable point. At any rate, Unamuno tells how France continued to be the main purveyor of German, English, and Italian ideas for Spain, and how Nietzsche came to be known on the peninsula because he had first been the fashion in France (III, 1095). To Unamuno, Nietzsche was one more French export, sponsored by snobs and dispatched to Spain in defective translations or by means of adaptations and extracts (VIII, 225, 1098, 1111; X, 111; XI, 70). Unamuno was unhappy about Spaniards who believed Paris to be synonymous with the rest of Europe, and who followed the vogues of Parisian *señoritos* by showing off, as they would new clothes, the latest Nietzschean ideas (VIII, 658).

Nevertheless, it was not the German philosopher himself that Unamuno criticized, but the ill effects of his misapplied ideas. He wrote that "poor Nietzsche has been beset by the sad luck of being misunderstood, and he has wreaked genuine havoc, at least among us in Spain, on account of that lack of comprehension" (VII, 803). Nietzsche contributed "more than anyone else to the fact that a number of fools think they are geniuses and figure they have lion-souls, just because they have learned his aphorisms. A legion of simple lambs who, through their herd-like spirit, have left the bulk of the flock" (IV, 851). The movement was, in Unamuno's recollection, "one of several formulas which was used by mental sloth to disguise itself." Among those who were carried away by the "little Nietzschean wind" that blew across Spain were "the most pitiful men, the most bourgeois in the core of their spirit, the most inoffensive, and the most weak"—men who were interested in "one more recipe for producing writings that would seem ingenious and audacious" (VIII, 1098).

If mediocre minds alone had been involved, Unamuno would not have been so troubled, but his frequently expressed concern for the future of Spanish youth made him watchful of possible corrupting influences. He found fault with the young intellectuals of the provinces, whose capricious tastes and lack of solid education led them to Nietzsche, whom they read "in some detestable translation [published] by a cheap, vulgarizing library series." What they should have been doing, he felt, was to labor over a German grammar in order to learn how to read Kant (I, 691). He believed that Nietzsche's popularizers had "tainted no small part of our youths, who have sought support from [Nietzsche] for their unscrupulousness" (IV, 478). The harmful effects could be seen first of all in the poetry of those "little chaps, more or less Arcadian, or more or less superhuman, who rhyme unequal lines in honor of their female companion of a single night" (IV, 613). These poets specialized in rare emotions and delicate artistry, and were identified as either Nietzscheans, anarchists, or *inactuales*, free from the conditions of the present (IV, 645). Their chief defect was a lack of spiritual restlessness; they quarreled among themselves, yet had no critical judgment. And "they gathered around Nietzsche. And everything is falsehood. And what most of them need, is to eat. And after eating, to sleep. And it would be just as well if they never woke up" (V, 863). This picture is distorted by Unamuno's own tastes in poetry, which were never very adventurous, for when he read someone like the traditionalist Rusiñol he would exclaim with rapture, "What balm such poets are after one has read all those Nietzscheans who have sprung up like mushrooms in the sun after a rain!" (V, 605). As early as 1899 he welcomed the appearance of a romantic and sociological novel because it represented a counterbalance to this unhealthy trend, and it seemed to him that "our literature is beginning to become infested with a fake Nietzscheanism, one of posing and affectation" (V, 541).

Nietzsche's popularity among unbelievers and philosophical illiterates also annoyed Unamuno (IV, 850; VIII, 1102), but not as much as the adverse effects which took place in philosophy. In this area the activity was dilettantesque, "with more literature than philosophy, or with a certain scientificist pseudophilosophy and not a scientific one. Spencer is known better than Stuart Mill, and Nietzsche is read more than Kant or Hegel" (IV, 806). Although Unamuno was unable to establish a causal relationship, he attributed the rise of Nietzsche's reputation to a sharp decline in philosophical investigation, due partly to the diversification of interests, and partly to a prevailing ignorance of genuine philosophy (V, 875).

In a related area, Unamuno also lamented the widespread ignorance of Christian thought. Since young men had read nothing about Jesus, they were quick to deny Him, "adhering to the most superficial vulgarities which some Nietzsche might utter in reference to Him" (X, 134). The German's attacks on Christianity gave him his greatest prestige in circles where religious knowledge was judged useless, and where intellectual sloth was termed freedom. "Some dolt who never read the complete Gospel in his life, much less meditated on it, and who stands aghast at studying the masterpieces of Christian spirit, waxes enthusiastic when Christ is called a thief of energy, and His religion a religion of slaves. And with this the poor wretch thinks that he is now released from bondage" (V, 875).

No single man can be credited with having introduced Nietzsche to the Spanish reading public, but Unamuno points to the essayist Maeztu as among those who contributed most to the German's wide acclaim (IV, 478). Yet Unamuno did not extend his esteem for Maeztu to less talented followers of Nietzsche, such as one deceived acquaintance who believed himself "free of all transcendent illusion, when in fact he lived on illusions and phantoms which were suggested to him by that unfortunate poet-dreamer" (IV, 850). On the contrary, these disciples discouraged Unamuno from pursuing an active knowledge of the philosopher, for, just as Unamuno was never deterred from reading an author because of the latter's enemies, so too did he claim that "the writers whom I don't read on account of their admirers is legion. What man of judgment who knows the Nietzscheans here in Spain, and I extend this to France, is going to be moved to read Nietzsche?" (IV, 630). On the contrary, Unamuno predicted a gradual demise of the facile radicalism and studied arrogance of the movement, which he compared to the ridiculous poses of romanticism (IV, 647).

The question of how far Nietzscheanism actually did spread goes unanswered in Unamuno's account, for his estimate varies with the degree of antagonism injected into a given remark. Since his hostility was directed not so much toward Nietzsche as toward an eclectic group of radicals who rallied under a name that epitomized their iconoclasm, the issue of what "Nietzschean" specifically meant becomes confused. Unamuno blurred the distinction still further by classifying "Hellenizers," "neopagans," "anarchists," and "Nietzscheans" as interchangeable subgroups of a category of shallow intellectuals who were trying to be different (IV, 939). As far as the extent of their presence in Spain is concerned, this was never determined. An occasional newspaper editor would exceed what Unamuno thought were the limits of liberalism by disseminating the German's views; but he felt that after a while the public at large would not take these views seriously, and that it would be a matter of waiting for youth to mature and novelty to wear off (IV, 696, 852).

In the meantime, popularized versions of certain ideas were not just misinformed; they were ludicrous distortions out of touch with the reality of Nietzsche's works. There arose, for example, from the many discussions of comparative culture, the myth of the superiority of the Teutonic nations, and Unamuno ridiculed those Spaniards for whom national regeneration meant becoming ferocious Anglo-Saxons: " 'Meat! Lots of blood-dripping meat; this is what we need. Out with the damned chick-pea! We must become carnivorous, like the strong races, the dominating ones! Let us learn from the Anglo-Saxons!' And in this key, the new faithfuls of Zarathustra continue to declaim" (XI, 71). A more serious charge, one still made, held Nietzsche accountable for Germany's militant nationalism. This notion was to gain wide acceptance during the first World War, and while Unamuno wrote consistently in opposition to German militarism—charging it with the moral responsibility for the war—he claimed that "the prophet of this war and of pan-Germanism was Hegel more than Fichte, and much more than Nietzsche" (VII, 356).

Most misconceptions about Nietzsche were due, of course, to the fact that he was not read directly. After all, slogans and key words did condense the meaning of some ideas, which was why they were coined in the first place. The problem was that misunderstandings occurred when writers tried to reconstruct the original ideas from the condensation, without previous knowledge of their context. Even Unamuno availed himself of clichés that either indicated careless thinking on his part, or else cast doubt on how well he knew Nietzsche. For the most part, he knitted a number of commonplaces into his prose with effortless skill, and they served his purpose well. He used them whenever he took a broad cultural position against destructive or nonreligious attitudes, and they expressed blunt anti-Nietzschean sentiment. With obvious indirection, he linked the "nefarious sect" of liberalism with the "leaders of impiety" and "several translated Germans" (II, 674). Upon finding a description of the Spanish character distorted by a dubious philosophical outlook, he complained that "one can see Nietzsche too easily beyond the pages" (V, 560). In the arts, Unamuno's reactionary views could no longer be termed conservative, and his opposition was consistent, whether the target was decadent literature or the "vulgarity" of a particular epoch, yesterday symbolist and estheticist, "today anarchist, Nietzschean" (VIII, 202; IV, 843; X, 361; XI, 822).[1]

If we are to believe his own statements on the matter, the extent of Unamuno's familiarity with Nietzsche's writings was minimal. He insisted that he never read such fashionable authors until they had gone out of style (IV, 630), and he recalled that on first meeting Maeztu the latter "was in the clutches of Nietzsche, with-

---

[1] On a number of occasions Unamuno attributed to Nietzsche the observation that Spain had "dared too much." I have been unable to trace the source of this idea, although it evidently impressed Unamuno a good deal: IV, 1132; V, 73, 102, 266; VII, 715; VIII, 720, 722; XI, 614.

out, I think, knowing him much better than I, who really have never known him very well and always indirectly. And at that time, when Maeztu and I met, I didn't know this Nietzsche in the slightest. Today, a little, but then, not at all" (V, 335). This remark of 1907 was supplemented in 1911, when he wrote that "I know little of Tolstoy . . . of Nietzsche, even less, a little book in French by Lichtenberg [*sic*] and fragments and odd bits" (XI, 168). Two years later he again insisted that "I do not know Nietzsche except for a little book in French by Lichtenberger and some scattered references, and this only recently" (XI, 740). In 1915, he specified that these bits and pieces were quotations cited in books, other long passages, and internal analyses (VIII, 1100).

These denials should suffice for us, and yet Unamuno did communicate a definite Nietzschean impression to his readers. In fact, his contemporaries were quite skeptical of his disavowals. Unamuno himself wrote that "what other people don't know the source of, must be due to the influence of Nietzsche. Even a number of things which I have written have been attributed to a Nietzschean origin" (XI, 740). Nevertheless, Unamuno's public image did reveal Nietzschean qualities. As Maeztu remarked, he was only capable of appreciating tortured and tragic men like Nietzsche and Senancour (V, 337). Similarly, the Basque journalist Salaverría felt that Unamuno wanted to imitate the German but that on finding he could not, he avenged himself with concealed rancor by calling him "poor Nietzsche."[2] Much of this is confirmed by Unamuno's own confession that an essay is "an occasion for pouring out one's soul" and that content is not as important as the pose representing one's emotions at the time. "I say Nietzschean things, I release ideas in order to free myself of them and to give birth to others, although they may be contradictory to the first, to the ones that really occur to me. Is it an attempt to be outrageous, to *épater le bourgeois*? No, it's just that I am this way."[3] These outbursts were temperamentally close to Nietzsche's own emotionalism, and Unamuno recognized this and remembered that he had read similar statements by the German on the subject (IX, 849; X, 77; XI, 175–76, 744).

As for other readings, there is no quantitative standard that will

[2] José María Salaverría, *Retratos* (Madrid, 1926), p. 139.
[3] *Epistolario a Clarín* (Madrid, 1941), p. 103.

determine an influence upon any author. Nor should we desire one. We know that Unamuno could quote Nietzsche, occasionally in the original wording, and quibble about translation (I, 956–57; VIII, 184, 1133). He was also appreciative of the man as a poet (VIII, 1136), and, accurately appraising the philosopher's style, he wrote that "of the little that I know of him in his own language, it appears to me as being a poetic prose, rhythmical, bordering on verse, and not lacking in energy in its short statements" (VIII, 1100). And yet Unamuno explained that he was not interested in Nietzsche because he found him unoriginal (except in expression), exaggerated, and inconsiderate of the feelings of his Christian readers (VIII, 1100). On balance, therefore, I would say that Unamuno read the philosopher perceptively, if sparingly, but became alarmed when the coincidental similarity of their character and style was interpreted as the effect of Nietzsche's influence on him. As a result, he became overdefensive in denying all but a minimum reading knowledge of the German.

What is really important is that Unamuno frequently identified himself with his anguished German colleague. He remembered that they were both professors of Greek, and he wrote that "the matter of Nietzsche's pedantry is very fair. I couldn't miss that pedantry because I am what Nietzsche was, a professor, and moreover, like him, a professor of Greek literature, or if you will, an official Hellenist. Except that it doesn't occur to me to dress up my ideas in Hellenic clothing" (VIII, 1104; IV, 767; IX, 79). Furthermore, he compared his own success with Nietzsche's fame and position in cultural history, thinking of himself as an unjust victim of being Spanish, and believing that his own works would have received their deserved acclamation if Spain had been more Germanic in her nationalistic mission. He wondered "what would be said of a Portuguese Nietzsche, or a Guatemalan, or even a Spanish one? He, Nietzsche, as an individual, was a defeated soul, but he belonged to a people of victors. And rest assured that an enslaved soul gains more in a master people than a master soul in a servile people" (VIII, 1131).

The foregoing comparison, which must have been recurrent in Unamuno's mind if at last he confessed it publicly, supports Salaverría's suggestion that Unamuno was envious, and explains why he might have minimized his familiarity with the philosopher's work.

Yet Unamuno sensed not only rivalry but a certain spiritual kinship with a mind tortured by the limits of reason. He found in Nietzsche his own effort to reconcile reason with life. Once, when Unamuno was told that he was too hostile toward reason, he answered, "yes, the idea of defending reason against my attacks is all right. And if I have attacked it so much—no doubt too much and not always with justice—it has been in order to defend myself against it, for it was attacking me. Because reason is a terrible thing! Nietzsche, whose heart tortured him all his life, could only free himself of it by losing it, by going mad" (VIII, 587). Thus Unamuno realized that they were both trying to exalt what neither had possessed: faith and will (V, 365).

Against this background, Unamuno's character analysis of Nietzsche becomes consistent. His review of the *Letters* reveals his insight into the philosopher, and how perceptively he heard "the Nietzschean whisper, without a trace of the lion's laughing roar" (VIII, 1137). He responded in part to the poet in Nietzsche, what he considered the true poet, slow to be understood and then only to be misunderstood. But looking for the man behind the words, Unamuno recognized him and found the encounter painful, "because a man, not a mere writer, is a mirror, and a mirror obliges us to see ourselves, to see our man—*ecce homo!*—and hear ourselves: and it is so painful to hear oneself!" He seized upon Nietzsche's words about people who talk and write in order not to remain silent, adding that it was probably in order not to hear themselves. Both men vociferated in public to drown out their inner voice of anguish. And both men were like the "professor of pathology who knows that he has cancer, that it is incurable, and who has to teach it in class" (VIII, 1136).

This is why Unamuno could sympathize so fully with "the great isolated" man who, like himself, "felt alone, alone on the top—or in the pit?—of a mountain, without air to breath" (VIII, 1136). As we saw in Part One, Unamuno was accustomed to this kind of solitude, and sought it because it was "necessary to plunge down into all the pits of the soul, even into those with boiling, poisonous slime" (V, 196). And this same intimacy was behind his ambivalent attitude toward the German. He called the latter a hypocrite, noting the discrepancy between *Ecce homo*, and the *Letters*, which unmasked the actor, "the man who invented the lion's laughing roar." But Unamuno also remembered the sound of his own laugh, for it too rang false in his ears.

There are numerous details which give color to Unamuno's mental portrait of Nietzsche. His tone of commiseration in so many passages is too steady to be superficial: "poor," "unfortunate," "great poet," "man of genuine merit," "sublime madman," "tragic bowels," "the no less venerable name of Nietzsche," "the mad lion who emitted sorrowful laughs of desperation" (VIII, 1002). Whenever Unamuno listed the writers whose inner strife engaged his attention, he usually mentioned Nietzsche's name (V, 328), although he pointed out, for example, that he preferred Carducci to the German (IV, 892), or that Amiel was more lyrical and intense (IX, 99). Compassion, however, did not interfere with his criticizing Nietzsche as one of the "systematic detractors of Christianity" (IV, 391), even though the system advocated was a "tragic and voluntaristic philosophy." Unamuno distinguished, therefore, between the man and his ideas, with the result that some statements praise and damn in the same breath: "transcendental egoism, which the unfortunate Nietzsche's genius has carried to imbecility" (VIII, 658).

Another dimension of the portrait has to do with intellect, creative faculties, and specific moral traits. Here, evidently, Unamuno's esteem for Nietzsche was based on having identified himself with the philosopher in several important respects. They were both isolated from the mainstream of history and had, consequently, the opportunity for the kind of "cloistered" meditation which their spiritual withdrawal could inspire. It was in solitude, in "moments of anxious truce, when visions of another world wound the spirit. . . . There are moments . . . of the most profound imaginativeness. It was not at the battleside that Nietzsche's poor, tortured spirit conceived the tragic occurrence of the eternal return" (X, 536). If the fruits of this contemplation were different for the two men, and tended to separate them, they were joined by their common circumstance, spiritual vocation, and artistic imagination. This was why Unamuno could accept in Nietzsche "what most people do not see, his disinterest, his greatness, the really Christian doctrine that lies hidden under the superficial paradox of the superman."[4]

[4] Joan Corominas, "Correspondance entre Unamuno et Corominas," *Bulletin Hispanique*, LXI (1959), 436.

Moreover, both thinkers shared a restlessness which Unamuno attributed to two causes: the lack of resignation in the face of losing individual consciousness, and the conflict between reason and emotion" (V, 328).

It was clear to Unamuno that both he and Nietzsche were helpless in their innermost selves. He realized that just as he had used will as a weapon against anguish, so too did Nietzsche summon the Antichrist for his own battle, but that in reality both of them were trapped by the paradox of their personal lives. According to Unamuno's interpretation, "Zarathustra is the *anti-self* of the unfortunate Nietzsche, who was weak and not a man of prey. Unhappy, sick in body and in spirit all his life, he dreamed of what he was not, of what he could not be" (IX, 78). Thus Unamuno excused him not so much for human failures as for human excellence: the sensitivity to life's tragedy and the imagination to disguise his irrational weakness by a method based on reason. Nietzsche was an "unfortunate poet-dreamer who, in order to defend himself from his inborn and never overcome weakness, invented the sophistry of strength" (IV, 850). It was possible, therefore, for Unamuno to say that "one can still sympathize with Nietzsche's soul, even while abominating his teachings, and have affection and admiration—both children of mercy—for that tortured spirit who lived in perpetual struggle with the Sphinx, until the latter's look consumed his consciousness, robbing him of reason" (IV, 851–52).

There is no doubt, then, that Unamuno was willing to separate the emotions that he and Nietzsche experienced from their intellectual results. In spite of this, however, a certain hardness overcame him when he began to probe with psychological depth. He searched for concealed motives behind Nietzsche's exposed feelings, and unwittingly displayed his own in the process. For just as Unamuno's spiritual identification with Nietzsche influenced his judgment of the latter's emotions, so too did his estimate of the philosopher's motives reflect the hidden motivation behind his own attitudes. Unamuno said, for example, "I have always believed that Nietzsche was a man who was dominated by fear, by the fear of completely dying, a fear that made him invent the idea of the eternal return, and a fear that made him attack Christianity, since he was unsuccessful in being a Christian" (IV, 851). Essentially, this describes how Unamuno dealt with his own fear, except, of course, for the fact that his solution was agonistic faith instead of the eternal return. As for Nietzsche's fear of Christianity, it is not explained by Unamuno, but it is somehow confused with the notion of rancor, as if the fear of an object were by some compensatory mechanism converted into hatred of it. Whatever the process, the contradiction between the original sentiment and its later form was termed hypocrisy by Unamuno. He accused Nietzsche of repressing the genuine state of his spirit—the fear that his "sickly consciousness," his "hypertrophic self," would not persist forever—by professing a joyous love of life which his fear could not allow, and which made his eternal return a "strange and sorrowful fantasy" (VIII, 1104). Since the mainspring of these ineffective devices was the fear of death, Nietzsche presumably turned with hatred against Christianity because it was incapable of helping him.

At this point, Unamuno's ambivalence crystallized. On the one hand, he declared his belief that Nietzsche "always was what he ended by so obviously being, a complete madman" who "suffered among other madnesses . . . envious pride or prideful envy" (VIII, 1102). At the same time, these satanic sins fascinated Unamuno, and he was startled by the boldness with which the German dared to defy God. Nietzsche was envious of Christ, he said, an assumption no doubt true, but made nevertheless on the basis of Unamuno's own knowledge of himself. He too wanted to be God, as did all death-fearing men, and so it was natural that Nietzsche's "Luciferian," "Cainite" characteristic would strike a responsive note ("What a tragic and grandiose envy he had of Christ! And of himself!" [V, 266]).

The idea of the self-envying man—and Unamuno included himself in this category, along with Paul, Augustine, Calvin, and Pascal—merges here with the notion that resentment and self-hatred are finally externalized in the form of hostility toward another object. It is interesting to speculate as to whether Unamuno's admiration and displeasure toward Nietzsche did not stem from his own inability to take the final step of defiance. He might have been speaking of himself when he wrote that the philosopher "was not sure whether other men would come to adore and to deify him. And he dreamed of nothing less than apotheosis. Poor man!" (VIII, 1102). Either out of resentment at Nietzsche's courage, or anger at his own lack of it, Unamuno lashed out at the philosopher's slanders, "for he was a master at them, since he spent his life slandering. He slandered Socrates, just as he slandered Christ, he, who wanted to be a Socrates and a Christ" (IV, 771).

But Unamuno refused to acknowledge that Nietzsche's impiousness was courageous, and by an inverted method of reasoning depicted him as a "poor man mad with weakness," an "antitheologian—which is another way of being a theologian," and "a man too weak to defend and avenge himself against his weakness, [who] began to exalt strength and implacability against the weak" (VIII, 1097, 1102). This evaluation was logical, in that Unamuno started from the premise of hypocrisy and worked backward from Nietzsche's outer show of strength to his inner weakness. But let us not forget that Unamuno also suffered from the discrepancy between his public and private selves. Therefore, since there was no objective evidence to support his character analysis of Nietzsche, it is hard to avoid the conclusion that he was projecting his own conflicts upon the German. The frequency of Unamuno's insistence on certain features in Nietzsche's profile is striking because of their resemblance to the Spaniard himself. And when he referred to "this thinker with so true a theological root, whose irreligiosity is an acute form of religion; this poor spirit tormented by metaphysical and religious anguish, by the frightening problem of individual destiny and immortality," it is hard not to see Unamuno's own spiritual portrait etched alongside of the German's (III, 513).

# 8 THE PSYCHOLOGY
# OF VALUE FORMATION

*Nietzsche once* said that the lonely man is eaten up in crowds by the many, and in solitude by himself (MA, II, #348). This observation summarizes perfectly the psychological problem which obsessed both him and Unamuno throughout their lives. Nietzsche's analysis of this question follows a pattern of existential-ist personality structure that is highly similar to what Unamuno himself outlined. That is, there is first an unexpected moment when man ceases to observe himself in the old subjective way and suddenly sees himself as a stranger who somehow looks familiar ("He who would see himself as he is, must know how to *surprise* himself, torch in hand. For with the mind it is as with the body: whoever is accustomed to look at himself in the glass forgets his ugliness, and only recognizes it again by means of the portrait painter" [WS, #316]). He begins to doubt which his true self is, and asks, "Am I another? Strange am I to Me? / Yet from Me sprung?" (J, II, 757). Then, as the cleavage deepens to where it becomes the spectator-performer duality, the question of authenticity grows more acute, and Nietzsche inquires of himself, "Art thou genuine or art thou only an actor? Art thou a representative of the thing represented, itself? Finally, art thou perhaps simply a copy of an actor?" (G, II, 948). Increasingly, the actor grows more independent of the contemplative self, but he carries out his performance in service to the latter. That is, since the contemplative situation can never repair

131

the personality split, Nietzsche as philosopher concentrates on the "I am" and its anguish, saying that "there are free insolent spirits which would fain conceal and deny that they are at bottom broken, incurable hearts—this is Hamlet's case: and then folly itself can be the mask of an unfortunate and alas! all too certain knowledge" (NCW, II, 1058).

The consequences of this situation follow those that were already described in Part One. That is, character transformation becomes a possibility, because "active, successful natures act, not according to the maxim, 'Know thyself,' but as if always confronted with the command, 'Will a self, so you will become a self'" (MA, II, #366). There is still, however, the philosopher's dilemma of making contradictory statements that are conceived in good faith by his opposing selves. Yet for Nietzsche, this was less a dilemma than an intellectual requirement: "When we have first found ourselves, we must understand how from time to time to *lose* ourselves and then to find ourselves again.—This is true on the assumption that we are thinkers. A thinker finds it a drawback to be tied to one person" (WS, #306). One effect, however, of harboring interchangeable selves is that any given conviction will be undermined by the judgment of another, submerged self. Nietzsche expressed this in words that foreshadow Unamuno's satanic self: "Thou knowest it well: the faint-hearted devil in thee, which would fain fold its arms, and place its hands in its bosom, and take it easier:—this faint-hearted devil persuadeth thee that 'there *is* a God!'" (Z, II, 429). This demon will play whatever ethical role is considered "immoral" at the moment, for its task is to subvert the idea advocated by the rational self. When a nature turns inward, what happens is that, due to social interests, "powerful instincts are prevented from venting themselves outwardly, and strive to survive harmlessly inside in conjunction with the imagination. The need of hostility, cruelty, revenge, and violence is reverted . . . the instincts are thus transformed into demons with whom a fight takes place" (WM, #376).

By instinct, Nietzsche meant anything that comes naturally to the organism and which would ordinarily manifest itself without undue interference from conscious psychological mechanisms. Since he considered instinct good, he must have, and did, view consciousness adversely. He traced human consciousness to the necessity for communication, saying that it "does not properly belong to the individual existence of man, but rather to the social and gregarious nature in him." Thus it followed that "it is only in relation to communal and gregarious utility that it [consciousness] is finely developed; and that consequently each of us, in spite of the best intention of *understanding* himself as individually as possible, and of 'knowing himself,' will always just call into consciousness the non-individual in him, namely, his 'averageness' " (FW, #354).

But consciousness is not only superfluous to the individual's existence as an individual; it perniciously makes him aware of his natural life principles as well. This leads to the appearance of moral scruples, which are *"the coming to consciousness of the values* which guide action." Consciousness betrays a certain morbidness; it is "a sign that the real morality—that of action, is going to the dogs" (WM, #423). Once this condition hardens, all the symptoms of the impurity of action and idea appear: distress, vacillation, hypersensitivity. A morbid nature of this kind is, for Nietzsche, incapable of greatness. Indeed, "genius lies in the instincts; goodness does too. One only acts perfectly when one acts instinctively" (WM, #440). What is necessary is "absolute *innocence* in bearing, word, and passion, a good 'conscience' in falseness." When this purity cannot be achieved, the duality of selves begins to emerge: "It is the sign of a *broken* instinct when man sees the motive force and its 'expression' ('the mask') as separate things—it is a sign of inner contradiction" (WM, #377).

As a result of this structuring of personality, Nietzsche was led to a series of postulates concerning self-knowledge. He declared that he had always felt "an inconquerable distrust of the *possibility* of self-knowledge, which has led me so far as to feel a *contradictio in adjecto* even in the idea of 'direct knowledge' which theorists allow themselves:—this matter of fact is almost the most certain thing I know about myself. There must be a sort of repugnance in me to *believe* anything definite about myself" (J, #281). Based on the impossibility of self-knowledge is the conclusion that "Know thyself!" implies "Cease to be concerned about thyself! become objective!" (J, #80). That is, the fundamental fact to know about oneself is that the self is unknowable, but that it is the means by which one can turn outward to know the world. Hence, while Nietzsche dismissed introspection, he did not rule out psychology, and, indeed, asserted that "we psychologists of the future are not very intent on self-contemplation: we regard it almost as a sign of degeneration when an instrument endeavors 'to know itself.' We are instruments of knowledge and we would fain possess all the precision and ingenuousness of an instrument—consequently we may not analyze or 'know' ourselves" (WM, #426). Nietzsche did not, however, conclude absolutely that the individual may not ultimately know himself, but said rather that his duty is toward the objective world: " 'Know thyself' is the whole of Science. Only when man shall have acquired a knowledge of all things will he be able to know himself. For things are but the boundaries of man" (M, #48).

So much for the "healthy" spirit that overcomes its divisive condition. But there is still the social self that remains, as part of this condition. This social self is the source of anguish for the man who senses the fraudulent nature of his external acts: "The most painful feeling that exists is finding out that we are always taken for something higher than we really are. For we must thereby confess to ourselves, 'There is in you some element of fraud—your speech, your expression, your bearing . . .' and this deceitful something is as necessary as your usual honesty, but constantly destroys its effect and its value" (MA, II, #344). In the case of a public figure, a writer, let us say, the projected image is what others accept as being the true man. When this happens, the writer begins to wonder, as did Unamuno, "whether he must not maintain this phantom of himself for the benefit of his fellowmen" (MA, II, #330). Thus, he becomes victimized by his audience, who accept him as a "whole" man without realizing his inner contradiction. Nietzsche called this the "saddest destiny of a prophet: he has worked twenty years to convince his contemporaries, and succeeds at last, but in the meantime his adversaries have also succeeded—he is no longer convinced of himself" (MA, II, #193).

The foregoing is Nietzsche's concept of personality as found in his writings. We cannot judge the extent to which he suffered from the problem, although Unamuno had his own opinion on the subject. Certainly Nietzsche was able to comprehend the condition in its most acute form, that of the actor as a man. He wrote that "the actor finally reaches such a point that even in the deepest sorrow he cannot cease from thinking about the impression made by his own person and the general scenic effect; for instance, even at the funeral of his child, he will weep over his own sorrow and its expression like one of his own audience" (MA, I, #51). Nietzsche was anxious to eliminate this vexing psychological state not so much for moral reasons or in order to be rid of anguish, but because it was the major obstacle to the kind of spontaneous vitalism which he advocated for the future. The superman, as the embodiment of this type of freedom, would be completely natural in the sense that his actions were to be total, hence, unreflective.

It does not matter whether Unamuno did in fact read the passages just cited. Since he was living the same problem, he could easily recognize its symptoms even from a general reading of Nietzsche. This was what he found irresistible about the philosopher, in contrast to other, perhaps more favored, writers. Unamuno's own work contained a similar analysis of existential psychology, and in passages dealing with Nietzschean themes it is clear that he was aware of the German's central psychological difficulty. Moreover, there were other similarities. Both thinkers spoke of the "psychic need" of freedom which impelled men to release their pent-up ideas by writing. They found the practice of "intellectual continence" to be both injurious and risky, because it would exacerbate the inflamed condition of the mind and the volatile ideas therein (XI, 175–76; FW, #93). Unamuno repeated this idea on other occasions, each time with a new variation. Observing that the unventilated idea stifles both itself and the mind that conceives it, he said that "if one didn't express those ideas, they would rot on him within, embittering his consciousness" (IX, 849). This meant that to free oneself of an idea was also to discharge one's responsibility toward it. By removing the weight of an idea and placing it in the public domain, the thinker nullifies its claim upon him, for the idea then is no longer his. This is particularly important in terms of consciousness (or conscience), since the mind can then shift positions without being embarrassed by thoughts that are neither discarded nor espoused, and yet are still occasionally believed to be valid.

Another psychological problem shared by Unamuno and Nietzsche was the writer's social self, and the extent to which he belonged to his audience more than to himself. Their question was whether the social self was not really an image which the public

created and obliged the writer to cultivate. This was how Unamuno described his own feelings about the matter: "I sit down with
my writing paper, take a pen, and say to myself, Another article!
And in this exclamation there is a kind of bitterness. . . . Another
article with which to be earning one's living, and keeping one's
signature fresh, renewing it in the readers' memory!" (X, 77). He
goes on to speak of Nietzsche, although the point about his need to
remain in the public eye is sufficient for us. There is no doubt that
Unamuno suffered from the duplicities of consciousness. How else
can we explain—to take but one example—his self-righteousness in
affirming: "I hate with all my soul the literary bohemia, which has
among other minor vices, the vice of hypocrisy, of pretending. I
know a literary figure who, without liking wine, began to drink
until he got drunk on it, for no other reason than to maintain his
reputation as a literary figure" (IV, 610); and then the contradiction to the foregoing, when he confessed in an article on writers
and their public: "Some people assert they have never seen me
laugh. And of course I assert that I have never seen myself laugh,
because when I laugh I never look in the mirror. I am afraid of
knowing myself. A question: How would comedians and actors act
if they were to see themselves reflected in a mirror while they were
acting? And nevertheless, how many times does one not act to himself!" (IV, 633).

In a similar vein, just as Nietzsche referred to being devoured by
others when in a crowd, and by himself when alone, so too did
Unamuno think of these operations upon the personality in terms
of the spectacle of the self. However, he complicated the process
by means of self-conscious irony. He added to the alternatives "to
devour or to be devoured" a third possibility, "to devour oneself,"
which, by means of ironic consciousness, was made synonymous
with "to make fun of oneself." Thus, he slyly suggested, "devour
yourself, and since the pleasure of devouring yourself will be confused with and neutralize the pain of being devoured, you will
reach a perfect spiritual equanimity, ataraxia. You will be nothing
more than a mere spectacle for yourself" (II, 968–69).

The point is that self-contemplation eventually adopts an ironic
perspective, and here lies one major difference between the two
philosophers. Nietzsche remained serious, whereas Unamuno cultivated his secret irony. If the terms "good" and "bad" faith were

used, we would have to say that Unamuno acted in bad faith, because he took seriously, in turn or alternately, his contradictory selves, which is to say that he found nothing serious within himself except his irony. Nietzsche, by contrast, acted in good faith, for he intended to overcome the personality split by renouncing all but the unconscious impulse. It is interesting to observe the mechanism which prevented Unamuno from taking the step that would have committed him irrevocably. He had always said that "I bear within me two contradictory principles which fight and destroy each other." He differed from Nietzsche in wishing for Christian principles to triumph, and so he wrote that he would be better as "an implacable debtor or a meek creditor. Meekness, meekness! Everyone celebrates the lion, even the tiger, and makes fun of the poor hare" (II, 715).

Unamuno was intrigued, however, by types such as Lope de Aguirre, whose "diabolical awareness of his evil" placed him beyond the common criminal and within the category of fallen angels (V, 196). By the same token, he was impressed by Nietzsche, whose audacity could not be measured by ordinary means. One is tempted to ask how strongly he envied the German, especially in view of his characterization of Artemio A. Silva. This victim of a self-eating personality ends in a state of moral neutralization, with the springs of action paralyzed by indecision. "Artemio's inner battles were between his man of efficacy and his man of morality, between the egoist and the deist. . . . his cynical self pushed him to the most implacable acts . . . but his other self, which we shall call hypocritical, held him back" (IX, 285). Bearing in mind that Unamuno was an activist, we must consider Artemio an ineffective figure beside a Don Quixote and even a Lope de Aguirre, both transcendental heroes invulnerable to the judgments of traditional values. Similarly, Nietzsche's hero of the future was the individual who could surpass common morality by eliminating the "ethical self," namely, that fragment of the ego whose consciousness evaluates its own actions. Which brings us to the superman, to be discussed later.

Unamuno's skepticism toward philosophy resulted from his having recognized the limitations of reason. Because of this, he was led to adopt extra-logical techniques that were unacceptable to traditional philosophers. In this respect, he and Nietzsche met at the crossroads of modern irrationalism. Unamuno saw in Kantian metaphysics the failure of reason to function in any way except as rationalization: ". . . it would seem as though the idea of metaphysical victory is something like moral triumph, which is never lacking in anyone physically defeated. Remember Nietzsche's idea: 'You must search out your enemy and wage your war, a war for your thoughts! And if your thoughts succumb, your loyalty should nevertheless sing victory' [Z, II, 312]. And that victory sung thus, is metaphysical victory" (XI, 367). According to this interpretation, metaphysics was nothing but man's instrument for justifying himself by affirming a priori the rightness of his behavior regardless of fact. As a result, it was only "natural that the defeated man devise the philosophy of defeat, and the victor that of victory. And it is cruel to make the vanquished accept the victor's philosophy, or the victor accept that of the vanquished" (III, 961). And to this Nietzschean sounding judgment he added elsewhere that "instead of saying 'I want this, and I want it because I want it, without knowing why I want it,' or if he knows why, saying truthfully why he wants it, man invents a lie in order to justify his desire, and he fights for his lie" (III, 1003).

Although Unamuno looked no further than the motives and prejudices behind a philosopher's rational thought, Nietzsche suggested that beyond them lurked instincts which affected the thinking of all philosophers, and, even more profoundly, that it was the unconscious which guided intellectual activity (WM, #423; J, #3; FW, #333). A given philosophy was in itself nothing more than the "confession of its originator, and a species of involuntary and unconscious autobiography" (J, #6). But even if Nietzsche adopted Unamuno's level of analysis, he could say of philosophers that "a prejudiced proposition, idea, or 'suggestion,' which is generally their heart's desire abstracted and refined, is defended by them with arguments sought out after the event. They are all advocates who do not wish to be regarded as such, generally astute defenders, also, of their prejudices, which they dub 'truths,'—and *very* far from having the good taste or the courage which goes so far as to let this be understood" (J, #5). Unamuno was prepared to confess this too—out of sincerity, not courage—and in fact he defended his right to rationalize his feelings. But he was unwilling to take the final step urged by Nietzsche, which would have placed him outside the limits of morality and freed him of the obligations imposed by a self vitally interested in the values that it was rationalizing: *"To recognize untruth as a condition of life:* that is certainly to impugn the traditional ideas of value in a dangerous manner, and a philosophy which ventures to do so, has thereby alone placed itself beyond good and evil" (J, #4).

The reasons for Unamuno's inability to do this are the same ones that prevented him from solving the problem of personality. He could never give up the desire to possess a single self and the sentiments that went with it. It did not matter *which* self, as long as it was a self in which Unamuno truly believed at the time he was composing his essay. Hence his determination to safeguard the right to contradict himself. Nietzsche, on the other hand, did very much "doubt whether a philosopher *can* have 'ultimate and actual' opinions at all; whether behind every cave in him there is not, and must necessarily be, a still deeper cave: an ampler, stranger, richer world beyond the surface, an abyss behind every bottom, beneath every 'foundation.' Every philosophy is a foreground philosophy. . . . Every philosopher also *conceals* a philosophy; every opinion is also a lurking-place, and every word is also a *mask*" (J, #289). Unamuno would have agreed that ultimate opinions were impossible, and even that every word was also a mask. But his particular anguish consisted of the wish that these conditions might not be so. He fought to overcome them, yet always discovered new ideological abysses and deeper caverns of personality, while hoping that one of these would turn out to be sheltering the real and permanent self. Nietzsche, in contrast, placed himself beyond the need to identify himself with a specific position, except, of course, that of standing outside of an ethical framework altogether.

If we further explore the question of various selves and their conflicting ideas, we discover that what invalidates a particular idea is not man's reason but his vital interests. Let us bear in mind the entire anti-rational critique of *The Tragic Sense of Life,* and consider Nietzsche on this point. He argues that something which I formerly held as a truth I might now deem an error. But this error was once as necessary to me as my present truth is now. My former self claimed as true what my new self repudiates, and since I am always another person at successive stages in time, I must necessarily contradict my other positions at every moment (FW, #307). This view undermines the traditional notion of personality as a special set of characteristics that remain relatively consistent. And, indeed, Nietzsche proposed self-transformation, and the relearning of values, thus making it imperative that character be subordinated to the individual's power to reject his former attitudes, and to be distrustful of all that might be fixed in him (FW, #296). By applying this rule to philosophers, Nietzsche discredited all systematizers, and proclaimed that "the will to a system shows a lack of honesty" (G, II, 946). By the same token, those who are able to feel both sides of a dispute, those whose multiple perspectives place them beyond the valuations of good and evil, are most apt to acquire knowledge. Thus, the wisest man would be the one richest in contradictions (WM, #259).

Unamuno came close to this gulf of protean perspectives, but never entered it, although he understood that his self-consciousness was carrying him dangerously near. He had reckless moments of recognition in which he saw that values were amorphous after all, and he shouted, "We must corrode. And we must confound. Above all, confound, confound everything. Confuse dream with waking, fiction with reality, the true with the false. Confuse it in a single mist. The joke which is not corrosive or confusing is worthless" (II, 968). The element of humor or mockery is significant since Unamuno not only admitted his histrionism, but, like Nietzsche, converted the actor's irony into a discursive and analytical method. Even when profoundly serious matters were discussed, this was the technique used. Thus, he said that whenever "the eternal humanity which sleeps in the depths of our spiritual bosom rises to the soul's surface shouting out its yearnings, we either appear mad or we pretend to be so, in order that our heroism be forgiven. Thousands of times a writer uses the artifice of pretending to say in jest what he feels quite seriously" (III, 856). As Nietzsche expressed it, "the philanthropy of the sage sometimes makes him decide to pretend to be excited, enraged, or delighted, so that he may not hurt his surroundings by the coldness and rationality of his true nature." And again, "men of profound thought appear to themselves in intercourse with others like comedians, for in order to be understood they must always simulate superficiality" (MA, II, ##246, 232). As I indicated in another context, Unamuno knew intuitively that Nietzsche was acting, and even called him a rationalist who, by "hypocritically pretending to be merry," invented the eternal return, which was nothing but "a tragicomedy or comitragedy" (XVI, 227, 450).

In less subtle but more identifiable ways, the two men used persuasive stylistic techniques to move their readers. They both employed an imagery based on biological references. Unamuno was fond of shocks, irritations, impressions. He defended passion, word-plays, and paradoxes as worthy of the best tradition: that of Paul, Pascal, and Nietzsche (VII, 433). And he explained that this method arose from two needs: to convince himself as well as others, and to relieve himself of the discomfort of "writer's secretion," the flow of ideas which demanded a written outlet (XI, 744). Nietzsche coincided in these and in similar respects, giving first importance to passion as the intellectual's motivating force (WM, #387), recognizing that the illogical is necessary and often good for man (MA, I, #31), and proposing that the etymological methods of the philologist be employed for philosophical analysis (GM, II, 797). Most decisively, he stated the tragic sentiment of life in Unamunian terms: ". . . how greatly we would like to exchange these [religious] ideas for truths which would be just as healing, pacifying and beneficial as those errors! But there are no such truths; at most philosophy can oppose to them metaphysical appearances (at bottom also untruths). The tragedy consists in the fact that we cannot *believe* those dogmas of religion and metaphysics, if we have strict methods of truth in heart and brain; on the other hand, mankind has, through development, become so delicate, irritable, and suffering, that it has need of the highest means of healing and consolation . . ." (MA, I, #109).

These, then, are the three elements common to both thinkers mentioned thus far: the critiques of philosophy, the techniques of analysis and expression, and the psychological estrangement of the thinker from his thought. But there is a fourth component of Nietzsche's methodology which we must understand in order to identify the specifically Nietzschean character of Unamuno's valuations. This factor can be termed antithetical or inverse reasoning. It consists of making all perspectives reversible, so that a transvaluation of values is achieved. The observer tries to see how things look when they are turned upside down: "It is a matter of arbitrariness with him, and pleasure in arbitrariness, if he now perhaps bestow his favor on what had hitherto a bad repute . . . 'Cannot *all* valuations be reversed? And is good perhaps evil? And God only an invention and artifice of the devil? Is everything, perhaps, radically false? And if we are the deceived, are we not thereby also the deceivers?' " (MA, I, #3).

Nietzsche's basic stratagem, as exemplified in *The Genealogy of Morals*, was to view "healthy" concepts from the standpoint of the sick, and, conversely, to evaluate "decadent" principles from a healthy standpoint (EH, II, 1071). But there were more refined approaches. He also thought by means of antithesis, despite his reputed contempt for dialecticism, and even considered his absolute skepticism as being akin to Plato's teaching of "the reverse" (WM, #409). For Nietzsche, however, this reverse consisted of the ambiguous interpretation of human motives and actions. This had to be done in such a way that we might view a given motive as resulting in any one of a multiplicity of actions, and a given action as being caused by any one of a multiplicity of motives. By this method, traditional moral judgments would be rendered absurd, which was precisely Nietzsche's intention.

Let us take, for example, these two statements: (a) "Whether man conceals his bad qualities and vices, or frankly acknowledges them, his vanity in either case seeks its advantage thereby" (MA, I, #313); and (b) "To have no wish to offend or injure anyone may as well be the sign of a just as of a timid nature" (MA, I, #314). In both instances, the purpose is to establish a motivational basis for the statement. Thus, there is no interest in cause-effect relationships, because their ambiguity makes this sort of judgment meaningless. In (a) there are two equally valid results from a single motive, and in (b) a single result can have two equally valid causes. Although the logic involved here is more subtle, it did not concern Nietzsche. What is important is that these two value analyses indicate his lack of confidence in valuations structured on causality. Instead, he concentrated on the intention of the agent, which means, ultimately, a volitional criterion. It is pointless, therefore, to build a frame of reference arising from the result, because this result is important only insofar as it is a function of the agent's motivation. For the same reason, it is also pointless to go beyond the motivation. In this light, the following aphorism is the most subtle expression of inverse reasoning: "One does not attack a person merely to hurt and conquer him, but perhaps merely to become conscious of one's own strength" (MA, I, #317). The result is morally inconsequential. The action is simply an instrument in the service of the agent, and what remains of significance are the various aspects of volition: purpose, desire, awareness. With this in mind, let us now examine some of Unamuno's value judgments.

# 9 THE ETHICS OF AMBIGUITY

*In discussing* the Nietzschean implications of Unamuno's moral values, we should make it clear from the beginning that his overall value system falls safely within the Judaeo-Christian ethic. There is no doubt that Unamuno would have repudiated Nietzsche's transvaluation if he had been confronted with a choice between it and this tradition. Nevertheless, there are a considerable number of instances where Unamuno makes some dangerous suggestions about value judgments, and these are what I propose to study here, in the light of what has already been said. In doing so, I would point out that the issue here is not to arrive at a comparative analysis of specific values, because this would prove fruitless. Since Unamuno's basic premise is Christian love, there is no common point of departure by which to compare him with Nietzsche. What *is* important, however, is what is characteristically Nietzschean in Unamuno's method, critique, and psychology of moral judgments.

By "characteristically Nietzschean," I mean the operation of a moral revaluation on the basis of human psychology. Whether we read *Beyond Good and Evil, The Genealogy of Morals,* or *The Will to Power,* this same principle is at work. The critique of Christian morals is based on the psychological observation that resentment of the strong by the weak causes values like humility and sacrifice to be treasured. The herd morality of a slave people is motivated by the need for a consolation and compensation against the more powerful. Love, therefore, is not an objective value but a rationalization made law, designed to protect the interests of its legislators. As such, this moral value represents a will to power and an instinct for survival, both as strong and as repressive as any master morality might seek to become. What counted, in Nietzsche's analysis, was not the condemnation of a particular ethic but the importance of transcending all ethics. This is the meaning of transvaluation. Nietzsche opposed utilitarian values as well as Kantian imperatives, Christian tenets as well as Socratic ones, and at the same time he borrowed from them all whatever suited his purpose. In other words, he strove to affirm the self openly, without the veil of a moral creed to hide his motives. His new valuation was nothing more than the psychological dissection of every ethical position.

This, of course, was plenty, and it led to innumerable interpretations in the subsequent history of ideas. Even in Nietzsche, the method was only the beginning, and we have come to credit his ideas much more than his methodology. When we talk about Unamuno, however, it is the Nietzschean psychologizing, and the ruthless probing for motives that we must take into account. Unamuno's fundamental attitude toward ethics was irrational. For him, rationalism in moral philosophy was futile, and if attempted, became absurd. It imposes a rigorous pattern of behavior which conditions the spontaneity of human nature, an inference quite in keeping with Nietzsche's doctrine of instinct. And its worst form, moral theology, forces action into a harness of consistency, with the result that man betrays himself by exchanging sincerity for a consistent appearance. Above all, "ethical intellectualism" is a category external to the structure of man's conduct, and "to be consistent almost always means to be a hypocrite. And this eventually poisons the very wellsprings of inner moral life" (III, 1047). The nature of this inner moral self will be examined below, but if we accept its existence for the moment, we can see that it stands against the cold rational morality of the system-makers.

What Unamuno was suggesting was that two contrary approaches to morality existed. On the one hand was what he called "egoism," a "coldness of heart" which he violently opposed in its major forms: "ethical science" and "monastic morality." The antidote to egoism was "egotism," Unamuno's term for the kind of human behavior that upheld emotional standards over scientific ones. This subjectivism did not, however, rule out the social application of values. Indeed, it refuted the selfish interests of solitude, and with regard to Christian values, it made of "the entire morality of submission and quietism an immense paradox, or rather, a great, tragic piece of nonsense" (XVI, 409). Unamuno wished to judge men by their interaction with other men, and he found it absurd to speak of morality or consistency in isolation.

Nevertheless, Unamuno was concerned with preserving the vigor of the "inner moral life." And yet if each of the interacting selves adhered to its own inner morality, how could this not result in anarchy? Unamuno's answer to this was again a matter of semantics. He distinguished between anarchism and panarchism, favoring the latter as the proper ethic to embrace. Panarchism converted the Christian ethic from an inhibitory code to an individually aggressive morality that stopped just short of anarchistic freedom of action. If utter license and anarchy were odious, so too was abject submissiveness. Unamuno rejected the idea of "neither God nor master," but he did substitute the concept "everyone gods and masters all, everyone striving to become divine, to become immortal. And for this purpose, dominating others" (XVI, 407). In other words, anarchy was indeed godlessness for Unamuno, but when it is suppressed by Christianity, the latter turns into something just as bad. Rather than allowing Christianity to incur the contempt of a slave morality, Unamuno argued for panarchism. It was better to encourage everyone to dominate, or at least to try, as long as this effort represented a struggle for divinity and immortalization. Of course, this unorthodox view of Christian ideals raises the question of how moral it is to impose the self, and I will come to this problem in a moment. The point now is that even within a Christian framework, value judgments are made to appear untenable when they are absolute or rationalistic. And this was because such judgments have little bearing on the private needs of the individual human being.

The irrationalism characterizing Unamuno's approach to valuation led to a methodology that dispensed with logic in favor of antithesis. By ignoring the conventional search for an unequivocal idea or answer to an issue, Unamuno allowed himself to entertain antithetical or even paradoxical statements in which both elements were recognized as true. For example, if he constructed a polarity between Tolstoy's morality of renunciation and Nietzsche's imperative to strive, he saw no need to resolve the opposites or to synthesize them. He simply set them side by side with the explanation that life itself "is woven with antitheses and antinomies." Thus, "one can profess and even practice two moralities—two? is there more than one?—at the same time, and strive by resigning oneself and resign oneself by striving" (XI, 169).

This technique of viewing a situation as a composite of opposing positions was modified when Unamuno dealt with moral judgments. Here, he held that an entity is only knowable by its antithesis, or at least by the cause which precedes it. An act, for example, is said to be a sin because a law exists which prohibits it. The act in itself is neutral; what makes it sinful is the prohibition. A case in point is a scene in the novel *Peace in War*, where Pérez "did not know of sin except by means of the law. He would not have known liberalism if the law had not said: liberalism is a sin. Sin, taking its opportunity from commandments, renewed in him his blood's rebelliousness, because without the law the sin would not live. Juan Pérez lived without law for some time, but when the commandment came, sin revived . . ." (II, 676–77). A sin, therefore, even a political sin, is not a quality of the act. It is an independent judgment about that act. Moreover, the sin's existence can only be determined by the prohibition that forbids it to exist. This prohibitional factor, while not exactly an opposing quality, is close enough to it to be considered antithetical at least as far as method is concerned. As for the blood's rebelliousness, it is identical to the "inner moral life," a concept that will require our attention again in another context.

The same technique of opposites produces some disturbing results when applied to a proposition that states only one of the two antithetical elements. This kind of statement takes a clear-cut ethical position, and is not meant to be ambiguous or to suggest the opposite view. And yet Unamuno infers this antithesis by reading into the statement and assuming contrary motivations. Thus, he undermines the validity of the judgment or of the position adopted. A good illustration of this method occurs in *Abel Sánchez*, where Joaquín's maid receives his violent blasphemy with Christian humility. Joaquín judges her refusal to react in kind not as a virtue, but as arrogance, and when the maid denies this, he shouts, "Do you see? It is the hypocritical arrogance of not recognizing it. She is practicing exercises in humility and patience at my expense. She is taking my fits of ill-humor as a hair shirt to exercise the virtue of patience." If we analyze the maid's situation, we find that there is only one visible position: the act of humility. The moral judgment of this humility is, of course, virtue. But Unamuno is saying that the only reason such virtue is visible is that it stands in contrast to an opposite value which may not be apparent but which exists. If Joaquín had not been present to exemplify arrogance, the servant could not have been judged as having acted with humility. Not to recognize this is truly to be arrogant, for without Joaquín the maid would be deprived of her moral advantage. Thus, the apparently self-sufficient position of humility is converted into one term of the antithesis humility-arrogance, or, virtue-sin. But, we must ask, if this humility can only exist as a function of its opposite, what is its ethical merit? None, says Joaquín, who protests that he is "being used as an instrument in order to gain merits for heaven. This is hypocrisy!" (II, 1063). And, as we have noted, not to recognize the true nature of humility is itself the worst kind of arrogance.

Unamuno knew very well that he had cast Joaquín in the role of revaluator, and, years later, he proclaimed how vastly superior in morality Joaquín was to all Abels (II, 1006). Unamuno was arguing for a new ethical perspective, one that would see behind every gain someone else's loss, and behind every evil a compensating good dependent upon it. "Good" men were really evil because they caused "evil" men to suffer, and "those who believe themselves to be just are usually a bunch of arrogant people who are going to deprive others by the ostentation of their justice. Someone once said that there is no greater scum of the earth than honest people." This reversal of Christian values was made, however, with an ulterior Christian motive. It was wrong in Unamuno's eyes for any mortal to cause his fellow man pain. For this reason, he conceived of hell as an idea alien to the spirit of Christianity. He even wrote that "the Abelites have invented hell for the Cainites because without it, their glory would turn out to have no taste. Their pleasure consists of seeing, while [they are] free of suffering, other people suffer" (II, 1042). In spite of Unamuno's non-Nietzschean moral purpose, therefore, the net effect was to impiously question traditional value judgments. Moreover, it discredited any valuation made outside the framework of antithetical reasoning.

The final aspect of Unamuno's attack on absolutism is his inquiry into the means by which goodness is achieved. Here too, the answer is that the temple of virtue is supported by a pillar of vice. Stated bluntly, Unamuno found that one man uses another man as a stairway to heaven, cultivating his neighbor's weaknesses in order to increase thereby his own supposed merits. Unamuno wondered whether it was not perhaps "a nefarious doctrine to hold the tacit belief that in order for good men to act, evil men are [also] necessary, that there be offenses in order that forgiveness may enter, poor people so that charity might exist, and iniquities to foster meekness" (IX, 148). If this is truly an ethic of instrumentalism, then its worth must collapse with the removal of the instruments. Nevertheless, wickedness forms an integral part of life and human nature, and it can never disappear. Therefore, we must concede that the so-called "unvirtuous" also possess virtue—and not just negatively, but in a direct structural relationship to the realization of "goodness." Unamuno seems almost to be saying of this morality that by our appearance we manage to "grieve our neighbor, to arouse his envy, and to awaken feelings of impotence and degradation; we endeavor to make him taste the bitterness of his fate by dropping a little of *our* honey on his tongue, and, while conferring this supposed benefit on him, looking sharply and triumphantly into his eyes." But these words, which sum up so well what Unamuno has been saying, were in fact written by Nietzsche (M, #30).

Unamuno's revisionist attitude toward ethics constituted a deeper radicalism in method than in value. Nevertheless, his particular conception of what the Christian ethic entailed often led him to a transvaluation which obscured his Christian intent. Let us take, for example, the traditional interpretations of the roles of Cain and Abel. These roles are reversed as soon as we consider Cain's remorse as a suffering equivalent to the death of Abel. That is, the slain victim is borne by conscience and memory within the killer's mind, and continues each day an implacable, deadly assault. Abel, therefore, is the evil one because of his psychological murder of Cain. And the latter cries out, "Abel is killing me. Abel, what dost thou to thy brother? He who becomes a victim is as evil as he who becomes the executioner. To become a victim is a diabolical vengeance" (XII, 828).

Thus, Unamuno did not find it morally perverse to consider the slayer as a victim of the slain, since the latter had in fact executed a kind of punishment on him. Indeed, there was no difference between the brothers: they are both victims and victors. True Christian judgment, based on compassion, must therefore dissolve the conventional moral distinction between the two. That is, "the executioner believes himself to be the victim. He bears within him the victim's corpse, and this is his sorrow. . . . I love Cain as much as Abel . . . . And I love Abel as a possible Cain, as a Cain in desire. . . . How much does honesty weigh upon the honest! As much as vice does upon the vice-ridden" (XII, 859–60). Thus, good and evil become reversible functions, each one, like "faces of the same figure," presenting a separate guise, yet always part of something greater.

But Unamuno also believed that good could result from evil. One such case is the enforcement of justice after a crime has been committed, and in other situations "peace springs from war, and the punishment of theft [follows] theft. Society must take crimes upon itself in order that its constituents be free of both the crimes and their remorse." Consequently, just as Cain's remorse turned into a force for good, so too "this fact of social remorse, ordinarily so unnoticed, is the prime mover of the species' entire progress" (IV, 323). In this form, reversibility is used as a genetic principle that finds the origin of one value to stem from the negation of its opposite.

This method of reversible valuation contains still another factor. As the preceding quotations reveal, there is a contrast between collective and individual moralities. Individuals are absolved of their sins when society takes these sins upon itself, usually in the name of progress. The result is that what exists as a prohibition for individual men receives sanction as a value for the group. If this is true, the question arises as to whether such an arrangement can be considered "moral." Unamuno did not think so, and he cited a number of examples to support him. For instance, an army organized for destruction has to punish breaches of discipline because if it doesn't, it may be destroyed itself. Similarly, the morality of a band of thieves forbids thieving among the practitioners of theft. In these cases, the prohibitions depend upon repression, and so even though they are stated as laws, their "ancestry and lineage" are false and immoral. Therefore, Unamuno felt that he had to choose between these "Pharisee" societies—and he included our general society—and individual criminals. The groups, he argued, concealed the morally illegitimate values that they adhered to. And he confessed to feeling "inclined to pardon and even to love the Roque Guinarts, because in them there is no duplicity or falseness. Their bands appear just as they are" (IV, 323). By this remark, Unamuno did not intend to uphold criminal action just because it is committed openly. But the contrast with the supposed moral virtue of an injured society was quite clear. Social morality was built upon a dubious principle which, if examined, proved no more contemptible than the disguised use to which society put it. Indeed, Unamuno went so far as to declare that "every class of human justice stemmed from injustice, from the need which the latter had to sustain and perpetuate itself. Justice and order were born into the world in order to maintain violence and disorder" (IV, 322). If this were so, how could this morality be admired?

Whether we find them convincing or not, the foregoing examples show how Unamuno turned traditionally "immoral" results into the sources of morality. Moreover, he did this while converting traditionally "moral" precepts into the results of immoral forces. Such valuations, unorthodox in their analytical form, are equally radical in substance. If vice can engender virtue, it is just as possible for vice to conceal itself with virtue. Normally, we call this deception hypocrisy. But what about cases where the virtue is practiced hypocritically and no one is the wiser? It is then necessary to explore the motives behind the virtuous act, and learn whether this act is performed with virtuous intent. Unamuno illustrated this point by taking the episode in *Don Quixote* where the priest and the barber lock the knight in a cage in order to save him from his madness. Their deed was attributed by Unamuno to "envy disguised as charity, the envy of sane men who cannot stand heroic madness, envy which common sense has erected as a leveling tyrant" (IV, 211). And elsewhere, he called envy "the inner moral infection of the monasteries" (IV, 423). In both examples, the moral surface reflected an image of virtue which did not convince Unamuno. He questioned the compatibility of action and thought, refusing to make a judgment on the basis of the deed alone. Nor was he able to regard values, in this case charity, as absolutely good regardless of how they were practiced. On the contrary, he made them suspect by doubting the agent's motivation.

It is interesting to note some of Unamuno's variations on the game of motive-guessing. It occurred to him that a man might adopt a virtue not for its own sake, but because he was too weak to do otherwise. If so, then a virtue like humility could be interpreted as the external form of the inability to be strong. Thus, if we were to ask hypothetically, "Why should man be less than God in displaying his glory?" Unamuno could imagine the outcry of the virtuous: " 'Satanic arrogance!' cry the impotent ones . . . all those grave men infested with common sense" (III, 696). And Unamuno's own reply was that these self-styled moralists ought not to judge their fellow men, but the morality which their own disguised weaknesses had created. To be sure, he knew that the "impotent ones" would not do this, and he found the reason to be that they lacked the courage to face their real impulses. "Cowardice," he explained, "means not giving in to one's natural bent, and not ignoring the voice of conscience" (XII, 228). The moralists were cowards because, in effect, they were substituting ethics for energy. What was worse, their cowardice led them to false valuations. They evaluated men and deeds from the standpoint of moral criteria that had little to do with their own ethical natures. Their cloak of morality was so threadbare, that it would have been more respectable to shed it completely, revealing in total honesty what lay beneath. Instead, these timid ones examined the condition of other cloaks, without realizing that their own needed mending. And so Unamuno asked them, "Why do you go about trying to redeem your neighbor, if you are so in need of your own redemption? Let each one regenerate himself and we will all be regenerated. Purify your sight, and you will purify the world in your eyes" (XII, 228).

With this recommendation, Unamuno set forth a personal criterion for value judgment. Moral standards are least sound when they are set up on an interpersonal basis. Although this may sound somewhat dubious, the reason is quite apparent. When the individual is judged in a group, he maintains his moral appearances, which are a social fact. However, this fact need not correspond to his essential moral character, his inner morality, so to speak. In other words, he might not be the same man in solitude that he appears to be in the group. A good illustration of this duplicity can be found in Unamuno's story about Artemio A. Silva. This man had a successful moral behavior, and yet "no one thanked him for his justice or imputed it to be good." The reason was that his good works were not the result of good intentions, but faulty courage. Some people knew that "he did not have the courage to be evil," and he himself realized that he was "a coward for good and a coward for evil" (IX, 287–88). That is, he could not live up to his inner morality, the one that reflected his true self. Of course, part of Artemio's trouble was that he could not develop a consistent, true self, and we spoke of this difficulty earlier in the book. But the result was that whatever desire he had, it did not receive a corresponding support in deeds. He committed himself neither to good nor to evil, but followed expedience in every situation. His behavior disregarded the truism that "morality is not profit," and this was his undoing. For Unamuno, at least, it was corrupt to derive any gain from the moral approval of society. Moreover, Artemio was incapable of affirming himself from within, without reference to social standards. His "angelic self" warred against his "demonic self," and neither impulse won. Rather, they were both vitiated, his tendency for evil neutralized by cowardice, and his "angel . . . corrupted by the failure of his devil" (IX, 287).

Unamuno's story has two corollaries. The first is that conventional morality esteems a value because it is socially valid, and not because of its intrinsic worth. And second, the more a conventional virtue contrasts with its opposite, the more highly it is esteemed. Both of these ideas were rejected by Unamuno. Their chief flaw was that they honored appearances and efficacy, and neglected the agent who was responsible for how the act appeared and operated. According to this standard, to give charity is a virtue, regardless of whether the donor feels compassion or not. In other words, the judgment has to be made on the basis of appearances. What Unamuno objected to was the fact that this standard made no demands upon the agent to be virtuous in thought and feeling. Even more serious was the fact that the agent created a certain inequality between himself and the recipient of his good deed. That is, he placed himself in a superior position by demonstrating his ability to do good, and he thereby forced the beneficiary into the inferior role of having to accept that good. Unamuno's logic, of course, is spurious if not silly, and yet it is persuasive in terms of his inverse reasoning. If the value arouses feelings of inadequacy or obligation in the recipient, why should this be considered a moral act? Why be grateful or approve morally of such acts of kindness, whether they are bestowed by a man on an animal, by God on man, or by one human being on a fellow creature in need? And if the benefactor was not emotionally involved in his good deed, why, then, should he be invested with the aura of virtue?

Quite apart from the inner morality of the agent, we must also consider the contrast between virtue and its immoral opposite. As we saw, a value gains in esteem as it stands opposed to its antithesis. However, this contrast also plays up the evil of sin in a humiliating way. That is, its immorality is pointed out by a comparison to what is good, and not on the basis of what is bad about the sin. This adds shame to the condemnation, subjecting the sinner to the pain of debasement and humiliation. For example, Unamuno told of a conversation he had with a respectable lady in which he explained how the perfections of the virtuous unfairly made the imperfect feel inferior and ashamed. He argued that just as paganism reached its height with physical nudity, so too should Christianity culminate in the nakedness of the soul. The lady reacted with horror, exclaiming that if it were not for clothes, how could deformed people, and others who had something to conceal, live? And Unamuno replied, "Much better than now, madam! The hunchback is worse off dressed than naked. His suit only torments him with his hump, and makes us suppose that it is greater than what it is in reality. As soon as our eyes became accustomed to the naked man, we would understand bodily deformities" (III, 996). And all of us, added Unamuno, have our peculiar deformities. The point is that we are prevented from understanding moral defects by the comparative or interpersonal standard of Christian ethics. If the individual standard of morality suggested by Unamuno were followed, all of the injustices now visible would disappear. There would be only one absolute: forgiveness. All valuations would be based on this, rather than on pre-established levels of moral achievement. And as a result, there would be no need to measure anyone's worth on the relative measure of someone else's accomplishments.

From what has been said, we may conclude that evil is a useless concept whose meaning can be influenced by factors of varying quality and origin. One such factor is the value judgment that has been wrongly constructed, and this was pointed out earlier in the discussion. Similarly, personality and sincerity are two more influences that reduce the usefulness of evil as an ethical concept. Let us turn now to a fourth factor, the relativity of good and evil, and see how Unamuno regarded it.

Unamuno's notion of evil was realistic and clinical. He wrote that "action liberates man from evil sentiment, and it is evil senti- ment which poisons the soul" (II, 1077). This comment is signifi- cant because it is so typical of how Unamuno approached all problems from a humanistic point of view rather than a doctrinal one. His suggestion here is that rancor is a feeling that should not be classified as a quality of man's spirit. It is an alien condition, due to a toxic accumulation which must be discharged before spiritual health can be restored. Once this foreign material is expelled, the individual reverts to his characterological goodness. So much so, in fact, that he is even capable of pity and love for the victim who had been the object of his vented hate (II, 968). The liberating act which Unamuno refers to is in fact the expression of evil, in this case the outpouring of hatred. But the act as such is beyond valua- tion, because it is purely instrumental. That is, it merely affords the occasion for the individual to purge himself of rancor by getting rid of it. Any judgment that considered such an action to be evil would, of course, be correct as far as traditional morality was concerned. However, it was a shallow judgment in the eyes of Unamuno, in that the moral traits of the agent's personality were deliberately ignored. The norms of good and evil are found in the psychological realm—character, spirit, soul—and not in any field of action. Morality is not a behavioral science. For Unamuno, a mode of conduct was an extension of personality, but not always an expression of the qualities of that personality. An outward act might have bad social consequences, and still not reflect evil in the heart of the man who committed it. Naturally, to the tradition- minded moralist this position is unacceptable because it frees the agent from his responsibility. And yet for Unamuno this was pre- cisely the issue. Thus, he speculated about the difference between social conduct and the basic moral fiber of the individual, revealing quite radical ideas in the process.

Unamuno often thought, for example, about how certain perni- cious forms of animal life could illuminate the problem of human ethics. Did the bee sting in order to hurt man or to be rid of its venom? Can a viper infect itself with its own poison? (IX, 740,

284). His answer in both cases was that the harmful substance had to be ejected, or else the secreting organism would itself be injured. The liberating act is, therefore, not a matter of malice but of self-protection. Moreover, the action might even turn out to be socially beneficial. Unamuno reasoned, by reverse analogy, that just as bees convert their honey into venom for defensive purposes, so too might man's bitterness also be rendered sweet. He felt that there are certain "days of philosophy, that is, of poison, when poetry, honey, departs from us or grows sour," days of "defense, of preparing the poisonous and protective sting," when one feels "a furious desire to sting them, those outside in the world, with venom made of honey, and what happens is that the venom turns to honey. . . . There are days when man wants to be evil and he cannot. He wants to wield injustice and he pours forth compassion" (IX, 737–38).

We are asked, then, to accept the notion that external behavior is usually equivocal in its moral effect. It may be a force for good or for ill, but it is never symbolic of the agent's moral nature. It is to this nature that Unamuno ascribes all criteria for ethical orientation. And when it was overlooked by moral standards, he merely dismissed the value judgment. Unamuno knew that this would "scandalize timorous readers," but he was more concerned about the personal sources of action than with the external deeds themselves. He felt that it was important first to maintain the moral soundness of man's character, and he was convinced that "the commission of a sinful act purifies us of the terrible desire for it, which was eating at our hearts." In other words, to repress evil thoughts is infinitely worse than to act them out, because man's essentially good nature is destroyed by the venom accumulated by such repression. If this happens, the result is that he is lost to himself, and he becomes a moral blot on the community of spirits. If he releases this evil, however, he reverts to his original goodness, and he may also discover the virtues of repentance and love along the way (III, 810).

Unamuno pushed these ethical limits even further than the idea that evil provides a catharsis. He conceived of instances in which an injurious act may not be considered evil at all, because it was not the individual's purpose to do harm. This "purity of intention" is, in its highest degree, innocence. But innocence here is understood as complete naturalness, as animality. There is no malice in the attacks of a wild animal, and therefore the consequences of its acts cannot be considered evil. So too is saintliness the purest form of spiritual innocence, and those who achieve this state have reached an animal purity which sets them beyond moral reproach. Even if "one of those saints stung, clawed, or devoured someone . . . it would be with as much purity of intention . . . as the viper stings and the tiger claws and devours. Grace returns them to pure nature" (III, 831–32). This very Nietzschean view is related to the problem of consciousness, which we analyzed before. He who acts without being aware of himself is so fully integrated a personality that there is not the slightest element of self-contemplation to detract from the completeness of his act. Hence, there is no room for the kind of moral judgment that occurs between Artemio's warring selves. Action is so complete and reflexive that it is carried out with animal innocence. Evil enters only when some extraneous contemplative factor destroys this purity by making room for the analytical self-awareness that divides the personality.

Here, then, is a psychological genealogy of morals. From consciousness man derives his conscience. If he is oblivious of the latter's voice, it is because he has not adopted the critical awareness of himself, and cannot perceive any discrepancy between his thinking and his acting selves. "He who has no awareness of doing evil is doing no evil," says one of Unamuno's alter egos to another, "because the intention . . . ." And then the other alter ego interrupts: "Intention! Do we know our own intentions? Do we know if we are good or not?" (II, 756). But the very nature of the Unamunian monodialog is itself a negative answer. We do not know if we are good because we do not know which of our selves is the real one. Thus, we are capable of conflicting intentions, for "every good man carries within him the seven cardinal virtues and their seven opposite vices, and with them he is capable of creating all kinds of agonists" (IX, 422).

By this, Unamuno did not mean that there is a clear alignment of virtues and vices pitted against each other, or that there are unequivocal good and evil selves within one man. This is not the problem. The ethical dilemma occurs when the judge is disengaged from the motivations that are involved in the situation which he is about to judge. If the evaluator of an action is not in sympathy with the purposes of the action, and that action happens to be traditionally "immoral," then the judge's valuation will condemn the act. Guilt, therefore, is not determined by the external deed, but by how aware the agent is of being disaffected from it. This refers, of course, to the state of self-awareness, where judge and agent are one and the same person. Hence the criterion of the harmony of intentions. Man is guilty only to the extent that he feels himself to be guilty. "When one commits a pernicious act, believing in good faith that he is performing a virtuous action, we cannot hold him morally guilty. And when someone thinks that an indifferent or perhaps beneficial action is evil, and he performs it, he is guilty. The act passes, the intention remains, and what is evil about the evil act is that it corrupts the intention, because by doing evil knowingly, he is predisposed to continue doing it. His conscience is darkened. And doing evil is not the same as being evil. Evil darkens the conscience, and not only the moral conscience, but the general, psychic one" (XVI, 414).

However far this reasoning carried Unamuno from Christian thinking, it is interesting that he used a traditional rhetoric to express it. He chastised the Pharisees for favoring the carnal man over the spiritual man. Whereas one may *do* good, the other can *be* good, and it is this essential goodness, rather than any phenomenological one, which Unamuno's religion demanded. Here too, awareness of intention is more closely linked to character than to action, and the value judgment is affected accordingly. Unamuno warned that "if, when desiring evil and filled with harmful intention, you do no harm out of some cowardice, or if, out of fear of being evil you are honest, no matter how justifiable, your evil intention will embitter your soul. . . . Learn to hate sin as much as you commiserate and love the sinner, because hatred of evil is in inverse proportion to hatred of the agent of this same evil. As long as you do not reach the state where the sight of the poor wretch who committed a horrible crime can draw the loving cry of 'poor brother!' from your breast . . . you will not be radically good, completely a Christian" (III, 133).

Unamuno did not deny the existence of evil, but he defined it in terms of events divorced from their source. His idea was that a man's act becomes part of the phenomenal world, and once its separation from him is complete, he is no longer held accountable for it. This is the only tenable position for Unamuno to have held, given his absolute principle of unreserved Christian love. He would not adhere to the "miserable juridical criterion of judging a human act by its external consequences and the temporal harm received by the one who suffers it." He suggested instead that "a harm inflicted with holy intention is worth more than a beneficial act when rendered with perverse intention." And yet whatever definition Unamuno had of "holy purpose," he allowed no room for a dogmatic meaning. On the contrary, there was "something more intimate than what we call morality, and it is no less than the jurisprudence which eludes the police. There is something more profound than the Decalog, which is a table of laws . . . . There is a spirit of love" (IV, 135–36).

This attitude is decidedly more Quixotic than realistic, and Unamuno would have shuddered with us if he had thought of it in a practical sense. Nevertheless, he insisted that evil had to be considered along with intention, and that the evil-doer need not be bound by his deeds if he undergoes a change of heart. To illustrate this point, Unamuno cited an interesting seventeenth-century play by Tirso de Molina, *Condemned for Lack of Faith*. The story involves a pious hermit who envisions his own damnation, abandons his virtue, and is in fact damned for his lack of faith. Contrasted to him is an outlaw whose life consists mainly of wrong-doing, but who is saved at the last moment by repentance. Clearly, the play was intended as a dramatization of profound theological concepts—grace and faith—but Unamuno seized upon the more immediate morality of the situation to strengthen his own view. He surmised, no doubt correctly, that the average reader would be startled by the apparent injustice of the play's ending. And he wrote, "So this is repugnant to the moral sense? To Sancho Panza's, yes. To Don Quixote's, no." In other words, there was a case to be made for a Quixotic view of evil, one which would eschew the practical sense of morality in favor of another criterion.

Unamuno went on to suggest that the immediate standards of justice and reward are not always seen in the proper perspective. Recalling how Nietzsche revaluated such standards, he remarked that the German "caused a stir in the world by writing about what is beyond good and evil. There is something which is not beyond but within good and evil, in their common root. What do we, poor mortals, know of what good and evil are as seen from heaven?" (IV, 327). Looking at this statement from our own standpoint as readers, it would be foolish to quibble with Unamuno about whether values are beyond, beneath, or within good and evil. It does seem as if Unamuno changed the phrase simply to avoid identification with Nietzsche's extremism. But the fact remains that he stepped beyond the ordinary limits of valuation anyway. It is, of course, true that Unamuno's criterion continued to be charity, and that he remained safely within the Christian tradition in this regard. Nevertheless, the very mention of Nietzsche in this context suffices to point out Unamuno's fundamentalism within the margins of moral orthodoxy. He diverted attention from his radical or Quixotic position by contrasting it with Nietzsche. In turn, this obscured the fact that it is almost as audacious to excuse a man from his moral duty on the basis of Christian love as it is to do so on the basis of Nietzschean strength. In both cases, the valuation is made without reference to the nature of the deed or to the agent's responsibility.

This raises the question of whether anyone knows what the true moral perspective is. Unamuno himself doubted that such a perspective could be found. His skepticism was due to the idea that the self was ambiguous, shifting its criteria at certain moments of self-awareness. But his doubts also stemmed from the fact that he feared wrongly judging his fellow men by the use of arbitrary standards. Unlike Nietzsche, Unamuno fell back on love for determining his ethical orientation, and he never abandoned this fundamental approach. At the same time, he was just as concerned as the German in seeking valuations that were more faithful to life than to abstract concepts. For example, Unamuno posed the problem of a beautiful woman dying of hunger, and he declared that if she did not exploit her beauty she would end by losing it. In other words, she would be better off prostituting herself for the sake of life, than dying for the sake of an anti-vitalistic morality. But—objects Unamuno's interlocutor—according to this idea one cannot live by morality. Of course not, replies Unamuno, because "morality is not for living. . . . Ethics is for dying and economics is for living. . . . And the man of talent is the one who knows how to live, and not the one who can dream . . ." (IX, 896–97). This vitalism represents Unamuno's basic attitude toward the problem of finding a moral perspective. There were, however, several complications.

In the issue of moral vitalism we cannot ignore the fact that living fully includes facing the contradictions that are produced by personality. It must consider also the extent to which values may be incompatible with the absolute perspective of Christian ideas. This incompatibility, as well as the contradictory personality, helps to determine Unamuno's moral relativism. His distaste for consistency, to take one example, is the result of having accepted the principle of contradiction, and this in turn influences the bent of his relativism. Given the contradictory nature of the self, an absolute ethic will inevitably be violated, either tacitly or openly. In fact, this is constantly the case, so much so that there are two moralities operating in our lives. "One is the behavior we ask others to follow with respect to us, and the other is the one we wish to follow with respect to them." In other words, we require an absolutist ethic for others, and a vitalistic one for ourselves. When our own desires are not at stake, we define a good man as someone who is "as it suits the rest of us that he should be, but who none of us would like to be. A good man is a man who is good for others." That is to say, we set up a code of behavior for our neighbors and expect them to act consistently with it. We call this consistency "moral," but it is not the goodness of such conduct that interests us at all. What we want is that they remain faithful to the image that we have formed of them. We are not asking that they be good, but "that they be consistent toward us, that they don't some day go ahead and do what we didn't expect them to" (III, 1045). On the other hand, this absolute code of behavior goes against our vital interests, and we adopt a more personal ethic for ourselves. But, since there is no honest justification for the double standard, Unamuno rejects its entire formulation. It is hypocritical for us to demand of others a behavior which we ourselves will not maintain. And to codify this demand under the guise of an absolute moral system is indeed presumptuous. But worst of all, any code of action or mode of thinking that requires this kind of inflexible conformity goes counter to man's psychological nature, and must therefore be rejected.

Unamuno took this point a step further when he found that even granting that consistency were possible, there was no assurance that Christian morality was the only true code. To believe this, in fact, constituted a serious error in judgment, because "the most terrible thing is that we not only demand consistency of others, but that it be according to our understanding of [the term]." Unamuno discovered no better example than Saint Augustine's belief that pagan virtues were not real but apparent. That is, he interpreted Augustine as saying that pagans were not virtuous in the Christian sense, in spite of having performed the same good deeds as the Christians, because they acted on standards or ideals that were different. Unamuno protested this view with the comment that "the greatest lack of humility and excess of arrogance and presumption is not that of the ancient pagans, but that which says: 'He who does not do good for the reasons which I believe that it should be done, does not do it with perfection. He who does not apply this principle [of mine] to his virtues has only apparent and false virtues' " (III, 1047).

Although this criticism is aimed at the complacent absolutism of Christianity, it can be extended to any system based on a single ethical perspective. And here Unamuno hinted at the complete dissolution of value standards. Whereas he first regarded the act and its consequences as irrelevant to morality, he now wonders whether even motivation is a reliable standard. His criterion had previously been motive rather than consequence, and personality rather than performance. Now, however, his criticism of Augustine indicates that even motives vary, and that a given act can come about for many reasons. Thus, he reached a position of moral relativity, whereby all perspectives would be admitted as long as they did not violate the most basic of values: love. This in itself might be considered to be a Christian position, and, in any event, it is not a Nietzschean one. At the same time, it is important to note that Unamuno was willing to dispense with the Decalog, as well as with social justice, for the sake of this love. We may safely conclude that this standard of valuation was a radical departure from the traditional purpose of ethics, namely, to safeguard social order and obedience to authority.

If Unamuno's use of love is quite un-Nietzschean in the matter of valuation, his insistence on a psychological explanation of values comes very close to Nietzsche's point of view. Both philosophers begin their analysis of motivation with the idea that man spontaneously seeks to exalt and immortalize himself. Furthermore, they both admit that this impulse is traditionally identified as the deepest root of sin. And yet neither of them feels that the sinfulness of this effort diminishes the heroic, or even the holy, quality of a life motivated in this way. Saints too, as well as heroes, strive for eternal or temporal glory in order to gain the personal rewards of their effort, and not because of their pure devotion to goodness. If they sin by the ambition and boldness of their desire, the sin is profoundly human. On the other hand, their heroism is truly admirable, because it stems from the effort to transcend human limits.

In his praise of heroism, Unamuno was prepared to face the fact that "what is superhuman about perfection touches on the inhuman, and descends into it" (IV, 95). He saw the hero as motivated primarily by individualistic aims which are expressed in the forms of Quixotic or Satanic rebelliousness. Not only did he refrain from censuring this kind of life, but he took a Nietzschean step in the opposite direction. Recognizing that traditional moralists would condemn such rebelliousness, Unamuno inquired into the motivation for *their* judgment as well. Thus, he turned the tables on the accusers and accused them of dubious intentions. Indeed, he thought that their valuations were just as much the product of their inner needs as were the values they had damned. As unheroic and unoriginal men, they hated people who possessed the imagination which they themselves lacked. What they called "dangerous, daring, impious ideas are only the ones that never occur to poor men of routinish wit." This was where the source of all moral orthodoxy lay: in the envy and resentment of the superior qualities of the few. The majority of men are "vulgar, commonplace spirits [who] fail to distinguish themselves, and since they cannot suffer others to distinguish themselves, they try to impose on them the uniform of dogma, which is a soldier's fatigue dress, so that they may not be distinguished" (II, 1057-58).

Consequently, Unamuno argued that we ought not to have any illusions about prevailing ethical standards. They are prompted mainly by the desire to restrain and to regiment. Thus, the standards are like all other codes of behavior in their common psychological origin. They all rationalize personal motives, and none can claim superior merit. On the other hand, if we must find merit in them, let it be on the basis of the superior motivations of the select minority: the Cains, the Don Quixotes, and the Roque Guinart-type outlaws. These figures never conceal their purposes, since hypocrisy is absent in them. On the contrary, "those who are called arrogant, who do not conceal the belief in their own superiority, are among the citizens most useful to their country and to all of their fellow men, and among the most fruitful in good things" (III, 1004). The only reason they are condemned for affirming their individuality is that the vast majority is not capable of the same self-assurance.

Let us bear in mind that in comparing Unamuno with Nietzsche, it is not the degree of iconoclasm that is so important, but rather the technique used in forming value judgments. Unamuno's axiological method is a more striking innovation than any particular anti-Christian statement he could have made. If his moral perspective is more traditional than Nietzsche's, his method is just as radical. Both men looked behind a given valuation in order to track down its psychological roots. And it was this habit which ultimately stripped the entire ethical code of its objectivity, and, consequently, of its claim to providing disinterested and fair value judgments. Indeed, Unamuno showed a truly Nietzschean suspiciousness when he approached formulations of this kind. He scrutinized them for traces of secret attitudes that might belie the actual judgment. He could not accept, for instance, the praise men bestowed upon his own work, because he felt that "when they praise certain things about me it is only to tacitly vituperate me for others." So too, in general, "when you hear someone eulogizing, you should ask: 'Against whom is that directed?' " (IX, 707). On another occasion, Unamuno maintained that the learned man cannot forgive the genius for being the object of his erudition, since he in turn would never be studied by his learned colleagues (III, 908). And once he even stated that those who cloister themselves from the world are really carrying worldly thoughts with them in their hearts (III, 809).

In all of this motivational guesswork, there is the insinuation that ethical postures are the fruits of duplicity. The moralist fights against the very evil that he harbors within him. Unamuno most frequently illustrated this idea by his critique of ascetic ideas. Pointing to the sin of pride, he noted that its repression in the ascetic man is usually accomplished by means of a deeper pride hidden within the man himself. For proof, we have only to observe "the precautions which the professionally humble have always taken in order that their humility not be turned into arrogance."

Unamuno observed how frequently "the masters of spiritual life, on commenting upon the idea that the humbled man will be exalted, warn us that humbling oneself with this in mind—in order to be exalted by having been humbled—is the most refined kind of arrogance" (III, 807; II, 355). Since they are professional moralists, they are excessively aware of their own feelings with regard to ethical values. And this self-consciousness concerning their virtue tends to destroy their sincerity. What is worse, if they are genuinely humble, their recognition of this virtue within them might awaken the sin of pride. On the other hand, if they are trying to break their pride, the abstract value of humility is useless to them. Instead of externalizing their pride and ridding themselves of it, the principle of humility forces them to suppress pride, and keep it dormant within them. Thus, the moral abstraction serves only as an intellectual reminder of what should be, without remedying the actual condition.

In this sense, ethical principles are formulas that do nothing positive, and yet retain potentially negative effects for everyone. They are not necessary to the virtuous man, for he already has his virtue. If he accepts them consciously, however, he may grow aware of his virtue and thereby cease to be sincere. On the other hand, these principles prevent the unvirtuous man from expelling his vice and being free of it. And finally, the zealous defender of the principles might become intolerant when he sees them challenged by other values. Thus, they turn into dogma, and inspire hostility against more vitalistic moral values.

# 10 THE SUPERMAN

*There is* probably no idea in modern thought that has been more misunderstood or bitterly contested than Nietzsche's concept of the superman. The very word lends itself to ambiguity, although its connotation of human perfectibility was clear even when Goethe made use of it in *Faust*. When the term gained currency in Spain, its emotional impact was due more to the various inferences drawn from the notion of a "super" man, than to an intimate knowledge of Nietzsche's philosophy. Unamuno first used the word in 1896, and he continued to use it for thirteen years before questioning its semantic validity (III, 361, 446–47; VII, 492). When he finally did, several variants of the term had made their appearance, and Unamuno quipped that his "head [was] befuddled with this business of the *superhomo, superhombre,* or *sobrehombre* of Nietzsche, which is a kind of future, and no more lucid than he [is]" (V, 880–81; VIII, 1095). But instead of choosing the least obscure of these neologisms, Unamuno created still another word to convey the idea of a future perfect man. He noted the progressive "Romanization" of the form *Uebermensch,* and announced that in an "effort to create something too, even if it is only a word, I have created the word afterman (*trashombre*) to translate the Nietzschean term." In part, this represented Unamuno's petulant response to the futurism of Marinetti and the essayist Gabriel Alomar, whose program he countered with the term *trashumanismo.* But broadly speaking, the word called attention to the generalized and often inaccurate associations which were made in reference to Nietzsche's concept.

Without doubt, *sobrehombre* was a convenient word for Unamuno, provided that its linguistic components summarized his ideas faithfully. The trouble was that since his theme was always *el hombre*, Man, the latter's meaning posed many more difficulties than the prefix which modified it. For example, Unamuno wrote in 1903 that "the man who bends his neck to fortune without struggling against it is not a genuine man, is not one of those who aspire to the superman," and in a footnote to this in 1917 he said, "Today, I wouldn't even use this expression about aspiring to the superman. . . . I would rather adopt the [term] of *man* pure and simple, or, if fitting, more-than-man (*más-hombre*)" (III, 597). Thus, even though Unamuno concurred with Nietzsche's wish for a perfect man, he keenly felt the inadequacy of any expression that might represent this ideal. And since he was interested in concrete men rather than in Man as a hypothesis, he could not accept, and perhaps even resented, Nietzsche's satisfaction with the term's etymology. At any rate, Unamuno wrote: "Bolívar was a man, a whole man, a man complete and true, and to be a whole man is more, much more, than being an *Uebermensch*—I will leave it in German for greater obscurity—a mere Nietzschean abstraction, one of those who wants and presumes, but never succeeds" (VII, 308).

With respect to the prefix "super," the philologist in Unamuno was just as distracted by its ambiguities as his German colleague was precise in the original choice. When Nietzsche had decided upon the term, he was aware of borrowing a word long established by literary usage. He chose it knowing that it implied a spatial order of existence, or a gradation of levels, among demigods, heroes, sprites, and demons. Unamuno, on the other hand, had a temporal orientation based on the history of human progress, and so he was affected by the negative moral connotation which a "super" man conveyed at that time. Thus, he cautioned in one dialog: " 'But take care, lest what in the insolence of your usual solitude you believe to be superhuman, really doesn't go beyond the subhuman or infrahuman.' 'No. None of this above or below. No spatial relationships. Just temporal ones, before or after. Either prehuman or posthuman' " (IX, 774). This is exactly the idea that we saw earlier in the temporal concept of the self. Unamuno thought of human development as a process of fulfilling the self in time, without this causing some selves to be superior or inferior to others. Thus, when he once referred to an "anti-superman" as an "abortive man" (II, 501), he meant just this kind of temporal evolution, which, if unfulfilled, would be comparable to the loss of an embryonic human perfection.

Unamuno also departed from Nietzsche's original idea by accepting the popular misconceptions about superhuman strength and harmful advantage over other men. He drew a distinction between the right of each person to actively protect his individuality, and an outright aggression for the sake of expanding the self. He stated that "there are times when to invade is to defend oneself," but he did not consider this to be an act of encroachment upon other selves. "In contrast to Nietzsche's man of prey and of domination, in contrast to the *Uebermensch*, the superman, who only maintains his personality by imposing it and absorbing those of other people, there rises man: he who is no more nor wishes to be more than a man, but a complete man—*the right man in the right place*—who allows other men their places in the sun" (VIII, 862–63). Therefore, if the term superman was important, this was because it denoted a new concept of *man*, and not because of any undue significance in the adjective *super*.

Nevertheless, this was begging the issue, and Unamuno knew he could not dispense with the troublesome prefix altogether. But instead of emphasizing the superiority of one man over another in terms of power, will, and morality, he took *super* to mean improvement with regard to civilization and culture. Thus, he was able to use the rhetoric surrounding the word superman without referring either to the latter by name, or to Nietzsche. He wrote, for example, that "to humanize is quite a lot, but to civilize is more. To civilize, to make civil—if you will, to citizenize—is to superhumanize. To us, humanity seems to be everything for man. But for him, civility is more. It is more than everything because it is the future which never stops being fulfilled. It is the ideal" (I, 792). The difference, then, is that Unamuno shifted attention from the interests of the individual to a wider field of human activity. Despite his well-known individualism, when he confronted the concept of superman he was more concerned with cultural amelioration than with safeguarding individuality. This does not deny his constant emphasis on the self. But it does redefine the superman to mean humanity, that is, civilization as the sum of its human parts.

Let us note, however, that Unamuno saw the limitations of the superman idea insofar as it concerned improvement of the species. In one satirical dialog he depicted a cat, named Zapirón, who points out the vanity of man's calling himself the culmination and crown of the animal kingdom. The skeptical cat sees not a hierarchy of species, but a number of separate animal republics, so to speak, a variety of groups with dissimilar evolutionary potential: "Now men have invented that idea about the superman. Very well, then, the ideal of the dog should be the superdog or 'supercanis'; that of the cat, supercat or 'supercatus,' and not man" (IV, 513). Zapirón not only reasons like a man, but he is talking about the individual human condition. In other words, he balks at the idea of a generic application of the superman concept. Its usefulness does not go beyond the individual and social levels, and its biological implications are best ignored.

So much, then, for the epithet itself. The word superman created problems for Unamuno because he found its Spanish equivalent to be overextended in implication. If he had negative feelings about the concept as a whole, they took the form of deriding the word, since there were other aspects of the idea which he himself endorsed and would not attack. For this very reason, Unamuno discredited the reputed originality of the superman concept, reminding readers that Nietzsche had ideological antecedents: Renan's desire for immortality (VIII, 1002); Havelock Ellis' study of evolution and children (IX, 648); Darwin, Stirner, and even Saint Paul (X, 97; VIII, 658; III, 513). Moreover, Unamuno dissociated himself from those contemporaries of his who were supposedly influenced by the superman notion. Why he did so will presently become clear. Admitting that all members of the Generation of 1898 had plunged into anarchism and "unchecked individualism," he identified himself with the Spencerians rather than with the Nietzscheans, although both groups had been looking for self-identity and individualist standards.

In drawing this ideological distinction, Unamuno declared that "some of us were nourished on the Spencerian formula of 'the individual against the state.' Others were sustained by Nietzsche, and, in search of the superman within themselves, discovered the man. They discovered themselves . . ." (V, 421). This clear-cut division of allegiances is, however, specious because no purely causal relationship had existed between the values by which Unamuno's contemporaries lived and their previous reading experiences. They recognized in literary form the many kinds of subjectivism that they were already feeling in mixed measure, and they used names and slogans in order to publicize their affiliations. Unamuno's statement is particularly misleading—and significant in illustrating the epoch's complexity—for it groups him with socially oriented contemporaries rather than with psychologically minded ones, in spite of the fact that he shared the latter's interests also, and, indeed, subsequently rejected Spencer.

One reason for Unamuno's unwillingness to link himself with Nietzsche was his aversion to the anti-Christian overtones suggested whenever the German's name was mentioned. Basically, he approved more of what he termed spiritualism than he did of the idealism of the superman concept, although this preference is by no means conclusive. If we consider Unamuno's religious moments, it is clear that whenever there is a choice between salvation for the individual or for the masses, it is always the hero who is sacrificed to the general good. We see this at the beginning of his career in the essays concerning cultural purism, and at the end, in the novel *Saint Emmanuel the Good, Martyr*. Even in the one instance where Unamuno contradicts himself, his paradoxical phrasing does not nullify this fact (XVI, 173). He stressed the people rather than the hero in this way in order to reaffirm what he called Spain's "spiritualistic naturalism." We need not be put off by this heavy phrase, nor by its opposite, "idealistic realism," which Unamuno rejected. Quite simply, he was contrasting the spiritual and the irrational as against the intellectual and the conceptual. And, as a result, he seemed to be choosing the mystique of the masses over the abstract idea of the superman.

The main difference between these two alternatives is that idealism depends on reason whereas spiritualism involves the irrational consciousness. Moreover, ideas function socially and can be communicated, while spirit is private and incommunicable. And finally, "the human ideal is fulfilled in earthly life, and is the archetype of man, something like the superman, Nietzsche's *Uebermensch*, being the Christ of the Earth. Whereas human spirituality has its sights fixed on heaven, in another life, in Christ dead and resuscitated. Idealism is of this world, is pagan, is Platonic, is of the Renaissance. And our Castilian spiritualism was mystical, medieval, and of another world" (XI, 587–88). Nevertheless, this contrast of idealism and spiritualism is really a masterpiece of sophistry, for the two terms are reversible in meaning. If spirit is a private and inward experience, does it not also involve man's collective redemption in Christ? And if the ideal is a Platonic abstraction, does it not take a concrete, individual form as well? In other words, aren't these terms simply artifices designed to help Unamuno take sides in the hero-masses issue, when in fact he favored them both?

There is good evidence to believe that Unamuno did approve of the superman idea, even though he wished to avoid being associated with Nietzsche. As we saw in Part One, his constant stress on the self in contrast with the group indicated how he felt about rescuing the individual from oblivion. Even more pertinent, he oddly chose to refer to Nietzsche's superman as "the Christ of the Earth." This fact is extremely important, particularly because the phrase occurs in a statement which purports to extol Castilian spiritualism rather than pagan idealism. Unamuno could have used this bold epithet only if he attached positive value to what the superman stood for. Indeed, he not only recognized that "the human ideal is fulfilled in earthly life," but he yearned that it might be thus fulfilled. Thus, to call the superman a terrestrial Christ meant that he affirmed the material world as well as the spiritual one. Moreover, we must remember that he regarded Don Quixote as a Christlike figure (IV, 367) and also as a hero who redeemed the people. This is not a contradictory interpretation, but one which served different purposes at the same time. It made possible the affirmation of the individual and his values—in a word, heroism—and it also safeguarded the group, doing both of these things on the material and spiritual levels simultaneously.

The point is, therefore, that Unamuno held an individualistic view of the social structure even while being concerned about the collective welfare. And he was alert to the needs of the material world at the same time that he affirmed the eternal values of spirit. His problem in making the superman idea fit into this world-view was that it would cast a Nietzschean shadow over an otherwise Christian position. The belief in the superman was not necessarily incompatible with Christianity unless the latter was regarded as an obstacle in the path of the superman's appearance. While Nietzsche did regard it as an obstacle, Unamuno did not. However, Unamuno was reluctant to be identified with the German for moral reasons, and not because he thought of the superman as an Antichrist. He found Nietzsche's attack on Christianity to be repellent, but, as we saw, he could conceive of some material value resulting from a terrestrial Christ in the world. In this respect, as well as in the question of genius, he came close to Nietzsche. Unamuno felt, for example, that it was necessary to remove oneself from the people, and to "withdraw from them for the benefit of the masses themselves. He who has reached some pinnacle must extend his arms and shout out from there, calling the others to the pinnacle, and not descend on the pretext of showing them the way . . ." (IV, 437). Once again we have a mixture of feelings, a desire to protect the hero against the amorphous populace, and an equally strong wish to elevate the latter. However, Unamuno inclined more to one side than the other.

His defense of aloofness from the people rested on several assumptions. One was that the individual's independence had to be safeguarded, and that his values, point of view, and freedom of action demanded respect. Unamuno took a relativistic approach to the question of individualism, admitting the rights of all perspectives and even justifying violence as a means to protect them. He wrote that "I try to be right in my way. There is the wolf's way of being right, and the lion's, and the eagle's, and the fox's, and the hare's, and the bee's. . . . And when the wolf devours the sheep, saying that he does it to defend himself, that it is in defense of his life, he is right. He is right in the wolf's way, of course . . . . . And there is the rightness of the person who defends the sacrosanct individual, the rights of man, which are superior to every social law . . ." (IX, 858). The potential immorality—from a Christian standpoint—of this attitude is quite obvious, although Unamuno never went so far as to advocate a pattern of conduct on the model of Zarathustra's program. On the other hand, Unamuno's choice of animals indicates how deliberately explicit he intended to be in calling attention to the possible violence of individualism.

The second assumption in his defense of aloofness was the idea that equality among men is a fiction. It is true that Unamuno attacked those social movements which fostered the notion that only antithetical relationships could exist in society: master or slave, conqueror or victim (III, 174). Moreover, he never abandoned the ideal of human dignity, and he declared that we must not tolerate a situation where "the desperate bourgeoisie goes in search of a god that can chain the working people to machines while it launches forth to reach the 'superman.'" Nevertheless, Unamuno discovered "much that is authentic and valuable" in the superman notion, and although he judged it to be a "farfetched daydream," he also deemed it a "magnificent daydream when understood correctly" (III, 446–47). He condemned instead the sterilizing effect, which he feared, in socialist leveling and its "triumph of the median" (III, 683). And, just as his satirical supercat was contemptuous of democracy (IV, 508), so too did he feel that superiorities and inferiorities existed in every aspect of existence. In fact, it was "the duty of brotherly love among peoples for each one to impose upon the others what he feels to be his superiority, and to resist an imposition which he feels in any way to be an inferiority" (III, 683). Thus, equality was a myth in any context, whether individual, class, or national, although the criteria of individual selectivity and eliteness could be applied within the bounds of Christian ethics.

If Unamuno gave his approval to the superman concept as it affected the individual, he did not extend this approval to the Spaniards as a people. He was familiar with the dangers of self-exaltation, and he bitterly criticized young nationalists in Spain who "wished to be convinced that they were an Arian species, a superior and aristocratic race" (I, 1105). He also rejected, as did Nietzsche, the idea of racial homogeneity based on physical characteristics that purport to identify a people, and he denied the racial superiority of Germans and Anglo-Saxons over Latins. In an impassioned moment, Unamuno derided "all those crazy mystical doctrines concerning races and the superiority or inferiority of one over another. A people that spends the years contemplating its navel and trying to persuade itself that it is a superpeople, and pretending to ignore or despise the rest, is a lost people" (VIII, 1097; III, 197; IV, 756).

On the other hand, while Unamuno followed Nietzsche in denying a gradation of racial excellence among nations, he did link the success of a nation to the active presence of a genius among the people. In an interesting essay on "Natural Men and Spiritual Men," Unamuno developed the notion that the genius is the spiritual voice of the people. His thesis was that a nation's ignorant folk are capable of being illuminated, but that they need the help of a visionary, who recognizes the intuitional bond that exists between them. Thus, the genius appears as "an individualized people," a dreamer, hero, poet, or prophet who has somehow intuited and expressed the inarticulate sentiments of the common folk. This does not mean that he has no intimacy or personal qualities. But, as Unamuno describes him, he is so filled with himself that due to "pure personality [he] becomes impersonalized" (III, 854). In other words, his basic personality is characterized by those spiritual qualities which permit him to commune with the people, and this communion dissolves the barriers standing between them. Thus, the fullest development of the genius' powers makes him become impersonal at the same time that he is fully himself. As the embodiment of all people, he is impersonal, but this impersonality is the proof of his personality.

Although Nietzsche did not conceive of the genius in this way, the idea of a "vital genius" does form the premise of any transcendental view of man (III, 443). In order for the individual to aspire to a superior state, there must be no marked qualitative distance between him and this state. That is, he must be, and he usually is, potentially able to rise from his everyday condition to a higher level. But, what of the common man who is no genius? Here Unamuno reverts to one of his basic philosophical positions, namely, the enduring value of the people regardless of how unspectacular their lives may appear in the march of history. If the hero, or genius, rises above the masses to make his mark on history, he does so only because beneath the surface of historical reality lies the deep bedrock of intrahistory, which is the foundation of all events. The people live unheroically, but their fundamental experience of life, the unchanging joys and sorrows that recur generation after generation, make up the permanent tradition of human existence. This is intrahistory, and the hero of external events is fortified by its eternal substance. Having been moved by this intrahistorical undertow, he can lead the masses beyond themselves, uplift them or enlighten them "even if only for five minutes."

Nevertheless, Unamuno was realistic enough to understand the limitations of this kind of human perfection. And so he avoided placing undue favor upon the individual at the expense of the people. At one point he stated that "the man within, the intraman . . . is more divine than the afterman or the Nietzschean superman" (X, 911). By this, he meant that if a choice must be made, the "natural," intrahistoric man is of greater value than the "spiritual" man of genius. He felt also that this choice was correct from the standpoint of progress and social evolution. Accepting the mistaken idea that Nietzsche's superman was a descendant of Darwinian theory, Unamuno decided that there was less room for individual improvement than for collective change. In this respect, he reflected the optimism of certain social doctrines current around 1895. He doubted whether men could individually advance much further than they already had, especially with regard to the strides which the social organism was expected to make. And so he asked, "Are we really moving toward a superman? Is man the germ of a species superior to himself? Perhaps individual progress . . . as such, has a limit . . . and if we suppose a limit to individual organic perfectibility, the social organism [still] keeps on perfecting itself, for it is perhaps in its infancy" (VII, 803).

If Unamuno hesitated to predict further improvements in the human condition on anything less than a social scale, he was quite unreserved in giving credit to the individual for the probability of such improvements. In fact, he was so concerned about individualism in general that he feared the superman concept because it could put a limit on personal development. The prospect of greater emphasis on social evolution did not cause him to worry over such a loss. But, considering how the genius enjoyed a personality only insofar as it was impersonal and characteristic of the people, Unamuno did worry about the effects of aspiring to the superman. He reasoned that the greater the transcendence which the ordinary man achieved, and the closer he came to the "spiritual" state of the genius, the less of an individual he would become. It seemed evident that "perfection is acquired at the expense of personality, and that the more perfect or archetypal a being is, the less personal he is. With this let us see . . . whether it behooves us to aspire to the superman . . . and whether to achieve such perfection we are each of us to renounce our personality" (II, 600; X, 100). Unamuno did not mind the idea of an extraordinary being who might lead the masses out of their "natural" state. Indeed, in some vague sense this might even be in harmony with his dream of social progress. But if the superman was to become a useless archetype, or even an impersonal abstraction, then it would be better to turn man's transcendent impulse to a more vital area. Unamuno's superman, in other words, could not be totally antisocial.

Another area of Unamuno's interest in the superman involved the question of the will to power. In large measure, his frequent disavowal of Nietzsche was due to what he and many others felt to be an overemphasis on the superman's physical strength. Although this is only one of several qualities indicated by Nietzsche, Unamuno's contemporaries in Spain seem to have stretched it out of proportion. Slogans such as "be strong," "blond beast," "master morality," and passages urging war, dangerous living, and acts of plunder (FW, #283), tended to be isolated from their contexts, or else were juxtaposed with the Darwinian idea of the struggle for existence. In either case, the issue of the will to power became inflammatory, making discussion of its implications unfair to the original idea.

Unamuno, however, gauged the notion of power and strength by several standards, and managed to present balanced judgments for the most part. When one of his characters gave the advice to "be one of the strong," this meant not only to act but to be able to think, and to do both at the same time (II, 507–8). Another character found himself suffering from a conflict between meek and severe tendencies, and observed the animal world in order to decide which quality to cultivate. He chooses meekness because he learns that the nobility customarily attributed to strong animals is a fallacy, and he argues that both strong and weak animals are creations of God (II, 715–16, 739–40). In these two examples, Unamuno's position is that strength is an important value when social action is at stake, but that in the moral realm its value is negative.

On the other hand, there is an interesting dialog of an ambiguous nature, featuring Roque Guinart—the outlaw in *Don Quixote*—and a judge. Guinart convinces the judge that the world is made for the strongest and most disciplined men, those with the greatest "will to power." He answers the question "Does the wolf have less of a right to live than the sheep?" by outlining a persuasive defense of strength. Unamuno's intention in this discussion is deliberately evasive, leaving the reader impressed with the argument in favor of immorality. Unamuno himself condemns the outlaw's defense, but he does so very briefly. At the same time, he grants Roque Guinart a typically Unamunian style of reasoning, as if an alter ego were speaking in one of his monodialogs: " 'And you even theorize about crime!' 'Of course . . . . We have intelligence in order to justify our acts . . . . I needed to defend myself.' 'Killing someone in order to rob him is self-defense?' 'Why, sure . . . I was defending my mode of being, my personality, my character. Either I am me, my dear sir, or I cease to be. I have defended my spirit, my transcendent character, my reason for being' " (IX, 824–25). The diction has a familiar ring, and, indeed, the ideas are Unamuno's very own. In reply to Guinart's statement, he does use the counterarguments of Christian sentiment and conscience. But the fact remains that he has allowed the outlaw's defense to carry greater persuasive force.

Unamuno not only found the outlaw type attractive, but he transferred the latter's willpower to a number of his own personages. One of these was Doctor Montarco, whose madness becomes a form of sanity and whose arrogance is a natural trait of genius. Unamuno's point, however, is that this arrogant manner is really the external form of the will to immortality. Montarco declares that "the man who tries to impose himself on the rest is seeking to save himself." Then, after referring to the ferocity of trapped flies, he remarks that "it is not the instinct of conservation which moves us to action, but the instinct of invasion. We don't work to maintain ourselves but to be more, to be all. . . . Yes, the appetite for divinity: 'You will be like gods!' . . . All or nothing! . . . The struggle for life, for survival, rather, is offensive and not defensive . . ." (III, 690–92, 1101). In this connection, Unamuno refers to Darwin and Rolph for scientific support, but his vocabulary of the superman is mixed in with their terminology. Passages of this kind do not always allude to Nietzsche by name, but Unamuno seems to have had him in mind whenever he phrased ideas in this way.

A good example of this failure to name the German occurs in *The Tragic Sense of Life*, although the allusion is quite obvious. Once again, the issue is the will to immortality, a concept which

Unamuno embraces while bitterly denouncing the Antichrist in the same breath. What is interesting about the passage is the fact that it retains Nietzsche's terminology even though his antireligious sentiment is condemned. Both he and Unamuno had the same purpose: the supreme affirmation of the self. However, Unamuno also yearned for an eternal afterlife, and so he needed a theological argument, whereas Nietzsche did not:

There you have that thief of energy, as he clumsily called Christ, who tried to wed nihilism with the struggle for existence, and who speaks to you of valor. His heart asked him for the eternal All, while his head showed him Nothingness. Desperate and mad to defend himself from himself, he cursed what he most loved. Not being able to be Christ, he blasphemed against Christ. Blown up with himself, he wished to be unending and he dreamed of the eternal return, a wretched solution for immortality. And filled with pity for himself, he abominated all pity. And there are some who say that his philosophy is for strong men. No, it is not. My health and my fortitude impel me to perpetuate myself. The other doctrine is for weak men who aspire to be strong, but not for men who already are strong. Only the weak are resigned to final death and substitute something else for the yearning for personal immortality. In the strong, the desire for perpetual life vanquishes the doubt about achieving it, and their life's overflow spills into death and beyond it. (XVI, 178)

This sensitive passage shows how well Unamuno understood himself and Nietzsche, and why he resented the latter's volitional strength to deny God. In attacking Nietzsche, Unamuno was also attacking himself, for he too wanted to be Christ. He too was "filled with self," and contemplated nothingness. Unamuno called Nietzsche weak, but if the criterion is endurance, then Unamuno was the weaker. That is, if endurance is the ability to suffer an eternally recurring condition in order to exalt this suffering— which is what the German philosopher meant—then Nietzsche was the stronger, and Unamuno, having understood this, turned resentment into a refutation of Nietzsche's idea.

The trouble with denials of this sort is that Unamuno felt bound to criticize Nietzsche whenever the subject of Christianity was involved. However, whenever the focus changed to a non-religious matter, Unamuno readily accepted the mystique of imposing the self and appropriating everything that is not the self (III, 1041; IV,

112). In one essay, he named Nietzsche, along with Pascal, Kierke-gaard, and Senancour, as having an attitude with which he felt in especially close sympathy; the wish for a persisting individual con-sciousness. He went on to describe the "great inner tragedies" of these men, without trying to distinguish moral or immoral, Chris-tian or anti-Christian positions. Their tragedy was Unamuno's own, "the struggle between the heart, which asked them for indi-vidual eternity, and the head, which denied it to them" (V, 328). Moreover, the issue was mainly how the superman fulfilled this desire, and whether God played any meaningful role. In Nietzsche's philosophy, of course, the superman does not need God. In fact, God is an obstacle to the superman's evolution. On the other hand, Unamuno's superman "plays with God" (IX, 774), and aspires to achieve His immortality. This is logical, because God has been created in man's image, so that the superman simply replaces Him by transcending his own finitude. As Unamuno asked, "What is God if not the supreme and absolute superman, the projection of man into the infinite? The vision of God sprang forth in the human consciousness, and of necessity it takes an anthropo-morphic form. Thus it is, and so it must be. The ideal must be for anthropomorphic man. And man is above all the depository of consciousness" (VII, 806; VIII, 1097).

This supernatural factor also complicated Unamuno's thinking in the area of progress. We know that despite shifts in emphasis he never ceased to support forward-looking social programs, and we have already talked of this with regard to the superman. If there ever was any negation of those programs for religious reasons, it was because Unamuno regarded this as a choice between the mate-rial world and the afterlife. He did not ever wish to deny the value of this life outright, but when he had to choose between it and the values of eternal consciousness, the latter came first. However, when there was no religious choice to make, Unamuno clearly affirmed this life and its social import. It is significant, then, that we should find the following passage in The Agony of Christianity, a book which discusses the conflicts involved in that choice: "And what is this idea of progress? Does history have a human, or better, a divine, finality? . . . For Christ and for those who believe with Him in the next world, this idea of progress makes no sense. In holiness one does not progress. . . . A Christian does not believe that progress aids salvation of the soul. Civil, historical progress is not the soul's itinerary to God. Hence, we have one more agony for Christianity. The doctrine of progress is that of Nietzsche's superman. But the Christian must believe that what he has to become is not a superman but an immortal, or Christian, man" (XVI, 523–24).

This is the best statement of Unamuno's attitude toward Nietzsche. Since he would not relinquish Christianity, all his evaluations of Nietzschean thought were made by the standard of the Christian afterlife. But when this standard was not at issue, he held the ideals of the superman to be valid provided they did not bear a Nietzschean label. Thus, it is not surprising to find a particularly enthusiastic declaration on behalf of material progress in 1896:

A new, specifically human type, a new live idea, allows a new world [to exist] on the ruins of the old one. A new man! Have we ever thought inwardly and seriously about what this implies? A new man, a genuinely new man, is the renewal of all men, because everyone gains his spirit. He is one more step in the painful ascent from humanity to superhumanity. The only purpose of civilizations is to produce cultures, and cultures to produce men. The cultivation of man is the goal of civilization; man is the supreme product of humanity, the eternal fact of history. How beautiful to see a new man surge forth from the debris of a civilization! . . . We must assist the secretion and promote the decomposing process. We must free culture from the civilization which is stifling it. We must break the cyst which is enslaving the new man. (III, 478–79)

It was precisely this new man, fully conscious of his condition, whom Unamuno continually posited as the man that yearned to be immortal. True, as his career developed, Unamuno's religious preoccupations overshadowed his earlier reformist activities. But it is always useful to remember that the Unamuno who strove to improve the social milieu was the same man of flesh and blood whom the religious Unamuno wanted to save and make immortal.

We cannot say, therefore, that a marked division exists in Unamuno's thought between social man and spiritual man. Such a distinction would be meaningless anyway, in outlining the profile of the superman. A Quixotic temperament, to take but one example, would be just as suitable for a superman as it would be for a spiritual hero (IV, 114). In fact, the means for reaching a higher level of humanity consists of trying to overcome one's material condition. In Unamuno's own words, "if man is to be the embryo of a future humanity more elevated than this one, a true human brotherhood, an embryo of the superman which Nietzsche spoke of, it is necessary for man to begin by emancipating himself from the land, making himself master over it instead of its slave. The entire history of mankind is a constant struggle to be emancipated from animality and from the land. We need a new, genuinely *new* man" (VIII, 70–71). This concern for the "natural" man springs from the conviction that in order to have true progress "it is necessary to naturalize humanity and humanize Nature." This does not mean reducing man to a state of nature, but rousing him to an awareness of nature, for "the superman will be he who reflects within him most exactly the entire life of Nature. This is why when I find myself tired, I seek solitude in Nature, and I wander through those Castilian fields . . ." (VII, 552).

Thus, it was possible for Unamuno to make a meaningful psychological identification between himself and the ideals of the superman, through the medium of the common man. Indeed, this enabled him to genuinely laud the superman concept as wholly desirable because of its relationship to inner awareness, a condition essential to Unamuno's philosophy of life. Once the individual became conscious of his intimate self, he transcended his "natural" state and in fact transfigured all that he saw with his own "internal beauty." "Man humanized nature at the same time that he became naturalized by submerging himself lovingly in it. And thus he becomes superhuman, raising himself above the man tied to the earth, and he supernaturalizes nature by making it his work. What a beautiful dream is the dream of the superman—which obsessed poor Nietzsche—in the bosom of supernature!" (VII, 492).

As we see, therefore, Unamuno's attitude toward a superhuman condition for mankind was neither unsympathetic nor anti-Nietzschean. It is true that he condemned the superman idea in social contexts where it threatened to destroy Christian morality with its all-inclusive egoism. And it is also true that he dismissed the prospect of a superman who would have no afterlife. But at the same time, Unamuno did envision a future man—whom he called "super"—who would achieve and surpass society's material goals, and then enter into a final spiritual phase. In this transcendental process, the individual would possess "time and strength to be integrated and live a human, or rather, superhuman life, once his directive labor were complete . . . ." Thus, Unamuno looked upon the present human condition as a preparation for the real humanity of the future. Mankind would emerge from a transitional period during which "the long struggle for the emancipation from brute animality" would terminate in the appearance of a "superman," and even a "superart." These ultimate qualities are not like the socio-economic perfections sought by the materialists and political reformers, but something much deeper. What they express is the "spontaneous expansion of a profound and really cultivated spirit, a profound *Te Deum* to Mother Nature humanized by human effort, by the extremely holy supernaturalizing work of man. It will be the age of the superman, the *Uebermensch*, which poor Nietzsche dreamed of among the dregs of his many selfish dreams. The age of triumph, not of the most brutish or the most clever, but of the most manly. Of those who bear in their breasts the most humanity, the most common substance. The most good" (III, 361–62).

# 11 BEYOND CHRISTIANITY

*Now that* we have seen Unamuno's interest in the superman concept and moral revaluation, we may conclude that his
modification of Christian values came closer to the Nietzschean
ideal than he cared to admit. What is puzzling, however, is that
Unamuno managed to convince himself—if indeed he was convinced—that the distinction he had drawn between his own view
of Christianity and Nietzsche's was truly radical. In fact, one of his
attacks on Nietzsche is unintentionally ironic because it criticizes a
number of attitudes that are similar to Unamuno's own views. One
irony is that Unamuno used the same epithet, "thief of energy," for
Nietzsche that the latter had applied to Jesus. He also described the
German's philosophy as an effort to "wed nihilism to the struggle
for existence," although Unamuno himself was advocating struggle
as a safeguard against annihilation. He further wrote that Nietzsche's "heart asked him for the eternal everything, while his
head showed him nothingness," a spiritual dilemma which was so
obviously Unamunian as to be trite (XVI, 178).

Looking closer at this identity of spiritual affliction, we find
several emotional differences between Unamuno and Nietzsche.
One of these was the way each man related to God. Unamuno
implied that, in contrast to Nietzsche, he had tried to become God,
whereas the German had rejected Him, and "cursed what he loved
most. Not being able to be Christ, he blasphemed against Christ." It
is here that Unamuno's quarrel intensified. Content that he himself
had never openly denied God, he never thought that he might have

harbored ideas quite similar to those attributed to the German. Thus, he showed little insight into himself when he wrote that Nietzsche was "blown up with himself. He wished to be unending and he dreamed of the eternal return," a solution which Unamuno found inadequate and "wretched." Both men were doubtless filled with self-pity, but it was clear even to Unamuno that Nietzsche "abominated all pity," whereas the Spaniard himself confessed his fears of death and his yearning to survive it. Inevitably, Unamuno must have realized and resented the contrast between an obviously "strong" philosophy that scorned sentiment and his own "weak" confessionalism. He rejected the idea that his German rival had offered a doctrine for really strong men, and he declared that "my health and my fortitude impel me to perpetuate myself. The other doctrine is for weak men who aspire to be strong" (XVI, 178). Either by a psychological blind spot or by deliberate rationalization, Unamuno avoided identification with Nietzsche on this issue, although he had done so on less crucial ones. It is difficult to explain in any other way the fact that Unamuno's descriptions fit both philosophers so closely.

A clue to this problem shows up in another of Unamuno's derogatory passages. This time, his statement was, "I must declare that Nietzsche's anti-Christianity was and is profoundly distasteful to me." And yet in spite of his disavowal, the reasons given by Unamuno were neither theological nor devotional. Instead, he argued from a humanistic standpoint that it was hypocritical to be anti-Christian because the modern intellectual, including the atheist, belongs to a "secular Christian civilization, and whether we like it or not, and know it or not, we carry Christianity in the marrow of our soul" (VIII, 1101). Therefore, he thought that it was impossible to "resuscitate the pagan concept and sense of life," as Nietzsche did, without falling into self-deceit or hypocrisy. This kind of argument, however, has very little to do with Christianity or its values, and it is important for us to note this. Unamuno placed his argument on a cultural basis, free of religious overtones. Not only did he forget the issues of God's existence, the nature of salvation, and man's duty to the Divinity, but he also hastened to defend Christianity in the name of culture rather than Christ. As a result, his deprecations of Nietzsche as the "systematic denigrator and slanderer of Christ" carry little weight except as emotional outbursts. Their practical effect is to distract the reader from a conclusion which is unavoidable, namely, that Unamuno only differed from Nietzsche in his aversion to the invective used to criticize the Christian religion and its God. Otherwise, the two philosophers had many more points in common that Unamuno was consciously able to recognize or admit publicly.

In addition to Unamuno's accommodation with the superman concept and his revaluation of Christian ethics, there were still other resemblances to Nietzsche. His revisionist ideas about Christianity extended to his outlook on history, and especially to the future prospects of man's development. In this area, Unamuno abandoned his individualistic perspective for a broader cultural view of the historical future. Although never forgetting the personal core of human existence, he made its tragic sense the yardstick of cultural destiny. Thus, when he undertook to examine the concepts of the eternal return and the struggle for life, it was done in the light of Christian civilization. And his reactions were largely positive, with a strain of Spenglerian pessimism running through them as a result of his customary doubts concerning individual immortality. It was as if something impelled Unamuno to invoke, from his own emptiness, the deeper abyss of existence and even history. Indeed, he was reminded several times of Nietzsche's observation about illnesses demanding more of whatever it was that made the patient ill (XI, 442–43, 108, 516).

There were several reasons why Unamuno was led from the central core of pain to a region beyond the frontiers of Christianity. One important reason was his deep sense of both nature and the natural spontaneity of man, a feeling which made it easy for him to reject religious dogma. Thus, in evaluating the kind of religion a hero might have, he approved of the fact that "Don Quixote's Christianity was much more inward, beneath grace, faith, and the merit of deeds, within the common root of nature and grace" (IV, 104). This unorthodox view granted Unamuno the spiritual freedom that he needed so badly, and allowed him many intellectual liberties that otherwise would have been forbidden, including his casual mentioning of Luther and Nietzsche in the same breath (XVI, 475). But even more, it removed the concept of grace from the theological realm and put it into a naturalistic context.

This brings us to the second reason for Unamuno's choosing a path that led him beyond Christianity. He not only saw religion as a natural experience, but he found it to be necessary as a social force. He even went so far as to interpret religious dogma in psycho-sociological terms instead of in the usual supernatural way. In one notable instance, the idea of the Immaculate Conception is given an anthropological derivation, and the entire problem of the Las Hurdes peasantry is focused in this direction. At the same time, Unamuno used a bit of sociology to refute the dogma of carnality as being an original sin (XVI, 556). Regardless of the validity of these views, they demonstrate Unamuno's secular orientation, and his desire for a social relevance in religion. He was, of course, quite aware of how radical this view was, and he feared undesirable comparisons with Nietzsche on that score. Consequently, he changed his own terminology in order to conceal his heterodox spirit, although the success of this stratagem is questionable. For example, he protested that God could not be "beyond good and evil" because "*Jenseits* is a Germanic formula of the progressivist Nietzsche," whereas "God is within good and evil and engulfing them" (XVI, 497). The effect of this distinction leaves much to be desired, although once again it is clear that Unamuno sought to call attention away from himself by attaching a "progressivist" label to the German.

We must recognize, therefore, that Unamuno's break with tradition is no less significant for his having refused to emulate Nietzsche's attacks on Christianity. We might say, in fact, that his negation of religious values was more subtle for its lack of violence. Nevertheless, the net effect was the same: a relentless critique of the Christian religion on the basis of its social and historical roles. The best exposition of this critique is found in *The Agony of Christianity*, whose main thesis is precisely the fact that religion has no real social relevance for man's future history. As Unamuno phrased it, the question was whether "Christianity can exist outside of each one of us." What he meant was that "Christianity is something individual and incommunicable," whereas "the truth is something collective, social" (XVI, 463). In other words, if we believe that man is best fulfilled when he has a social dimension as well as a private one, then we must face the fact that Christianity is basically uninterested in "communal understanding." Unamuno went on to develop the conflict between the otherworldliness of Christian doctrine and the material needs of mortal man, an issue we need not introduce here. The thrust of his argument, however, was to place religion in an unfavorable light with regard to social progress.

Unamuno also found Christianity to be historically problematic, and he thought he saw in the Nietzschean superman the embodiment of a practical solution. He defined history as an unending progression which, from a mortal standpoint, "lacks ultimate human finality, [and] is on the road to unconsciousness, to being forgotten." Unamuno then took Nietzsche as an example of how man tries to supply this human finality by striving for a terminal state of perfection, toward which his historical progress has been leading. This is a "superhuman finality, as Nietzsche would say, he who was the great dreamer of the absurd: social Christianity" (XVI, 466). The absurdity, of course, is that Unamuno should have misinterpreted Nietzsche in this way, seeing there what he wanted to see, and dreaming of the very religious materialism that he ascribed to the German.

If we look at the term "social Christianity," we find that its meaning is far from absurd, but that it does represent a contradiction in terms—at least for Unamuno. Basically, the Christian spirit is personal, not social, and the form which it takes in man is conflictive (*agonizante*) because he wants to give it cultural meaning. Therefore, Nietzsche's "superhuman finality" is the key to transforming the traditional Christian faith in a personal salvation. It is cast in the mold of what Unamuno called a forward-looking *pistis*, the "holy confidence in the ideal." However, this ideal was no longer individual, but rather a utopian fraternity of social well-being. Thus, the second coming of Christ would signify a renewed activity in the material world, and not a life of abstraction in a Paradise for souls. In this respect—and Unamuno was daydreaming, to be sure—Nietzsche and Unamuno become reconcilable. The latter set aside his private religious leanings as he redefined Christianity without regard to supernaturalism. And he ignored Nietzsche's anti-Christian invective in order to identify the "perfect Christian" with the "superman when he breaks the Gnostic cocoon in which he is enclosed and comes out from the mystic darkness in which he has abhorred the world, God's world, and in which he perhaps has denied life." This is Nietzschean philosophy as Unamuno would have written it: concilliatory, inoffensive, so-

188 Nietzschean Categories

cial. But as far as Unamunian philosophy goes, it moves away from the religious sentiments commonly associated with *The Life of Don Quixote and Sancho*, or *Saint Emmanuel the Good, Martyr*. And it brings Unamuno and Nietzsche together in their wish for a perfect human condition wherein "Nature will be grace" (XVI, 103).

We have then, this common denominator of social philosophy which we might well term "evolutionary utopianism." To a large extent, it satisfied Unamuno's need for a historical dimension in Christianity. But strangely enough, he was also fascinated by another Nietzschean idea which stands in direct contrast to it. He entertained the historical notion of the eternal return, a pessimistic idea because of its inherently destructive developmental cycle. It is difficult to see why Unamuno, who believed in increasingly higher stages of life, should have been attracted to this "circular conception of time," but we must count this additional inconsistency of his among the others. Nor was he interested in the cosmic implications of this theory, limiting himself to what it meant in terms of history. He understood recurrence to mean the historical repetition of the same or similar events and conditions, which undergo identical processes of change and development. As history repeats itself, its phenomena are different, but the processes through which they pass remain constant and renewable. Thus, different periods and generations are united by like patterns of culture, while humanity constantly returns to older forms of being. Unamuno accepted these ideas without comment, using them as light material for discussions of varying seriousness (III, 683; VI, 506).

On a different level, however, Unamuno was more emphatic in his reaction to the eternal return, and he considered it to be Nietzsche's most palatable idea because it had respectable antecedents. He related the notion to St. Paul's concept of reconstitution (*apocatastasis*), "the gathering together of the universal human consciousness" (VIII, 1002). But, by the same token, the linking of a pagan idea and a Christian one made it clear that Unamuno was interested in any theory which held out the prospect of immortality. Moreover, his sympathy for this solution of Nietzsche's deepened with the suspicion that it represented a desperate gesture on the part of a man whose personal anguish broke through the surface of the philosopher's objectivity. He surmised that Nietzsche had been turning weakness into pretended strength, while at bottom really consoling himself with the dream of "the eternal repetition of the same universal life." Since Unamuno shared this dream, he had only to alter the recurrence idea slightly in order to make it compatible with Christian immortality. This he did by bringing in the notion of a supreme moment of fulfillment, eternally repeated. Immortality was a perpetual state of living one ever-present experience. A Christian recurrence, then, would be an "eternal repetition of a moment of beatific vision" (XI, 539). This idea hardly sounds like Nietzsche, and yet Unamuno found the eternal return useful enough—and even innocent in its paganism—to be made over again along Christian lines.

On still another level, however, Unamuno showed himself to be ambivalent about recurrence. He ridiculed the theory while sympathizing with the theorizer, and yet there were times when the theory appealed to him and Nietzsche became the irritant. It would seem, then, that Unamuno made use of disparagement in order to reproach Nietzsche symbolically for some fault. He was annoyed, for example, by Nietzsche's blasphemy against Jesus, and he charged that "in order to cover up his hunger for immortality he invented the tragic buffoonery of the 'eternal return'" (VIII, 1097). But since Unamuno himself knew exactly what that hunger was like, he called the philosophical camouflage a "tragic" farce. This softened the bite of his ridicule and directed attention to the real question of why Nietzsche had conceived the idea of recurrence. However, Unamuno could not find fault with Nietzsche for wanting immortality. It was the German's blasphemy that bothered him. Therefore, he expressed his displeasure by disparaging the theory. Let us note, for example, that he placed Nietzsche in the same company with Seneca and Job, and referred to "that comic occurrence of the *eternal return* which sprang from poor Nietzsche's tragic inner recesses, hungry for concrete and temporal immortality" (XVI, 357). Thus, we may conclude that if Unamuno sometimes showed little respect for the idea, he did so out of compassion for the man, who so clearly failed to appease his hunger with it.

There is one more aspect to Unamuno's apparent ridicule of the eternal return. He was irritated by the fact that Nietzsche should have answered so irrational a yearning with so rational a concept.

Unamuno's own will to immortality was as passionate and as illogical as was his fear of dying, and he believed that by affirming this emotionally in his essays he had a better argument than any theological proof could have given him. For this reason, he found it incredible that Nietzsche should have tried to calm the same passions by inventing *"mathematically* (!!!) that poor imitation of the soul's immortality which is called the eternal return, and which is the most formidable tragicomedy or comitragedy." Unamuno became impatient with the hypothesis that, given the finite number of atoms in the universe, the combinations of atoms now existing must invariably repeat themselves forever. This was as irrelevant a fact as it was precise, and too absurd to be brought into a discussion about human consciousness and how to make it eternal. Even if the notion were taken seriously, it would still not satisfy Unamuno, because to live an eternal return would put him in "the sad situation of my not remembering any of my former existences" (XVI, 227–28). In answer to this shortcoming, therefore, he offered his own "comic" version of recurrence, and thus betrayed his continued interest in the idea. This version conceived of an unending universe which held a planetary system duplicated an infinite number of times, with Unamuno living a countless number of identical lives simultaneously. Although the idea was admittedly a joke, Unamuno repeated it in a serious vein later, when he modified Nietzsche's eternal but finite universe by making it subject to an Infinite Being (XVI, 364).

We cannot escape the conclusion, therefore, that Unamuno had a fundamentally serious attitude toward the eternal return in spite of his occasional mockery. The final proof of this is the fact that he saw many historical and eschatological implications in the idea. It entered his meditations whenever he tried, as he put it, to "prevent God from committing suicide in my consciousness." Nor could he dismiss the notion on personal grounds either. He was tormented by the loss of all the possible future selves that he might have been in the years gone by. That is, he despaired over the many different Unamunos that he might have been (*yos ex-futuros*) if he had chosen the other alternatives that were open to him, rather than the ones he did choose. Thus, he tried to turn back the course of time and recover in his mind what he once did have. He imagined the centuries in reverse order, proceeding "like the melody of a phonograph record playing backwards, and history with it," so that he could again live his life, "but from death back to birth." Thus, he linked his own biography with the history of the universe, envisioning a historical recession that extended back to the beginning of time, "when there was the Word, and then again to recommence the forward movement. Just like Nietzsche's madness, and almost the same!" (X, 533).

Far from being amusing, Unamuno's last remark reveals a kind of nervous embarrassment over his need for having created such a fantasy. And yet he repeated the same idea in another essay, once more modifying the Nietzschean cycle for his own purposes. This time, he asks what would happen if "the movie film of natural and universal history were reversed, and everything would live again in reverse order until the beginning of the world were reached, and we would begin anew." Unamuno found this possibility to be no less tragic or plausible than Nietzsche's, since they both dramatized the tragedy of time. If they had no firm basis in reality, they did have the mythic power to cure men of "the madness of life's dream." The remedy was to be sought in the eternal return, where the cure for "the anguish of present history is to cling to the anguish of eternity." Thus, Unamuno imagined two distinct currents running through life and the universe. He fancied that under the flow of ordinary existence that runs from yesterday to tomorrow, there "runs another current in the opposite direction." This was the dual structure of life, different from the cyclical recurrence of events but serving the same function. That is, the two currents act in a simultaneous process, a "weaving and unweaving at the same time," in which "the innermost pith of history is a counterhistory" (X, 536–40).

All of these imaginative reflections must be viewed from an extralogical standpoint, for they were not intended to communicate anything more than emotional states. Unamuno's rhetoric here, as in most places, is unanalytical and tends toward lyricism. He spoke of "feeling" history with the heart. And he made the heart analogous to an hourglass: just before turning over the empty glass, "the instant becomes eternity." So too, "between the systole and the diastole of day, the heart stops" and man intuits infinity. This was exactly what "Nietzsche's poor tortured heart" had sensed, and indeed, "he had at hand, at his heart's hand, the eternal instant." But man is doomed to go on, the heart must keep beating, and the sand will continue to run out. The anguished Nietzsche "did not rest for a single minute," and Unamuno himself, living his vision of the moment, felt that moment slipping into the past. And he wondered whether everything was not just a memory of the past: "The present has vanished; everything has become the past. That is, everything has become the future. There is no today: everything is yesterday. Everything has become tomorrow" (XI, 454–55; cf. IV, 397).

In the last year of his life, Unamuno remembered Nietzsche as a "tortured" man, a "dreamer," and a proponent of the eternal return. Writing movingly of a tranquil afternoon when he was resting in bed, Unamuno went on to speak of peace, the meaning of life, suicide. While waiting for "sleep and silence, the things which make old men young," he reflected upon the monotony of events and the fusion of history with legend. It was pointless, he said, to read the newspaper, for it prints the same items that it did yesterday, "and this indeed is a little eternal return, mirror of the tragic 'eternal return' which tortured poor Nietzsche." But Unamuno was already beyond desperation, and at seventy-one he understood that "tomorrow will be the same day, the age-old day." Thus, his compassion was for those "poor men who cannot fall asleep in peace" (XI, 492–94), whereas he, finally, had learned to face the terrors of time with equanimity.

In the final analysis, it can be said that Unamuno considered Nietzsche's eternal return to be a semi-mystical image that expressed, for them both, their anxieties about life and death. This was why he ridiculed Nietzsche's rational description of the idea, a presentation which he felt to be inadequate for such profound feelings. Nevertheless, we cannot as critics expect to understand Unamuno's metaphorical responses to the eternal return except insofar as they fall within the boundaries of our own subjective experience of the problem. The notion does have this kind of limitation. Unamuno himself used it as a means to experience his despair imaginatively, and not in order to acquire the truths of historical knowledge. For him, the idea had an emotional value rather than a cognitive one, and we are forced in great measure to accept his terms.

Although in the last few pages I have emphasized the contemplative and passive characteristics of Unamuno and Nietzsche, the fact remains that they will both be remembered for their activist philosophies. Unamuno frequently depicted life as "a mutual devouring" (II, 707), a description which, when placed in a historical framework, became "a long and sad struggle of adaptation between Humanity and Nature" (III, 379). So too did he feel that a similar struggle existed in the spiritual realm, one which was manifested by the constant attempts among men to impose their viewpoints upon each other (III, 705-6). And even in the biological sense, Unamuno verified human conflict in the "combative instinct of man" and his "psychic and physiological need" for war (IX, 716). These convictions, plus the "appetite for divinity, the hunger for God" which impelled man to impose himself on the world (III, 1041; see also p. 691), made it easy for Unamuno to accept other doctrines, like those of Darwin and Spencer, at least for a while.

Inevitably, the popularization in Spain of both the law of the survival of the fittest and the superman concept created a confusion in people's minds between Darwin and Nietzsche. However, this association of names gave Nietzsche the advantage of securing a greater tolerance among Spanish writers, especially because this was a violent sector of social philosophy. As far as Unamuno was concerned, struggle was not only the natural law of existence, it was an ethical law as well. Moreover, he carried this conviction to the realm of moral action, and stated bluntly that "the profound moral life is a life of mutual aggression and penetration" (III, 1123). There was always, of course, the tacit understanding that none of this could be undertaken with cruelty or malice, and we have already discussed this basic rule. For in general, Unamuno succeeded in adapting the violent aspects of amoral vitalism to the central value of Christianity: love. But in doing so, he allowed the adaptation to go beyond Christianity into a region where there was no clear line drawn between violence and virtue.

There were, nevertheless, several mental reservations which prevented Unamuno from fully supporting the struggle-for-life principle. One of these was his frequent quest for inner tranquility, and in 1895, prior to his having read Nietzsche, he affirmed peace to be the essence of man's reality (III, 274). By the same token, he later blamed Nietzsche for having misinterpreted the survival of the "fittest" to mean survival of the "strongest." However, Unamuno understood "strong" to mean something quite different from either Nietzsche's or Darwin's definition. To Unamuno, strength meant the possession of Christian resignation, humility, and patience, all of which constitute being "fit" and equipped with a "powerful weapon in the struggle for life" (III, 514). Which again led him back into the midst of the conflict.

For the most part, consequently, Unamuno subscribed to the idea that "the man who bends his neck to fortune without struggling with her, is not a real man, is not among those who aspire to the superman" (III, 597). This aspect of struggle acquires religious significance when Unamuno seizes upon the episode of Jacob wrestling with the angel, as we will see in Part Three. In later years, when Unamuno learned about Rolph's theory of excessive life energy, he modified his commitment to struggle as the life force behind evolution. Instead, he maintained that the struggle for life was to obtain not what is necessary but what is superfluous. Needless to say, this idea was even more radical, for it held that struggle is not defensive but offensive, and that a personality which does not expand by imposing itself upon others will eventually contract and shrivel up. The epitome of this doctrine, of course, was to be found in Nietzsche, and Unamuno called it, not surprisingly, the "poetic culmination" (VII, 336–37). In the end, therefore, he maintained a dialectic of force and freedom that almost always broke through the limits of traditional Christian thought.

PART THREE

# Comparative Culture

# 12 DEITIES AND NATIONS

*Without his* deep knowledge of the Old Testament, Unamuno could not have been as good a student of antiquity or of Christian theology as he was. His awareness of the Judaic heritage was a constant source of insight into most of the problems he discussed, a fact attested to by the innumerable uses he made of this heritage in his writings. Whether he was recording impressionistic reactions to Biblical themes in paintings, or giving a Biblical frame of reference to his ideas on women, marriage, and maternity, Unamuno demonstrated his thorough familiarity with the figures and events of the Old Testament,[1] although for a classical philologist he seemed scarcely aware of Hebrew, and he was quite inaccurate about Jewish religious practices.[2] So prominent is the body of references to Judaism in his writings, that their total number is at least commensurate with those alluding to the New Testament.

Unamuno's allusions to the Old Testament are, certainly, external proof of his awareness of the Jew. And yet it was not Jewish religion or culture in themselves which interested Unamuno. Rather, he sought the implementation of this special area of Western Civilization as an anthropological approach, as a method and mirror for understanding Spanish culture. In other words, Unamuno studied the Judaic tradition and used its premises, mythical structures, and ideology as models to create a parallel framework

[1] I, 721, 1080; II, 98, 207, 234, 611, 798; III, 257, 291, 411, 846, 1107; IV, 708; VII, 587–88; IX, 526–27.
[2] III, 324, 556–57, 561, 851; IV, 207–8.

for his basic preoccupations with Spain. His comprehension of Judaic culture refined his analysis of many Spanish problems. It is also true, however, that Unamuno was very aware of the role played by Jews in the unfolding of Spanish history. Thus, his extensive use of their tradition as a technique of comparative culture provides evidence of his esteem for that role. And in turn, this places him among the ranking Spanish intellectuals who have given renewed prominence to Semitics in the historiography of Spain.

One of the basic problems facing Unamuno in his efforts to understand Spanish civilization was the fact that religion was so deeply ingrained in the national character. Just as Unamuno's self-analysis had to deal with the relationship between man and God, so too did his cultural analysis have to assess a similar relationship between deity and nation. In this assessment, it was useful for Unamuno to establish clearly—and indeed, arbitrarily—the difference between the Spanish Christ and the Hebrew Jehovah. Although his distinction represented nothing new, the conclusions he drew bear repeating here as a kind of background to our discussion.

In the Old Testament, God's name is revealed in a dual form, thus corresponding to the two aspects by which He made himself known to the Patriarchs. These separate manifestations—justice and love—are binomially independent but theologically fused into the monotheistic God of Sinai, who tempered law with mercy. From historical and anthropological standpoints, the two aspects have important implications for the evolution of religious sensibility. But they are distinctions which Unamuno ignored in his characterization of the Mosaic God. The reason is not hard to find. Unamuno considered the God of Love to be a product of Christianity, whereas he looked upon the God of Justice, originated by Judaism, as an early and incomplete predecessor. He ranked charity as the highest of values because it was a reflection of divine essence, and hence the most perfect attribute that a psychologically fragmented man could aspire to. We have already seen evidence of this, as well as of the supremacy of love over justice, in Unamuno's writings. In contrast, the Old Testament portrays man in the first stage of his ascent to unselfish sentiment. It follows that the deity of man's dawning consciousness would appear as a reflection of humanity in its restless infancy. Thus, Unamuno saw a restive and ominous God, in keeping with the primitive character of the epoch.

Basically speaking, Jehovah's significance as a God lies in the role which He played as lawgiver. This role is inseparable from the harsh conditions suffered by the Israelites during the period of trial before they possessed the land promised to them. Their desert existence had made no imprint on the wilderness, for it was a way of life imposed upon them as a discipline by a militant, "conquering Lord of hosts" (I, 181–82). Their God, consequently, suited their nomadic life, since His warlike qualities corresponded to their tribal need to fight for a stable existence. Thus, the Israelites found their life experience extended in two directions. As tent dwellers, they bore the outdoor hardships forced upon them by geographic conditions. But at the same time, they were compelled to transcend topography by their Levitic leadership, who kept before them the ever-present Ark of the Covenant, which guarded the Law.

Here, then, was an interlocking relationship of open landscape, nomadism, aggression, and tabernacle, with each element shaping the destiny of the Semitic tribes. It was among these elements that Unamuno found a cultural symbolism for Spain. The landscape of barren Castile, the agrarian question, internal strife and fratricide—all were part of Unamuno's Spain, whose "bloody numen," as the poet Machado put it, was a just but severe God presiding over a primitive national condition. Unamuno even extended this idea to the intuitions he experienced while going out into the countryside, and of one such moment he wrote, "I greet this mountain peak, which is higher than its sister, the one I now stand on, and where once, before daybreak, when lying on the ground with heaven as my only roof, I found myself wrapped in a storm cloud. And it was then that I understood the God of Sinai" (I, 713). Sometimes he would try to create the illusion of pastoral tranquility in order to gain peace of mind, but it would be shattered by the reality of Nature's violence. At such times, he could imagine Jehovah, in the midst of natural upheaval, handing down the stone tablets that represented moral order. In this way, he linked the historical present to the mythological past, and located the sanctuary of eternal order in the center of natural unrest. Referring to one experience, he wrote: "As I watched the lightning bolts gird the huge peaks of Gredos, the God of my country was revealed to me, the God of Spain, just as Jehovah revealed Himself to the

Israelites while thundering and lightning on the crests of Sinai. The revelation of God descends from the mountains" (I, 510–11).

In this way, Unamuno was careful to situate the Judaic God in the wilderness. Moreover, he was just as assiduous in stressing the terrifying aspects of divine activity. Not only did God issue apocalyptic warnings of doom, invoking Nature in her most threatening guise, but Unamuno could even cite scholarly sources to prove how bellicose Jehovah was. Thus, Unamuno created a portrait of God in the image of primitive man. Yet this primitiveness did not imply one special culture, but tended, rather, to be supranational. That is, it was unfettered by history and the limitations of one country's experience. Consequently, Unamuno's Jehovah became supremely anthropomorphic, in that the set of emotions associated with Him was a reflection of the eternal forces at work in the human condition. By projecting man's basic psychological patterns upon a superior being, Unamuno imputed to these patterns a preternatural source. His technique is interesting to watch.

He began with the familiar setting in a wild and thunderous Nature. A hurricane blew, and "at night it seemed as if the darkness were moaning. Moaning or roaring? And I recalled those terrible words in the Old Testament about the whispering of Jehovah. It wasn't a whisper; it was the cry of grief, almost of anguish. You might say, the death rattle of His demise" (X, 775). This scene might awaken any number of different sentiments in us, but to Unamuno the mood that it inspired was one of dread. He found that Nature's indifferent violence lent itself to a variety of emotional interpretations. Her state of neutrality allowed Unamuno to infer any emotional condition he wished, simply on the basis of his own subjectivity. Whatever projection he made was based on an inner need, and it required an external support, a natural setting which became the *de facto* locus of the emotion in question. Unamuno did not see that the atmosphere of fear in this case had originated within himself, and so he began to explain it on external grounds. Hence his reference to a supernatural source.

If we pause for a moment, we can see how spontaneously Unamuno shifted his understanding of Jehovah from a cultural and geographical level to a private and intuitive one. Let us recall the sharp despair which was associated with some of the psychological problems discussed earlier in Part One. Although Unamuno relieved this despair by resolving the issue of personality, this was only one of his solutions. Another was to raise his personal anxieties to a universal level, watching for signs in Nature that corresponded to his feelings. When he found them, he adopted a religious outlook to help him cope with their effects. Thus, his reference to Jehovah's whisper being "the cry of grief, almost of anguish" really tells us more about Unamuno than about God. He made Jehovah serve as the deity for the exorcism of his own spiritual dread, and he attributed to Him his own human feelings. Let us also remember that Unamuno's underlying attitude in his religious moments was the fear of death. Since he was so aware of his mortal condition, he felt the proximity of death even more by contrast with the prophetic whispering of an eternal Being. God, as the creator of mortal men, was also their foil in their awareness of death and immortality. Thus, Jehovah became for Unamuno a symbol of inevitable destruction, the cause of man's spiritual terror, and a figure devoid of any sign of love (II, 802).

More than just a symbol, however, the God of the Hebrew patriarchs was a portrait-study of justice and strength, qualities which Unamuno deliberately sharpened to make them stand out against the gentleness of Jesus. Whereas meekness characterized Jesus in Unamuno's mind, awesome fear was the passion inspired by Jehovah. This difference in feeling is a central problem in Unamuno's religious existentialism. One of his basic concerns was how the concept of God in man's awareness was influenced by fear. He saw the evolution of this relationship between fear and man's image of God on several levels. Psychologically, it involved the most instinctive form of insecurity, in which the divine image appeared as a primitive god of vengeance. From an anthropological point of view, however, this fear appeared to shape a different image. He was now seen as a mountain god, an elementary cultural product stamped in the stereotype of "the terrible God of Sinai, thundering from His cloud-wrapped carriage on the sacred mount, and hurling lightning bolts" (III, 638). Unamuno did not, of course, place Jehovah among the ranks of local nature gods, but the primitive traits in this image do reveal certain vestiges of religious paganism. At the same time, Jehovah qualified as the father of Unamuno's Christian God because of the ethical quality of His divine nature. His purpose was not exclusively to seek retribution among generations, but to provide moral continuity as well, by being an eternal judge from one historical moment to the next.

Nevertheless, the Mosaic God was, for Unamuno, disaffected from man in feeling, and dictatorial in the matter of ethics. Missing was the spiritual communication later supplied by Christianity, a lack stressed by Unamuno when he pointed to the difference between "the God who punishes the sins of the fathers in the sons up to the seventh generation; the harsh, justice-seeking God, and the God of the Gospels, the Father of Christ, the God of forgiveness." The latter, of course, represents an improvement over the God of Sinai from the standpoint of humane qualities. But the Christian deity does not reveal any other divine attributes. In fact, there is a suggestion that the humanization of Christ marks the turning point in the way by which divinity had been manifested in previous religious experience. For example, Unamuno remarked that "the great originality of Christianity in the religious order is its having discovered the filial relationship between man and his God. God is the Father of Jesus, and Jesus is the Son of Man" (III, 638). In other words, the Hebraic experience produced a relationship of formal and emotional distance between man and the divine power. The great discovery of Christianity was that the same capacity for love existed in both God and man. This resulted in the creation of a new, human God, who appeared as the son of man and God at the same time. Consequently, the entire emotional motivation behind religion shifted from fear to love.

What we have said thus far can be summed up in broad existentialist terms. Unamuno's concept of Jehovah was formed in the image of man's terror of death and the unknown, while the notion of Jesus' salvation expressed hope in the human capacity for love. Mankind had projected its fears upon the Hebraic deity, just as now it projected its love upon Jesus Christ. Since man was afraid of the former, he could not love it, and consequently he created the latter in order to personify the love that he wished to see embodied in divine form. To support this view, Unamuno cited a passage from St. Augustine, which attempted to explain why man fears and loves God simultaneously: "He is something very different from me, and therefore I am frozen with fear. He is something identical to me, and therefore I am inflamed with love" (III, 638). In truth, the Judaic tradition had accomplished a similar synthesis by giving the God of Sinai two different names. But Unamuno, being a Christian, had to ignore the Mosaic God of mercy in order to reserve for Jesus the role of Saviour, and to retain Jehovah for man's darker fears.

If Unamuno's psychological approach to the Judaic God was complementary, his juridic interpretation was schismatic. He found that Moses and Jesus represented different law-giving attitudes, with the Decalog being antithetical to the Sermon on the Mount in its spirit of revelation. On this point, Unamuno's imagery is unmistakable: "From Sinai, a mountain wrapped in a continuous collar of lightning flashes and stormy uproar, Moses proclaimed the Decalog to his people. And from a serene mount in Palestine, an olive grove perhaps, sweet and scented by the sun, the holiest of teachings was poured forth over man" (I, 629). In Unamuno's mind, there was always something magical about Moses' powers, whether he was surrounded by Jehovah's glory, or was striking a rock with his staff to draw water (I, 267). On the other hand, whereas Moses made fountains spring in the name of a mighty God, Jesus had only to open his mouth gently "to let flow . . . the wellspring of his doctrine" (I, 629).

More important, however, than the distinct religious aura around each lawgiver was the purpose of the laws they promulgated. Jehovah's ethical message emphasized obedience to Him and to the Law. Jesus preached the love of man. This difference was elaborated in *The Tragic Sense of Life*, which maintains that the major contribution of the Christian ethos of love was the belief in immortality. A son of man becomes God, which is to say, immortal. In contrast, the book continues, "among the Jews there was no general or clear faith in another life" after this one (XVI, 186). This is why Unamuno considered Christianity to be the superior religion of the two. The Mosaic God required His people to obey commandments which involved the earthly, rather than the heavenly, kingdom. Thus, Judaism became a religion centered about God's demand for obedience and supremacy. Christianity, on the other hand, stressed its preoccupation with the future—and present—well-being of men. Its mission was spiritual and eternal.

Despite this evaluation of Judaism, Unamuno did trace carefully the emergence of Christianity from Judaic sources, and he depended upon his understanding of Jehovah to do so. He discovered that since Israel was unconcerned with immortality, its concept of God developed according to historical criteria. Israel had placed its faith in "a personal and live God, whose formation is His entire spiritual history." In other words, Judaism progressed with the needs of each moment, attending to its immediate problems without concern for transcendence. If it finally developed beyond the stage of other local cults, it never became more spiritual than its affirmation of an individual immortality. And this materialistic trait was the result of Jehovah's own attributes as a divinity.

One such attribute was evident from the fact that Jehovah had begun as one god among many and then became the national god of Israel. He was "so jealous, He demanded that they erect a cult to Him alone, and it was through monocultism that the Jews arrived at monotheism." This anthropological interpretation places Jehovah at one end of the religious spectrum, for His genesis is clearly "social and warlike." In the long evolution toward Christianity, this meant that there were at least two stages in the emergence of the Judaic God. In the first, as the Sinai deity, "He was adored as a live force, not as a metaphysical entity, and He was the god of battle" (XVI, 187). In the second stage, the prophets embraced Him as an intimate experience. Thus, Unamuno saw the absence of metaphysical qualities in Jehovah as a distinct advantage, for they would have stood in the way of the deity's future personalization. When the Hebrew prophets did experience Him personally, it was because they were able to transform His external qualities into a human intuition. Most important to Unamuno, however, was that this God was becoming more universal.

Actually, at this point Unamuno could see that Jehovah was virtually a precursor of Christ. He believed that Jehovah's love had a certain redeeming effect, because it stimulated man's faith in a personal God and in immortality. His idea was that the deity "did not love Israel because it was His son, but rather, took it as His son because it loved Him." Man took the first step in loving, "and faith in a personal God, in the Father of men, carries with it faith in the eternalization of the individual man, which begins to dawn in Phariseeism, even before Christ" (XVI, 187). The more of these personal developments that appeared in connection with the Sinai God, the more Unamuno found Him acceptable for a humanistic religion. Of course, a religion of this kind would seem to require few godly qualities, as distinguished from human ones. And, in fact, as Jehovah discarded sternness, militancy, might, and other awesome traits, He gained in esteem. Indeed, the only essential attribute of divinity which Unamuno seems to have required is immortality. All of the others have little meaning for the individual who is also yearning to be immortal. The reason for this is that Unamuno was not really interested in God per se, but only insofar as He would love man and make him immortal. This is why the Mosaic God was humanistically useless to Unamuno, since His love proved to be less than man's self-love and desire to live eternally. God became valuable only to the extent that He reflected man's existential concerns. Thus, the image of Jehovah rose in Unamuno's esteem as it gradually changed into an early reflection of Christ the man.

The Judaic and Christian deities evolved not only in relation to men, as we have seen, but also to nations. The uniqueness of Judaism as a national religion was decidedly of great significance to Unamuno, who was always more interested in the practical consequences of religion than in theology. This special orientation of the Jewish nation helped him to crystallize his own thoughts about the relationship between Christianity, Spain, and himself. He found in Judaism's God, land, people, and law, a cultural complex analogous to similar inseparable elements in Spanish civilization. All of his speculations were so interconnected that they formed a chain of themes which actually reflected the complicated cultural reality. For example, his reflections on Castilian geography led to associations with the Biblical myth of Cain. The latter, in turn, suggested to him certain ethical considerations and national characteristics. These brought him first to the ideals of Don Quixote, and then to human destiny on both a personal and an interpersonal level. From there, finally, he was led to the question of religious destiny, the role played by Jesus, and the spiritual effect of both on Spain. Each of these themes is enormously complex in Unamuno's philosophy. However, they are all tightly bound to each other, just as their counterparts in the Judaic tradition are also inextricably related. Most important of all, in the cultural experience of both Israel and Spain, the sacred and the profane were two sectors of the same existential sphere. Thus, whether in the collective memory of the

Bible, or in the private theater of Unamuno's consciousness, the hunger for immortality was the same.

One of the chief factors in this multileveled spiritual quest was geography. For Unamuno, the communion with the land which, in the Pentateuch, formed a brooding background, was in Spain a continuous source of introspective activity. The same identification of man and earth existed in both cases. The primeval beauty of the Canaanite landscapes and the Castilian plains mirrored, on the one hand, the harsh splendor of the Sinai God, and, on the other, the nuptial rewards of the ascetic God of the mystics. Unamuno found in the area around Santa Teresa's Avila, the Genesiacal majesty of certain Old Testament settings (I, 839). Elsewhere, the terrain had a tragic aspect, and the abrupt changes from desert to oasis in both Palencia and Palestine made them twin sources of unexpected fruition. But in general, the burden of labor and barrenness settled on the land, and "the terrible barren plain" was seen "as a tragic and petrified sea, from the bald mountain top of Christ of Otero," with its ground yielding a single, long-awaited harvest: "just one gathering. The miracle of Sarah, Abraham's wife" (I, 823). Thus, regional characteristics became transcendental categories when compared to their Biblical archetypes. And the history of a time-bound locality was made eternal when its fate was coupled to the desires of a divine power.

Time also failed to exert a lasting control over the inhabitants of the land, for "the history of the Iberian Abelite was to struggle against History." The mythic Iberian, graced with the aura of immortal struggle, reflects Unamuno's personal battle for eternal life. The peasant strives to get outside the framework of history, and his hope to recapture the pastoral idyll of Genesis forms the nucleus of Unamuno's complex mass of themes. On one level, it represents the terrestrial versus the Edenic concepts of agrarian life; on another, the problem of exile and nationality; and on a third, the alternatives of death and immortality.

Unamuno's coherent treatment of these questions is based on the mythos of Judaic religious nationalism. The Spanish Abelite, by means of his historic—and intrahistoric—recollections, maintains contact with the bucolics of Adam's paradise, refusing to relinquish the ground "next to the walls of Paradise, from which God expelled his first parents." His wish is "always to be within sight of the flaming sword with which the angel guards the path to the tree of life" (IV, 1138). The desire is based on personal motivation, but it also reflects a tacit appraisal of the physical qualities of the country he dwells in. Thus, we are reminded that the Spaniard has agricultural difficulties as well as a yearning for immortality. His very life is a blending of the historic and the eternal, with his individual destiny being tied to national circumstances, and then to a religious framework. For instance, an observer of the Spanish landscape might imagine how "yonder in the distance there sounds the clash of arms of the armies of Joshua and Gideon, who, in the plains of Canaan, battle for the promised land." In contrast, the Iberian Abelite "seeks only the resigned and sad peace of the barren land here, next to the walls of the forbidden Paradise" (IV, 1138–39). Yet there is no difference between the two images except in Unamuno's mind, which contains the integrated picture: the Biblical reminiscences evoked by the land, and the resigned Castilian shepherd who is a mythical counterpart of the Bible.

The foregoing scene is part of a complete essay devoted to supporting the ethical values of the Old Testament. Two of these values were, in Unamuno's opinion, protest and resignation, attitudes which reminded him of the figure of Job. A third value, the vanity of action, brought Ecclesiastes to mind. In the light of these attitudes, Unamuno began to characterize the Iberian peasant as an eternal "type." He depicted him as a passive figure standing in the shadow of Paradise, where "he learned that there isn't any new world, that it is all old and that History is a nightmare." This did not mean that the peasant abandoned hope for an afterlife, especially when his illusion helped to ease the geographical burden of his existence. On the contrary, he preferred the "pleasant dream of the Genesiacal legend, with which to brighten his siestas in the brush" (IV, 1139). But his tragic situation remained Job-like, and even resembled the plight of Jesus as a man who was abandoned by his Judaic God. This parallel was dramatized by Unamuno with great feeling. Just as Job and Jesus protested at God's apparent disfavor, so too does the Iberian lament his exile in the wastelands of Castile, lands which surround the Garden now shut to him. He cries out asking why God has forgotten him, "and the Lord, to prove to him that He has not abandoned him, rains hail down on his fields, causing the fiery sword of the angel guarding the path of life to shine out in the black sky." The object lesson here is that the Spaniard has no permanent hold on the earth. The land belongs to God alone, and if man complains, he is punished in the same way that the children of Israel were, when God banished them to the wilderness. The transgression varies in each age—original sin, blasphemy, or protest against the pain of existence—but the penalty is meted out through the "natural lands, God's lands" (IV, 1139).

These descriptions of man's destiny within a specific Iberian location are what make Unamuno different from the utopian writers. He considered it meaningless to abstract the human condition from its national context, and, by the same token, he was unable to evaluate a culture without also taking its inhabitants into account. However, he was not averse to generalizing about Spain's national character, even though it meant talking about a hypothetical Spaniard instead of specific people. When it came to examining the cultural implications of Christianity in Spain, this willingness to generalize was quite helpful. Unamuno was able to move from national religion to universalism by taking the religio-cultural vision of the Old Testament and comparing it with Christian Spain. Thus, he pondered the extent to which so-called Judaic traits had been assimilated by the Spaniard. He also sought corroboration for at least a partial Semitic influence, recalling that "there are those who say that we are proto-Semitic, that Berber blood, at the least, runs through our veins." This existence of Semitic traits was a debatable hypothesis, but it was the premise accepted by Unamuno in his analysis. Moreover, he distinguished between the Jewish Jesus of Nazareth and the Hellenized Christ, and he suggested that the former truly approached the Spanish character. In effect, Unamuno asked whether "we Spaniards have reached the New Testament? Could it be that we have remained in the Old Testament? Have we really reached Jesus? And more than reaching Jesus of Nazareth, who, after all, sprang from the Old Testament and is, as perhaps we are, a Semite, have we reached Christ, the Platonic Christ, the one who was baptized again in Greece?" (I, 491).

The weight of these questions lay less in the answers—for none were forthcoming—than in their use as methods of cultural analysis. As unsystematic as Unamuno was, his writings show the frequent use of certain standards or guides for his discussions. And often these standards did bear results, if not always conclusive ones.

A good example is the racial criteria that appear to differentiate one linguistic group of people from another. Unamuno himself was opposed to racial exclusivism among societies, as his essays on purism prove. He supported "the systematic deprecators of what is purist and native," and he echoed their shibboleth, "May they conquer us!" But he detected in both Israel and Spain an inclination to affirm the very traits that tended to keep them aloof from the effects of other nations. Thus, he approved of "that doctrine of anarchism and submission whose prophet was Jeremiah in the days of King Josiah, when he called for the Israelites to submit to the Chaldean yoke so that, purified by slavery and exile of their dissensions and inner vices, they might become the people of the Lord's justice" (III, 173). Thus, the parallel drawn between Jewish and Spanish national experiences went even deeper. Both nations sought to keep their identities intact, rather than submit to cultural assimilation. Their resistance to externally imposed changes led to militancy and fanaticism. But, in the end, they both failed as states because their puristic exclusivism clouded the meaning of Jeremiah's plea for submission.

What was the meaning of this plea, which Unamuno himself looked upon favorably? It involved the idea of submitting to God's universal kingdom, and forgetting about the compulsion to preserve a cultural identity. Significantly enough, Unamuno developed this idea best in his account of the death of Jesus. Against a background of political drama, he recreated the crucifixion as a civil tragedy rather than a religious one, in which the central actors clash over how important the State should be in their lives. The chief accusation against Jesus was the charge of treason. Pontiffs and Pharisees alike "condemned him to death for being an antipatriot" (III, 658). At that time, Israel's highest value had been embodied in the Maccabean fight for independence, and her citizens were dreaming of renewed revolt against Roman domination. Jesus lived "in conditions analogous to those of the Spaniards under Arab domination or under the Napoleonic invasion" (III, 659). His moral philosophy was a universalistic one, and it conflicted with the narrow national interests of his fellow countrymen. Thus, the latter feared in the growth of Jesus' influence a subversive danger more serious than any foreign threat could have posed.

Consequently, the issue became one of whether cultural survival depended upon the political orthodoxy of the group, or whether there were ideals higher than government in the concept of a nation. Of course, when the orthodox leaders realized what the issue implied, they felt threatened. They knew that Jesus was teaching a new philosophy that dispensed with nationalism. Thus, they posed a question designed to trap the rebellious teacher. They tried "to tempt Jesus, who was a Jew, one of a people conquered and subjected to foreign domination." The question put to him was whether tribute should be paid to the Roman invader. Unamuno's emphasis here on Jesus' nationality is important, for it makes the analogy with Spain more explicit. If Jesus were looked upon as Christ rather than as an ordinary citizen, Unamuno could not have used the episode as a practical mirror for Spain. As a Jew, then, Jesus' dilemma in answering the question was this: "If he said yes, he would appear as a bad patriot before his Jewish compatriots, as someone who was taking the part of his people's oppressor. And if he answered no, he would be reported to the Roman authorities for sedition." By pronouncing the famous dictum about rendering unto Caesar what is Caesar's, Jesus redefined cultural tradition according to eternal and divine standards. He maintained that it is possible to retain the purist characteristics of the group while also transcending the limits of time and space. In other words, by becoming internationalized in the limited political sense, the nation would be saved; but by coming into contact with the divine, it would be universalized. As Unamuno interpreted Jesus' answer, it was a "statement equivalent to saying: I don't have anything to do with these earthly dissensions over national independence or foreign domination. I have nothing to do with the Romans' dominating us in order to extend their culture, or we Jews being independent of them in order to maintain our collective personality. My kingdom is not of this world!" (III, 659).

The reference to "collective personality" must not be taken to mean that Unamuno held in low esteem the retention of unique cultural traits. It was possible to be a Jew without having political means, and even without having a physically existent country. And the fact was that Unamuno continued to be a Spaniard despite being forced to live in exile. Therefore, the judgment passed on any seditious national had little to do with his basic resemblance to the collective personality, or to his loyalty. Rather, judgments of this kind were usually based on concepts like "narrowness of race" and the "separation of civilization," views that grew out of a superficial understanding of cultural growth. As Unamuno said, paraphrasing the high priest Caiaphas, "it was fitting for one man to die for the people, rather than for the whole race to perish." But, added Unamuno, "Today the race of Caiaphas and Jesus, the Jewish race, is throughout the entire world without a country. Without a country? Without a country, no! Without land, without national territory. Because he who said, 'Render unto Caesar what is Caesar's'—money—'and unto God what is God's'—honor and spiritual reverence—gave us a spiritual fatherland, that of our race" (X, 649).

History has thus proven the Jewish priestly class to have been wrong in opposing Jesus, since its strongest fear, the loss of identity, was never confirmed subsequently. The state, on the other hand, reputedly the instrument for protecting that identity, was liquidated without further cultural detriment. Unamuno concludes, therefore, that any form of persecution for the sake of purism is without justification. This is why the crucifixion had, in his eyes, greater meaning for Spain in secular terms than as a religious passion. Basically, Jesus was an internationalist, a utopian who was executed so that "narrow Jewish nationalism" could be preserved. Like the proponents of the Spanish Counter Reformation, "the chosen people could not allow itself to be made to live in spiritual communion with the other nations, with the Gentiles" (X, 650).

At this point, the parallelism with Spain becomes decisive. The destiny of Israel during its political disintegration was guided by the same intolerance of heterodoxy that later gripped the Spanish Inquisition. Jesus symbolized the spiritual freedom of the humanist who sought to unite nations through a doctrine of moral universality. "The Jewish priests who led Christ to the Cross were fanatics. Centuries passed, and the Inquisition was established in Spain, and the Jews were expelled first, then the Moors. For religious reasons? No, in order to maintain a Pharisaic unity of race, to protect its homogeneity, which is the origin of spiritual, moral and even economic impoverishment, and death" (X, 650). The mistake of both Israel and Spain in their roles as persecutors was to confuse the external and the essential qualities of their cultures. There was a great difference between the institutional mechanisms of a nation, which rust away and can be replaced, and the permanent collective identity of the people (race), which can be assimilated without losing its internal and eternal uniqueness.

Here, then, was the lesson which Israel spelled out for Spain. When nations bind themselves to the material fate of the land and its administration, they lose their spiritual hold on the transcendental meaning of their existence. At that moment, religion ceases to play a role in their activities, although it is used as a pretext. In the case of Spain, it was a body politic that became "the leader of the Counter Reformation. The heretic was considered an enemy not of religion, but of the Caesarian fatherland. And it was temporal Power, Caesarian power, the secular arm, which tormented the heretics." And Unamuno added, in a reference to one conservative nineteenth-century scholar: "It is futile for Menéndez y Pelayo, who thought he was destroying what he believed to be a legend, to have created another legend. The black legend of the Inquisition is less black than the historical reality" (X, 650).

Linked to the above issues of rigid orthodoxy and religious nationalism is the question of militancy with regard to the law. For here, too, the interests of the cultural group become a pretext for exercising political legalism through the use of religious values. Once again Unamuno saw Caiaphas as the embodiment of diabolical principles. Being "the priest who was the most careful about the prestige of authority, he condemned Christ. And it was these very principles which later condemned Dreyfus in France and so many others elsewhere. It is the barbarous, inhuman, and unjust principle of *salus populi*, with health and people understood in the same way that quack doctors of salaried patriotism understand it" (IX, 951).

The point is that the religio-national problem, which was originally a Jewish phenomenon, can apply to any society that sets up an official orthodoxy at the same time that it seeks to preserve its cultural personality. The concept of the people's health is the central motive of what turns out to be a programmatical persecution. The main force in implementing this militancy is, eventually, the juridical system, a secular organ of the social body. Moreover, it acquires an enthusiasm which is fed directly by the religious forces acting upon it. Unamuno found this situation to be repugnant, and in a letter to his friend Angel Ganivet he denounced it: "To what monstrosities have we been carried by the infamous and vicious alliance of Christian Gospel and Roman Law! One [of them] has been the religious consecration which people have tried to give to militant patriotism" (IV, 1001). This meant that patriotic fervor had drawn strength illicitly from a realm which had nothing whatever to do with the materialistic purposes of political law. Again the Judaic tradition illustrated the point nicely, and not only with regard to Jesus' treason. The Jews had proven subsequently that a culture can exist without political values. That is, as a persecuted people scattered over many lands, they were able to transcend their particular geographies and "subsist better as a people by not forming a nation" (IV, 1001).

As Unamuno moved back and forth in history, he concluded that the Judaic fusion of church and state could ultimately have only unhappy effects. If that fusion had ever indicated any positive value, it was when humanism entered as a mitigating factor. Unamuno supported this idea by citing the presence of Fray Luis de León in an age of patriotic militancy. Fray Luis had been a sixteenth-century anomaly because his love of peace was out of place in the religious violence of his epoch. And yet temperamentally, he struck a perfect balance between the philosophical serenity of his spirit and the burning vigor of his intellect. His portrait seemed etched according to the tradition of the Old Testament, and then retouched by pagan idealism. To Unamuno, he lived "like Job, a master of misfortunes, his soul filled with the burning thirst for justice, with Hebraic prophecy, tempered in the serene temperateness of the Hellenic ideal" (III, 268).

Unamuno singled out both Fray Luis and Don Quixote as anomalous figures who symbolized the love of law and justice in a rigidly orthodox Spain. This orthodoxy would have turned justice into a stern rule under any condition, but when religion and statism were combined within a single culture, the results were pitiless. This was Unamuno's judgment of Spain's sixteenth century, and the reason why he condoned Don Quixote's freeing of the galley slaves. He also admired Fray Luis' rejection of both war and the harsh legalism that it produced. By the same token, there was a tacit acceptance of the need for severity, as long as it was restrained by love. Thus, Fray Luis represented a compromise before the unfathomable hardness of Jehovah, and the clearly erroneous militancy of the Israelites. Since God was inscrutable, His stern justice might well have concealed an equal measure of love, but the children of God, being mortal, had no right to display such severity. When Fray Luis spoke of war and law, he "shrank back on observing that the Scriptures use military terms, it seeming to him to be one of the profound abysses of God's secrets. In our Golden Age society, which chased after profit and caused wars with religious grief, Maestro León considered the Jews' greatest and original sin to be their worship of the golden calf, which, as it plunged them deeper into sin, led them to expect a warlike Messiah" (III, 271–72).

This evaluation is typical of Unamuno's general anatomy of Spain, whose inner landscape, as her physical one, was hewn out of the older and ruder sections of the Scriptures. The Golden Age was unenlightened in its fanaticism, brutal in its missionary enlightenment of the world. During such a period, Fray Luis "embodied the philosophy of the lamb in the society of wolves that he suffered in," for what the group lacked in moral rectitude and compassion, he atoned for through resignation and yearning. The distinction which Unamuno saw in him consisted of his advanced stage of spiritual development. If Christianity was the mature outgrowth and refinement of Judaism, then Fray Luis personified this maturity by combining "Lucretius' *pietas* . . . with a prophet's yearning." And if Spain had not yet emerged from the Old Testament storm into the calm of Hellenism, she could still aspire to the synthesis of Fray Luis, who, "classicist and Hebraizer, united the spirit of Greek humanism with that of Hebrew prophecy" (III, 274–75). The Spaniard was still tied to the material concept of his country, whereas Fray Luis had freed himself from his national circumstance. And in doing so, he had transcended the spiritual meagerness of such an existence in return for a universal cultural outlook.

# 13 RACE AND RELIGION

*Members of* the Generation of 1898 always approached the problem of Spain with at least a tacit definition of the Spanish national character. They envisioned the "soul" of Spain in many ways, but always within a loose homogeneity of group traits that were listed under the denomination of *race*. This was also true of Unamuno's attempts at a cultural portrait. In Unamuno's case, however, the descriptions have almost no trace of racial overtones of the kind that might suggest biological distinctions. And when it came to illustrating an anthropological point by using Israel as an example, he avoided references to the Jews as a race. In no sense, then, can Unamuno be considered a racist, as this term was understood at the beginning of the century. Nevertheless, for all his avoidance of the popular theories of his day in this regard, he did not show any hesitation in affirming certain permanent characteristics to be typically Jewish, just as he did for many Spanish traits.

Unamuno's references to Jewish traits are drawn along psychological and nationalistic lines. This is predictable, given his broad analytical purposes, for although the references themselves are sometimes trivial, their use as cultural norms is indicative of a basic approach. The very contrast is itself interesting. For example, Unamuno fell into the banality of stamping stereotyped traits into several of his fictional personages (IX, 357, 361). In one place, he remarked that "where Semitic blood flows, there is an overly carnal sense of virility" (II, 694), and elsewhere, for literary effect, he compared Jews and Carlists, stressing their beards, ragged black clothes, and surreptitiousness (II, 670). In another area, he referred to Jews as materialists, and as a people who demanded visible proof before believing in God (III, 1001, 1002). Because of its religious implications, he found the latter trait to be especially defective. But this aside, it was even more interesting as an example of how unique attributes existed which, when identified, could help to distinguish one group of people from another.

In one curious case, these unique attributes were made to point out the subtle difference between inherent cultural traits and national ones. Unamuno spoke of a priest that he knew, born of Italo-Jewish parents, who was abducted and baptized while still an infant, and who had retained his quasi-ethnic characteristics despite a lifetime of Catholic doctrine. This priest was "lively and sagacious, ingenious and enterprising," and "had another trait of the genuine Israelite, which was his facility for learning languages" (IV, 943). This particular trait and others like it are in themselves meaningless, but they do indicate the way in which Unamuno acknowledged the existence of national peculiarities. He believed that the qualities of biculturalism ascribed to the priest were culturally selective, and inherently transmissible throughout the generations. On the other hand, he dismissed exterior national characteristics as being irrelevant, because they did not necessarily survive when the individual moved to a new culture. What Unamuno did single out were traits that exceeded physical limitations and combined to form a psycho-ethnic heritage. The latter could be recognized by an observer without his having to seek biological proof of its racial origin.

Unamuno regarded the qualities just described as ethnic or cultural norms that characterize a particular people or group. The existence of these qualities was important to Unamuno because it confirmed for him a method that was valid for apparently different national situations. On the one hand, the method applied to a nation that still preserved its group identity after having been dispersed from its geographical home: Israel. And on the other, it applied to a nation that had a laminated cultural structure and a racially mixed background, behaving nonetheless as a consistent historical personality: Spain. The basis of the similarity between the two nations lay in the fact that their cultural traits were of an extraterritorial nature. This enabled Unamuno to state, in one passage, that "the Sephardic *Zohar* is set apart from monachal Catholicism by its manner of feeling love between man and woman with a profoundly Semitic sense" (VII, 436). And in another instance, referring to political Zionism, he said that "the Jews—whose colonies, . . . promoted by Baron Hirsch, failed because of the agricultural inability of a caste which was not born to till the ground, a caste whose descendants were shepherds who could not move their flocks from winter to summer pasture—devote themselves to being merchants, first traveling and later stationary" (VIII, 243).

These examples reveal the existence of permanent national norms that are not determined by geographical or historical factors. This suggests the workings of a collective heredity, so to speak, where a people's abilities and moral attributes are transmitted from generation to generation without regard to the effects of space and time. If national qualities endure, it is because they are viable at any time or place. Thus, when Unamuno once wrote of the peddlers of Hendaya who spoke Basque with a Jewish intonation (X, 814), the quality he described was unrelated to the people's territorial reality, but was highly colored by collective psychological factors. Rather than speaking of purely racial concepts, he referred to a kind of collective heredity, where group characteristics were rooted in the psychology of the people. These traits were also often linked to the land, although sometimes they transcended it. Indeed, during the years of Unamuno's own exile, geographical contact was the criterion that mattered least to his acute sense of national identity.

Whenever such persistently unique and permanent characteristics were dominant, the general tendency among writers of this epoch was to speak of "race." Unamuno, however, dismissed the term if it was being employed in this way. On one occasion he said that when "a writer affirms that the Catalonians are Aryans and the rest of the Spaniards are Semites or even less, it is certain that he doesn't know what Aryans and Semites are," because "the distinction is philological more than ethnological" (III, 619). This linguistic basis of racial identification was repeated on other occasions, and most eloquently in 1933 and 1934 when German nationalism violated the ideals of Unamuno's philosophy of civilization. His attack on the "barbarism" and "savagery" of Germany's racism was, of course, in good measure an expression of moral outrage, but it was also an affirmation of his cultural criteria. These standards included removing the concepts of biological anthropology from any essential characterization of a social group, the elimination of political structure from a culture's set of basic traits, and the subordination of national values to the higher good of universal confraternity.

This last principle, especially, rooted as it was in Christian charity, placed a religious idea and a social institution at the service of humanistic universalism. It seemed that Christianity's purpose was limited in its theological and ecclesiastical forms when compared to its benefits to all of mankind through the cardinal tenet of love. This was why the attempt to legislate racial purism and superiority was more than just ethically barbaric. It was culturally destructive too, tending to isolate the group and suppress its natural impulse to reach beyond itself and its present condition. As Unamuno exclaimed, "What, if not savagery, is all this about Aryans and the swastika, which is completely the opposite of the universal Christian cross" (VI, 944). The universal aspect of Christianity broke through the formal limits of religious thought and, through love, embraced other forms of spiritual and cultural idealism. Whereas Aryanism established racially homogeneous group values, Christian humanism encouraged the transcendental impulse of cultural activity.

That Unamuno feared racism for ideological reasons and not for practical ones is self-evident. He saw in the persecution of the Jews not an incipient menace to a group of people in Germany, but an attitude that bore long-term cultural dangers to the Spanish people as a group. There were no Jews in Spain, but there were myopic intellectuals, mostly "snobs and pedants," through whom "this racism and savage anti-Semitism are beginning to take root in our Spanish soil" (VI, 944). Thus, his motives for opposing this attitude were different. First, he saw no religious justification for anti-Semitism, since "Christ himself and his apostles, among them Paul, the apostle of the Gentiles, were—and are—Jews, and Christianity is as Semitic as it is Aryan. Or better, it is above Semites and Aryans" (XI, 1089). And second, even with the protests on the part of the "barbaric Teutonic racists and their pedantic disciples here," to the effect that their persecution was not religious but racial, the danger was great, because the horizons of their countries' vision were confined to narrow tradition. Moreover, the distinction between religious and racial persecution led only to confusion, because "many of the supposed Jews by race—and anyone knows what the Jewish race is anthropologically!—are not Jews by religion, but Christians of one branch or another, whereas the self-styled Aryans who persecute them are not of the Christian religion but [are] rather anti-Christian" (VI, 945).

At any rate, what mattered for nations was not their race but the cultural transcendency of the Christian religion. A good case in point was Spain's offspring in Latin America. Unamuno made it clear that the "Spanish-language nations—language is the blood of spirit—include very different material races," such as Jews speaking "secular Spanish," and "the descendants of Hebrews expelled from Spain. Not to mention those who remained here and assimilated into the common Spanish nation" (VI, 944–45). All of which was to argue that national exclusivism was a fiction when viewed historically, and a harmful absurdity when put into practice.

In general, Unamuno's opposition to purism was steadfast, beginning with his early essays against *casticismo* and continuing to the articles of his last years. Interpreting the Cain myth in this frame of mind, he identified the mutual hostility of shepherds and farmers as the distrust and hatred of the foreigner, an attitude which took the outward form of envy. To each group, the other was a stranger, and each thought that the way to preserve its inner cohesiveness was by expelling the alien. Unamuno imagined a social stratification of this myth, where an incompatibility of dissimilar groups existed between shepherds and farmers, rural and urban people, Spaniards and Semites, and Aryans and non-Aryans—in that order. Cain's act was sinful because it was committed against the folkways of a group to which he did not belong. The Jewish people, "a people of shepherds, initiated their historical legend with the murder of the shepherd Abel by his brother Cain, the farmer, from whose blood sprang the city dwellers" (V, 683). But, by the same token, "those of us who know Abelite peoples, cattlemen, know that the latter have persecuted the farmers due to envy. Such was done here in Spain with the Moors."

Thus, the question of race in the biological sense is never a real issue when a nation persecutes its cultural minority. What counts is its desire to expel the out-group for the sake of collective uniformity. The psychological reason, of course, is largely envy, but this only explains the cause, not the sociological results. Unamuno dealt with both: "And the expulsion of the Jews, who had stopped being shepherds of flocks to become shepherds of money stocks, was that not also a work of envy? And I don't mean Aryan envy because I don't know what that Aryan business is, nor do those poor simpleton racists with the swastika know" (V, 683). The forced exodus of Semitic minorities in Spain had the effect of ridding the culture of so-called alien energies which deflected the central thrust of the majority. What was really a social standardization aimed at refining the texture of the social fabric, took the guise of racial purification. In this light, there was little difference to Unamuno between Spanish purism and German Aryanism as far as cultural aims were concerned, although the difference in degree is of course obvious. In fact, the two were parallel, and Unamuno, being reminded of the similarity, tried to dissociate his own nation from the extremism of Germany.

The credibility which Spain had given to purism in past centuries was one source of the nation's difficulties, according to Unamuno. The Jews and Moors had been judged alien components of her culture, and were removed in spite of having fortified the central fibers of the social organism ("Toledo . . . for example, was as Judaic as Christian, perhaps more" [VIII, 709]). This neutralization of Semitic influences led to an ebb in the vital flow of the nation. After the Reconquest and the Romanizing Cluny reform, "the Jews and Moors were exiled, not in the name of God, whom we had in common, but in the name of a poorly or well interpreted theology that concealed low passions, and finally the Inquisition emerged. And this ghastly power, which sprang from so natural and native a root, stifled the very soul that gave it its start" (IV, 1085).

The distinction made here between theology and religion becomes a guide to foreseeing the consequences of maintaining purism as a cultural policy. What theology is to religion, purism is to a healthy cultural life. Both were artificial restrictions to Unamuno. Just as the spontaneity of religious life is suppressed by the systematic categories of religious philosophy, so is the vitality of a national group checked by the rigid definition of its supposed group characteristics. The result is narrow orthodoxy in one case, and ruthless conformity in the other. Both forms of dogmatism usually require scapegoats and purges in order to enforce their standards.

In this respect, the Jew has always been the most convenient and ubiquitous symbol of the threat to purism. Thus, what happens to the Semitic sector of a nation's anatomy is indicative of how a people has been dealing with its culture insofar as the latter naturally exists and develops. If there are strong puristic symptoms, then this development is bound to reflect a growing strain between the proposed cultural destiny and the general collective personality. That is, purism feeds upon an exclusivist pride in a civilization having homogeneous characteristics, and it sets up cultural goals that reject divergent traits, regardless of their contribution. The culture itself, however, has heretofore continued to thrive because it had never repressed its natural heterogeneity. When attention is called to the visible, even physical, attributes of the divergent subgroup, the culture is strained by an unnatural division of parts. If the traits of the subgroup form an independent culture within the larger civilization, then the degree of purism and alienation is accentuated. What we call racism is the militant exaltation of dominant group characteristics over the visibly different minority. In Spain, the Jew was placed in a difficult situation in this regard, because he was bicultural and hence seen as an ambiguous figure. The purist majority recognized those traits which differentiated him from the larger culture, choosing to ignore the features which assimilated him. Racism, therefore, became an administrative tactic in the service of broader cultural goals. Basically, however, it had a psychological origin in the collective will to self-perpetuation.

For Unamuno, consequently, purism was a moderate form of racism, and racism in his day had many nationalistic and cultural implications which have since disappeared from our definition of the term. One of the problems at that time was to specify exactly how the stranger in the group stood out from the homogeneous majority. And it was here that Unamuno located the fallacy of purist thinking. If it were true, as he believed, that the foundations of a culture are its cities, then the most characteristic attributes of that culture must be found in the metropolis, which by nature is heterogeneous. Moreover, the Jew must be a structural support of the civilization in which he participates since he, more than anyone, exemplifies urban life. "Civility," reasoned Unamuno, "genuine civil life, was born in these clusters of dwellings and in narrow, winding streets. The Jewish ghetto is the most genuine expression of city sociability" (V, 1105). In contrast, non-urban areas are the most likely to develop suspicion toward the stranger, because they are areas where individual rather than group dynamics prevail, and where cultural activity is at a minimum.

It is in just such a rural ambience that homogeneity turns into a cultural value, as the Cain myth demonstrates. The Abelites comprised a pastoral in-group, barely cohesive and yet a group nonetheless, which drove away the outsider, Cain. The fugitive, who advocated communal living, became a city dweller and eventually founded a civilization. Thus, cultural harmony was a matter of values and not racial uniformity. The fact that the murder of Abel was "the first act of fraternity" destroys the biological argument in support of that harmony. In other words, since it was brother who killed brother, the requirement for maintaining a harmonious group could not have been blood kinship. The incompatibility lay in the opposing forms of culture, one rural, the other urban. Thus, Cain's banishment can be interpreted as a flight from an alien culture, for he was "the one who first erected a city. . . . And in that city [Enoch], *polis*, civil and political life must have begun: civility and civilization. A work, as can be seen, of fratricidal man" (IX, 526).

Unamuno's thesis, therefore, was that purism and racism are absurdities in cultural theory because the very first cultures had conflicts even when they were racially homogeneous. At the same time, the prestige of purism arose in areas of minimum cultural development: among pastoral groups. Real civilization began in the city, and even more important, it prospered because the city had integrated heterogeneous elements. The nucleus of the civilization established by Cain was a haven for outcasts—fellow fugitives of the same temperament as Cain but of different blood. Eventually, the mixture of elements in the city, coupled with a similarity of values, resulted in a significant cultural activity. Therefore, any struggle among the components would have to be considered confraternal in a loose sense, if not really consanguineous. If purists were hostile to so-called alien parties, they were fighting a cultural battle in their own imaginations, and not in fact.

We have seen thus far that racism is the disguise which cultural purism takes in order to insure its group uniformity. Stated in religious terms, racism is the secular counterpart of orthodoxy, a militant affirmation of dogmatic ideals which may not be debased under penalty of excommunication. Purism does for society what orthodox religion does for the individual: it establishes a standard of conformity and practice which guards against the evils of alien values. Thus, sinfulness consists of the admixture of standards, and the violation of an established code.

Unamuno brought this theme into a long analysis of religious values when he wrote *Nicodemus the Pharisee*. This exegetical narrative is an eloquent and dramatic plea to rise above the narrow interests of nation and sect. Its central entreaty is that we embrace Jesus in universal brotherly love, and that "all of us become as one, the common and the distinguished, all those who are of Christ and not of the world, so that being all in one, we may be one in God" (III, 148). In order to expound this principle, Unamuno had to assert a number of axioms that reflected his thinking about many forms of human experience: the nature of good and evil, faith and reason, history and eternity, and freedom and action. He also deliberated on the roles of psychology, ethics, and metaphysics in relation to man's final destiny. In all of those areas, his ideas emanated from a single source—the man Nicodemus: a Jew, a Pharisee, an intellectual, a skeptic, and an Israelite citizen.

What made this New Testament figure a perfect example for Unamuno's exposition was the fact that he was a cultural product of Old Testament values. Nicodemus was less concerned with eschatology than with the practical concerns of living, whose ends require that rational thought be made supreme. Having come within the sphere of Greek influence ("an intellectual seduced by Hellenic culture"), his basic materialism was compounded by an additional skepticism toward all specific forms of immortality. His beliefs in this regard are vague, yet strong enough to resist Jesus' doctrine, despite the latter's disquieting appeal to man's weakness and need for reassurance. To Unamuno, the Pharisees were of one caste: "They are princes of the Jews, they have a history and a prestige, and the inner man, who finally awakens in them, hasn't enough strength to shake off the exterior, what the others have made them to be" (III, 129). Nicodemus' exemplary merit consists of the way in which he demonstrates how all men are locked within the prison of their cultural and personal limitations, captives of their formal religion, their nationality, and their individual selves.

They appear unable to be reborn spiritually, tied as they are to historical determinants ("I owe myself to my past. Even more, I am nothing but the result of my life"), and to their personalities ("But, how can I become another self, I myself, who am as I am and no other way?" [III, 130]).

This is Unamuno's Pharisee, limited by the rational and religious dogma that are set up to deal with the practical world. What is worse, however, is that the Pharisee rigidly directs his actions into moral categories which are unfaithful to his true feelings. It is one thing for Nicodemus to do good according to the ethical dictates of his religion, but this does not necessarily mean that he is a good man. To hate sin is a virtue, but one must have love for the sinner as well. Yet Unamuno believed that the Pharisee mentality was incapable of this act of forgiveness. What was lacking was a genuine morality arising from an inner psychological sincerity: "if you are honest out of cowardly fear of doing evil . . . your evil intention will embitter your soul." Indeed, as we saw earlier in this book, any mental reservation that lurks beneath a virtuous deed is reprehensible, and Unamuno even went so far as to suggest that "everyone who hates his brother is a killer" (III, 133).

True morality, then, occurs when thought and action exist in harmony. Nicodemus, however, is steeped in "Pharisaic moralism," and finds true Christianity beyond his reach. He narrows his field of vision to the strict allegiance to Judaic ethics, and he fails to see the possible goodness that may lie beneath an evil act. According to Unamuno, the Pharisee reasons that "if we succeed in preventing someone from doing evil, what does it matter if he doesn't feel goodness?" (III, 136). This attitude is grounded in pragmatic considerations: it is effective, realistic, and in keeping with the rationalist's knowledge that the mysteries of the soul, like those of the universe, are unfathomable and beyond the range of intellectual activity. But, asked Unamuno, is this not the unforgivable pride of a man who sets himself and his group above the others? And indeed, he depicted Nicodemus as the self-esteeming cultist, the skeptic who despised the poor and common folk and their unshakable faith in the irrational teachings of Jesus.

In addition to his cultist exclusivism and moral formalism, Nicodemus also revealed a lack of compassion in matters of justice. The Pharisee was unable to express true forgiveness because it demanded pure love, a sentiment which Unamuno assumed to be absent in the Judaic ethic. It was Jesus who taught that "only the good man truly forgives, not simply the honest one, because only the good man sees the heart of the offense and the unique justice of forgiveness" (III, 142). Nicodemus, however, was never able to renounce his ethical formalism. His conversion to Christian love would have been complete, had not Christ's crucifixion galled him into hating the people who killed Jesus. Reacting in accordance with traditional law, he demanded that justice be done to the people who had shouted their approval of the execution. Thus, the venom which accumulated within him was contrary to the sentiments and practices of Jesus, who himself had prayed on behalf of the multitude, saying that it knew not what it did.

Unamuno's indictment here, clearly enough, was not against Jews as a group, but against "fickle people who today receive the envied man with palms, and tomorrow demand the ignominious cross for him." Thus did he blame Nicodemus as a potential convert to Christianity who did not fulfill his mission of goodness. The Pharisee was a "distinguished man," but his sense of "repugnance" managed to "stifle the loving sentiment of compassion toward the prophet, that sentiment which might have produced immense pity toward the poor blind people who denied him [Jesus] by condemning him to death. For love and hate do not go together, even though the former is for the victim and the latter for the executioner" (III, 149). Thus, Pharisaic and Christian temperaments stood in exact opposition: one set up categories, the other dissolved them. One religion was rational, classified people according to similar values and actions, and distinguished logically between knowledge and ignorance, good and evil, distinction and baseness. The other religion swept away the barriers that separated men, and preached the supreme emotionalism of love, regardless of logic.

By pointing out these differences, Unamuno sought to call attention to the obstacles to real Christian brotherhood. It was important to note that the Pharisees belonged to the intelligentsia, because it indicated that religious differences had their class origins. If a man belonged to a respected caste, his sense of individual superiority set him apart from the masses. As a result, he cursed "not the sin in which he participated, but its ostensible ministers, the blind people." That is, Pharisees like Nicodemus found fault in the blind faith of the people, and yet never recognized that they themselves were guilty of the sin of pride. Consequently, "the Pharisaic morality of his hard shell stifled the Christian pity in his breast" (III, 149). More than this, the experience of Nicodemus as a single aristocrat reflected in miniature what was a collective attitude. The Pharisees, as members of an intellectual elite, recognized theological faith to be a rationalization, and so they rejected Christianity as dogmatic sophistry. Similarly, they thought of blind faith as an illusory state of mind, fit only for the masses. Their attitude was that the masses "perpetuate the fanaticism, hypocrisy, and deceit of vulgarity on earth. And they prevent the ministers of wise and distinguished men from seizing Jesus and taking him away to be analyzed and reduced to their rational reality" (III, 145).

Thus, Nicodemus unconsciously rejected Christ by nourishing an ethical rationalism that was contrary to the spirit of charity. At the same time, the Pharisees rejected Christianity by demonstrating how remote it was from logic and reality. They were not, however, unaware that Jesus' influence over the populace was increasing, and that his heterodox views and Sabbath violations were endangering the social order of the theocratic state. Quite the contrary, the Pharisees feared that if Jesus were left alone, he would convert all the people. This in turn would permit the Romans to conquer the land and destroy the nation. For this reason, which Unamuno felt could "never be sufficiently meditated upon," they decided to kill Jesus "as an anti-patriot, so that the Romans might not blot them out as a nation" (III, 147).

The event meant as much to Unamuno politically as it did morally, and his dramatic reconstruction of Jesus' entry into Jerusalem reveals how much more significant he found its social implications in comparison to its religious aspects. He sketched the scene in the festive market-place before Passover, where, beneath the communal preparations and "concealed by the gay hubbub, the struggle of passions was coming alive." Jesus enters the city at this moment, in full knowledge that Israelites usually flocked to Jerusalem at that time from all over the country. As he might have anticipated, the multitude receives him joyously as he rides in on his donkey. It would almost seem as if "the Galilean were pleased to proclaim himself God's emissary and light of the world, thus draw-

ing upon the Judaic nation the suspicious glance of the Romans"
(III, 147).

Consequently, the spiritual significance of Jesus' appearance
takes second place to the threat of a possible social disruption which
his teachings might provoke. As far as Rome was concerned, the
Pharisees' religious principles were of no importance as long as they
did not disturb the political status quo. This was why the Pharisees
turned the religious controversy over Jesus into a problem of protecting the Jewish nation and its well-being. They feared any
disorder that might incur the Romans' displeasure. Unamuno used
this interpretation to support his idea that Jesus was a political
subversive, a "promoter of seditions" (III, 144), who cared little
about what was rendered unto Caesar as long as God received His
due. It was this position which threatened the stability of the
theocratic establishment. Indeed, this seditious man was "lacking in
all prudence," for he could "very easily have provoked the mob at
the fair to any conflict that might give the Romans a pretext to blot
out the Judaic nation from its established place and cast it wandering over the earth" (III, 147–48). If Unamuno was speaking with
historical hindsight, it was not because he had Israel's Diaspora in
mind, but because he was thinking of Spain's own civil strife. As a
Spaniard, he saw that Jesus' tragedy was the means by which an
ideological war was avoided. Had Jesus been allowed to continue,
the vested interests of opposing groups would have come into
conflict. The prophet had brought tidings of transcendence, but
since his doctrine sought to obliterate the factionalism among men,
he fell victim to the very differences he wished to remove.

As we can see, the Pharisee mentality dealt with social realities as
well as religious forms. In Unamuno's essay, it also provided an
opportunity for discussing the question of faith. Here, as everywhere in his writings, faith is developed as an agonistic concept, a
principle which is molded by the opposing forces of reason. What
is new in this essay, however, is the fact that Unamuno makes
Judaism symbolize rational philosophy. He looks upon the Jew as a
rationalist rather than as a heretic, a believer who is always demanding proof for his belief and weighing all the arguments judi-
ciously. When Jesus came up from Galilee to Jerusalem, "the Jews
sought him out, arguing whether he was a good man or a deceiver."
This confrontation sharpened the distinction between the two reli-

gious positions. They began to enter into a wider social conflict, the disciples standing for spontaneity of heart, and the Pharisees representing measured control of will. And so a "grave discord was born in the people, because good men, allowing themselves to be led by their goodness," affirmed their faith in Jesus as the true prophet and Messianic figure they had been waiting for, while others, "clinging to a law that is deadly and a reason that is dessicating, adduced the letter of their scriptures to oppose the Teacher" (III, 144).

On this basis, the traditionalists thought that it was wrong "to cheapen the dignity of reason" by turning to illusory hopes for their spiritual consolation. Their philosophy was to create a "solace out of reason" (III, 145). Yet it was precisely this idea which irked Unamuno, who saw it as a dogmatic ossification of what was originally a vital and emotional faith. He felt that the original Judaic commitment, despite its differences with Christianity, had also been made quite irrationally, just as Jesus was now doing. Unamuno approved of this irrationalism, and he was dismayed by the direction which both religions had taken subsequent to their first flowering. In the same way that Judaism had hardened into Pharisaic formalism, so too did Christianity later become the monolithic structure so alien to the spirit of Christ.

In support of this view, Unamuno continued to analyze the Pharisaic mentality and the pitfalls of its narrow-minded rationalism. He interpreted the wanderings of the Israelites after their escape from Egypt as a test of existential faith. Their tribulations in the wilderness caused them to complain against God and Moses, who had led them from the comforts of Egypt into the barren lands of deprivation. As a punishment for this rebelliousness, God sent serpents down to kill them, and the frightened people ran to Moses, confessing their sin and begging forgiveness. Moses prayed to God, who told him to forge a metal serpent and fix it to the banner, so that whoever had been bitten might look at it and be healed. Unamuno regarded this episode as having a symbolic meaning with respect to religious skepticism. The case of Nicodemus was clearly apropos, since he too had been lost in the desert of sterile knowledge, where he tried to regain the repose of his former spiritual captivity. His "enchanted Egypt" had been the certainty of factual understanding, and his exile was the loss of tranquility and the need to appease his spiritual hunger and doubt. Almost unconsciously,

Nicodemus complained against God for his "strange uneasiness," his "sadness in the futility of all effort," and his basic condition, in which "his appetite for life being extinguished, he lives as if out of necessity, out of routine, cowardice, or fear of death" (III, 139).

Unamuno made this initial discontent analogous to the Israelites' plight in the desert, a misfortune that would disappear as soon as they embraced God wholeheartedly. But instead, both Israel and Nicodemus turned against the Deity, the former by grumblings that eventually brought on the plague of serpents, the latter by turning to God to accuse and deny Him. As a result, God punished the rebellious men by sending down real serpents in the wilderness, and metaphorical ones in the form of intellectual anguish. And so an appeal for relief was necessary in both instances, either to Moses, as God's agent, or to the Deity himself. Nicodemus goes "filled with hunger to confess his having sinned and to ask that the serpent biting and killing him, the cross crushing him, be removed from him." Thus, the metallic serpent is transformed into the Saviour's cross, "the cross of eternal sorrow," which is raised high for all to see, and for the spiritually stricken to look upon and be revived.

Unamuno's symbolism, therefore, is self-evident. Man must go through a period of doubt before his faith is confirmed. His pain must be such that no human resources can avail him, for only this will cause him to turn to divine help in spite of his disbelief. This is Unamuno's existential position. The return to God is polarized on an intellectual choice and an emotional need. The appeal to a superior being regardless of reason forms the basis of agonistic faith, and it becomes the mainspring of a vital religion. This was how Judaism sprang to life initially, and it was also the essence of incipient Christianity. What Unamuno cautioned against was their subsequent rigid forms (III, 138–39).

*Nicodemus the Pharisee* is an outstanding example of Unamuno's dramatic flair for making philosophical and even theological problems palatable to his readers. The narrative indicates how vividly he could discuss the relationship between reason and religious impulse. Unfortunately, the same cannot be said of another religious work, *The Agony of Christianity*, whose issues are treated quite drily despite their urgency for Unamuno. His handling of sources, the technical language, and the exegesis all suggest the earnestness with which he wrote the book. Since he was studying so fundamental a problem as immortality, he doubtless wanted no distractions, not even his customary sense of drama.

What is noteworthy for us in *The Agony of Christianity* is the question of what role materialism plays in religion. That is, to what extent the Christian religion contains a conflict between material and spiritual values, rather than a solution. This was the question asked by Unamuno, and the thesis which he set forth in answer to it was tragic in its implications. Fundamentally, he considered the misfortune of Christianity to be the fact that its dual heritage produced a basic incompatibility: the opposing eschatologies of Judaism and Hellenism. In these divergent philosophies, two irreconcilable concepts opposed each other: the resurrection of the flesh, which was "the Judaic, Pharisaic, psychic hope—almost carnal," and the immortality of the soul, "Platonic, pneumatic, or spiritual" (XVI, 478). This conflict was not only an individual problem for Unamuno, but it also troubled him as a Spaniard who felt certain ties to his countrymen. Was it enough, he asked, to worry about individual salvation, without also considering one's role as a citizen? If the social self were a valid aspect of one's total personality, how could the material values of society be reconciled with a spiritual life? Indeed, was it at all valid to conceive of spirituality and the State in the same context? The rigid separation of Caesar and God was affirmed by Jesus in order to insure devotion to spirit. Now, Unamuno proposed to consider whether religion could properly entertain material ends as well as spiritual ones. As his point of departure, he used the concept of immortality.

For the Jews, Unamuno argued, the nature of the resurrection was completely physiological. Therefore, it was a completely individual event. A hermit could "be carnally resuscitated and live alone with God, if this is living." Such a prospect might satisfy Unamuno if he were content to live outside the historical context of society, which is what solitude represents. But this kind of immortality would deny him his role as a Spaniard with a personality involved in the national life of his country. On the other hand, Christians believed that "immortality of the soul is something spiritual, something social." Since Unamuno's notion of "spiritual" and "soul" combined the material world and transcendence, this form of immortality would indeed be social. That is, spirit exists in the concrete world, not abstractly. Therefore, it cannot exist in isolation. The soul depends on the awareness of men for its immortality, on human memory projected into succeeding generations. Thus, spirit is properly a social phenomenon. Specifically, "he who makes a soul for himself, he who leaves a deed [behind him], lives in it, and with it in other men, in Humanity." And even more important, there is the temporal extension of spirit, which is "to live in History" (XVI, 478).

The foregoing explanation indicates how immortality can be a social condition, but it makes no judgment on the relative merits of Judaism and Christianity vis-à-vis the social man. In fact, it only highlights the "agony of Christianity," which is torn between the allegedly pure flesh and pure spirit of its theological antecedents. Unamuno understood this difficulty very well, and he realized that it made little sense to value the "Hellenic," "pneumatic" aspects of religion if his real concern was immortality within history. This in itself is a contradiction in terms, for it confuses atemporal and temporal categories. Nevertheless, Unamuno knew that the Christian tendency to Platonize Judaism had hindered the concept of the immortal historical man. But his real problem was that God did not fit into the picture. Unamuno wanted a religion in which man, not God, was at the center of the universe. And not an abstract man—since God would do just as well for this—but a specific man with a history, a culture, and a nationality. Modern Christianity embodied everything that was opposed to this ideal, and indeed, it had transformed Jesus into a model of self-denial. At most, Christianity had created a more personal God, but it had also made man's final destiny more abstract (XVI, 302).

Thus, the cultural finalities of human experience seemed to be neglected by modern Christian formalism, which emphasized God over the history-bound individual. But this was not true for Judaism, said Unamuno. In his eyes, "the Pharisaic people, in whom was born the faith in the resurrection of the flesh, waited and hoped for social life, historical life, the life of the people" (XVI, 478). The fact that Jews seemed unconcerned with abstract eternity, theocentric eschatology, or even spiritualism, helped to transform their religion into a humanistic ideal. The truth was that "the genuine deity of the Jews is not Jehovah, but the Jewish people itself, the chosen people. And they believe in their immortality."

Here indeed was religious health, thought Unamuno. The Jews lived for life, whereas the perfect Christian renounced life for monastic solitude, "which is impossible, if the human strain is to persist, if Christianity is to persist in the sense of a social and civil community of Christians, if the Church is to persist" (XVI, 511).

This was the terrible agony of Unamuno's religion, in contrast to the blessing of Judaism. He thought of "the Judaic preoccupation with physically propagating themselves, having many children and filling the Earth with them; their preoccupation with patriarchy" (XVI, 479). Regardless of how accurate this statement is—and, indeed, much of what Unamuno has been saying all along is questionable, to say the least—his interpretation is consistent. The Jews immortalized man through the persistence of the Israel nation. Their concern for the socio-economic aspects of religious law took precedence over metaphysical speculation. Whereas Christianity was anti-historical, Judaism exalted the historicity of Israel as a people. Christianity demanded a choice between incompatible alternatives: "either the resurrection of the flesh or immortality of the soul, either the word or the letter, either the Gospel or the Bible." Therefore, "pure Christianity, Evangelical Christianity, tries to look for eternal life outside of History" (XVI, 511). Judaism, by contrast, oriented its ideals around the fate of the collectivity, trying to guarantee thereby an unending projection of itself in time.

Unamuno wrote *The Agony of Christianity* while in exile in Paris, in 1924. At that time, he was concerned more with his country's socio-political problems than with religion, and he was disturbed over the impasse that Christianity had reached in solving Spain's and Europe's difficulties. It troubled him to admit that "it is not the Christian mission to resolve the socio-economic problem," or that "democracy, civil liberty, dictatorship, or tyranny have as little to do with Christianity as science does" (XVI, 513). He compared this failure with the frankly humanistic ideals of Judaism, and strained the point to prove his argument. That is, he set forth both the Jews' supposed "preoccupation with the proletariat," and the fact that "a Jew, Karl Marx, has tried to make a philosophy of the proletariat," as two modern manifestations of the earlier idea that "the Sadducean Jews, materialists, sought the resurrection of their flesh in their children. And in money, of course"

(XVI, 479). Furthermore, he perceived in the origins of Christianity a similar humanizing tendency, attributing to the early disciples of Jesus a keen sense of history. But whereas these men followed and understood the historical figure of Jesus, their successors later caused religion to enter phases that negated the values of temporal man (XVI, 478).

It was here that Unamuno recognized the religious nationalism of the Jews to be an agent for cultural preservation. In his distress, therefore, he stated the dialectical conflict of irreconcilable positions: "The agony of my country, which is dying, has stirred in my soul the agony of Christianity. I feel politics elevated to religion and religion elevated to politics at the same time. I feel the agony of the Spanish Christ" (XVI, 552). Unamuno had remade God in the Spanish image, yearning for the redemption of his nation. But in doing this, he replaced God with a temporal culture, thereby destroying the essence of Christianity.

# 14 THE JACOB MYTH

*If Unamuno* found beauty and emotional drama in other Old Testament myths, he discovered in the Jacob story a philosophical richness that enabled him to clarify several aspects of his own existence. Out of Jacob's eventful life, he selected three episodes: the fight within the womb, the ladder dream, and the wrestling scene with the angel. In none of these events did he abstract religious meaning from its existential context, and in all of them he singled out the myth's individual and human elements for explication.

More than the other patriarchs, Jacob projected the image of a real man: he was a shrewd brother, a father who sired twelve sons, and a weary dreamer. He incarnated the virtues of health, masculinity, and a practical sense of life. When he dreamed, it was as a tired sleeper, and when he awoke, he was an all-too-mortal man called upon to grapple hand to hand with God's emissary. This was how Unamuno imagined Jacob, and by means of this impression he was able "to intuit life's dream in a healthy and virile way" (XI, 618). He found a similar rendition of the patriarch in a painting by the seventeenth-century religious artist, Ribera, which he described with a good deal of empathy. In fact, his comments seem to be less a description of the canvas than a sensitive reliving of the scene itself.

Unamuno admired the appearance of this mighty "striver with God," and he was impressed by the detail of "the strong male figure's closed eyelids." Jacob's physical presence dominated the scene even in repose, seemingly powerful as he lay at ease, "full-blown with life, on the ground at Haran." Unamuno remarked on the tranquil strength of the Hebrew, reclining as he did with his head on a pillow of rock. From the latent energy of that out-stretched figure, Unamuno could infer a past and a future marked by activity. He noted the patriarch's "naked feet, which caressed [the earth] on their march," and with this and other vivid details in the portrait, he reconstructed the long day's journey of a shepherd through the country. Unamuno also thought beyond that moment of vital contact with the earth, to the time when Jacob would be given the name Israel. This renaming wrought profound changes in both the Hebrew and his everyday world, and it set Unamuno to meditating upon how it came to pass (XI, 618).

Jacob became Israel after wrestling with an angel until dawn, and this in turn occurred after his dream about the ladder. It was this dream that blurred Unamuno's impression of Jacob as a man, and led him to wonder how substantial a reality the Hebrew was. After all, what Unamuno saw and pieced together in the painting referred only to the physical world. Was it not also possible, in metaphysical terms, that this concrete reality might be lacking in substance, and that true reality was to be found in the imaginary world of the mind? This problem had always troubled Unamuno, as it had other Spaniards before him, among them Calderón. And yet Unamuno sought to reflect upon the "life-is-a-dream" theme in the figure of Jacob, and not Segismundo, the Calderonian hero. The latter merely personified the abstract form of the problem, whereas Jacob embodied the human experience of it, making Una-muno aware that the only solution was an interior one. Hence the importance of Jacob's dream. It was an event that unified heaven and earth, a yoking of illusion and reality that made irrelevant the question of which was which. This vision combined both realms within a single, personal intuition.

Thus, to Unamuno, Jacob's synthesis was essentially a mystical revelation. Returning to Ribera's painting, Unamuno noticed that the traditional opposites—night and day, dream and reality—were rendered pictorially by parallel chromatic symbolism ("With lights and shadows did Ribera create a dream of life"). Behind the shut lids of the patriarch, Unamuno perceived a "withdrawn look, the look which creates the world—dream is life—and which spreads a heaven of light over the shadow of the earth." The inward vision, with its perspective implanted in the physical world, had withdrawn sufficiently to allow the otherworldly light to enter with equal force. In the resulting fusion of both, "the entire visible earth, earth of earth, [became] heaven's mystical ladder." Indeed, it even seemed as if "heaven and earth embrace each other, and they are one and the same thing." Thus, Jacob is no longer just a plain man rooted to the earth. He represents the link to divinity, due to an inner perception which God had inspired in him. In his waking hours, Jacob separated the earth from the sky, but while asleep he discovered that "the sky is not above the earth and at a distance; the sky girds the earth, encompassing and sustaining it. One can see that the earth is the sediment of heaven." Which was "what our Castilian mysticism tells us," remarked Unamuno, who thereupon situated Jacob along the periphery of the Spanish religious tradition (XI, 619).

Despite the vague, poetic quality of these observations, Unamuno presents Jacob in a well-defined role. The patriarch is imagined to possess the kind of religious feeling that often existed during the Spanish Golden Age, as well as in the time of the first disciples. It was the same exaltation which orthodox Christianity lacked so grievously in later years. That is, it had ingenuous spontaneity, the personalism that defied codification, the Hebraic sense of prophecy which Unamuno detected in Fray Luis, and the unorthodox intimacy of Spain's mystics. In Jacob's case, the entire concept of experiencing God personally assumed mystic proportions. His wrestling with the angel was the external counterpart to the interior conflict which precedes mystical union. And his dream corresponded to the mystical vision itself. Unamuno argued for this idea by linking Jacob to the mystics in one of his discussions on religious contemplation. He explained that when struggle is one aspect of a religious sensibility, God's nature is projected outward in the form of a conquering spirit. Personal conflict takes place "in the center of the soul, as Santa Teresa said, in the most intimate part of the castle. That is, in the dark, where there are no windows to the world." Unamuno again repeated the symbolism of light that he had referred to in connection with Ribera's painting, and then wrote: "And we go on, like Jacob in his fight with the angel, asking God what His name is, from sunset to daybreak. Has there been a dawn and sunrise of knowledge for us?" (IV, 1123). Jacob's answer to this question was affirmative, for he emerged at daylight with the name of Israel, meaning "he who had striven with the Lord." And the mystics' answer, surmised Unamuno, was probably affirmative too, although their struggle resembled his agonistic faith much more than did Jacob's effortless contact with God. Unamuno and the mystics had sought out God, whereas God had come to Jacob without being entreated.

This difference was one of the reasons that Unamuno emphasized the wrestling episode, and related it to Spanish mysticism. He believed that the mystics were like himself, doubting God's existence and yet seeking Him incessantly. To prove this point, Unamuno quoted the entire dream of Jacob as it was narrated in Genesis (VIII, 491, 494). His contention was that the faith of Jacob and the mystics could not have rested on the bedrock of religious dogma. Jacob's ladder, the symbol of this faith and of divine communication, had its legs planted on solid earth (VIII, 492). Furthermore, Jacob himself "while sleeping, had his head resting on the hard rocks," and did not use the soft grass as his pillow. Therefore, it was man's natural condition, and not some artifice or dogma, which prospered his efforts to reach God directly. The man with spiritual needs never ceases to be a mortal being, and his physical body remains the center of religious feeling. Thus, hard earth becomes Unamuno's symbol for the origin of human faith. In order to "dream those dreams at the end of which we comprehend that God is here, on earth, just as much or more than He is in heaven, we must dream them with our heads resting on hard rock, on the earth's bone." And from this, Unamuno made Jacob the prototype of his "man of flesh and bone," whose existential condition is problematic, and whose spiritual awareness springs from his life's needs in this world.

Unamuno's stress on the physical basis of spirit extended to much of his imagery of Jacob's dream. Paradoxically, his concept of spirituality sounded quite materialistic. For example, he wrote that the "angels of God who ascended and descended the ladder had sprung from the bowels of the earth," just as "Jacob's dream sprang from the earthly recesses of his soul, from the latter's animal and earthy roots." These physical references are indicative of a central idea in Unamuno's religious philosophy, a concept which he called "spiritual naturalism." The idea holds that the purpose and content of religion are to enrich the spiritual dimension of man's material existence. Spiritual naturalism recognizes the nonmaterial aspects of reality, but instead of declaring them part of an ideal realm, it looks upon spirit as an extension of vital substance. Spirit is the creation of concrete man, and his religion must cultivate the means for experiencing spirit. At the same time, this philosophy was meant to benefit more than just individuals. Jacob was not only a man but the father of all Israel. Similarly, Unamuno was concerned not only with himself but with all Spaniards caught up in his nation's material and spiritual condition. Thus, he spoke of "our Spanish Jacob's ladder," meaning the procedure by which Spain, like Israel, could be immortalized. Within the frame of this ladder were the countless geographical and social factors which affected Spain's ability to transcend her present culture and endure as an eternal civilization.

Unamuno recast the foregoing allusions to Jacob into a cultural analysis that would apply to Spain's geophysical situation. He said that the nation's ladder "was very difficult to place on soft ground because we don't have any. It is carried out to sea . . . by the deluge of torrential waters that follow the droughts" (VIII, 492). Linking Biblical symbolism to the land's physical condition, he referred to the necessity for building on hard rock, and coping with the adverse climate and terrain. We are reminded that Jesus was a builder of houses, and that he spoke of constructing them on foundations of rock and stone. Unamuno then recalled that in some regions, men must live on arid sand and still dream of gaining salvation. Thus, Unamuno shifted from one symbolic level to another, integrating many kinds of human experiences and directing them into a spiritual mainstream.

When we take a backward glance at Unamuno's use of the myth of Jacob's ladder, we can see that factors such as geography, individual striving, and group aspirations are all lacking in one respect. Without the promise of divine help, it would be impossible to achieve salvation on any level. Jacob's dream offered the promise of such help, and Unamuno had felt that Spain, like Israel, expected as much. The Spaniard imagined his nation to be favored by God. Thus, "he believed that heaven was his due by virtue of an oath of inheritance, and he finds himself without a ladder to reach it.

Except for the ladder dreamt of by Jacob in dreams . . . . And with a stone as our pillow, sleeping on the ground in the solitude of our poverty, we dream of our heaven" (IV, 1132). It does not matter that there was no justification for this attitude, nor did Unamuno draw a perfect equation between Spain and Israel. But he did find it helpful to fit this Biblical mold around contemporary society, thus tying it to the ageless past, and identifying its aims with the eternal forms of history.

If the life of Jacob had wide social relevance for Spain, its personal meaning was just as profound for Unamuno the individual. The inner life of the patriarch was of keen interest to Unamuno, who had spent a lifetime defining his own concept of "substantial and essential man." He continued to speak of the difference between individuality and personality, but this time his frame of reference was philosophical, not psychological. That is, he no longer adopted the position which we analyzed in connection with the concrete and cerebral selves. Instead of dismissing men's names as being the shadow of reality, he affirmed them as indicating human essence. He adopted the nominalistic view that an object's name enabled it to be differentiated from the general mass of objects in the world. Names identified essences, and when it came to people, "the name is the man" (VII, 1079). In this way, the individual was drawn forth from the sea of humanity by means of his name. Nevertheless, it was not his individuality that stood out as much as his personality, for "the man who has become a name becomes a person."

This was very pertinent to Jacob's adventure with the angel. The wrestling scene symbolized his desire to master his world, to dominate his opponent by gaining complete knowledge and control of what he held in his power. For this reason, Jacob had to learn who the angel was. He demanded to know the angel's name in order to draw him forth from the unknowable night that surrounded them both. With great emotion, Jacob asked, " 'Tell me your name!' . . . And Jacob told him his own name so that he might be blessed" (VII, 1079). It was not the physical battle that was important, but rather the triumph of understanding and the transformation of names. Unamuno saw Jacob as a seeker of knowledge, a man constantly yearning for the unknown. When Jacob learned the nature of the being he had wrestled with, he could then ask for God's blessing. And he was blessed, by receiving the name Israel.

If we compare this passage written at the end of Unamuno's life with another composed almost thirty years earlier, the consistency of thought is astonishing. Citing chapter and verse in Genesis, he depicted an anguished Jacob in search of existential substance. He told of how "when Jacob crossed the ford of Jaboc in search of his brother Esau, he paused to spend the night alone, and he struggled until daybreak with an unknown person, with an angel of God or with God himself, and, filled with anguish, he asked Him what His name was" (II, 765). The match was heroic, and the outcome problematic. But the important question was what a mortal could derive from his encounter with the eternal essence of things. Therefore, the real issue was Jacob's name, because in those days "to declare the name of a living being was to declare his essence. The first thing that the Homeric heroes do is to give their names" (II, 765). And the spiritual energy required for this confrontation in any age is indeed epic, since it is an act of courage to seek out God and wrest from Him His name (XVI, 307).

Like Jacob, Unamuno asked about his own name and essence, a question which pulled him in many psychological directions, as we have seen. His problem was one of spiritual inadequacy, and it centered around the definition of his personality. Knowing the unceasing divisiveness of his mind, he rightly explained its cause as the quest for identity *within* the tensions of his existence. His definition of self, therefore, was in part characterized by a conflictive mental state, itself a major factor in his existence. At the same time, his self-definition could not exclude the nature of divine essence, since the ultimate goal of the self was to become as immortal as God. For these two reasons, the Jacob myth suited Unamuno's untiring efforts to grasp essential truths ("And my name, my human essence, what of them? Jacob struggled all night from sunset to daybreak with an angel, that is, a messenger of the Lord, and asked him not for peace, which he surely needed, but for his name" [X, 936]). Jacob really exteriorized Unamuno's internal conflict, and that of all agonistic figures, by striving with another being. He reflected Unamuno's method of self-definition, which required a certain awareness of the perfect being, God. Since Unamuno himself was finite, this was the best method of determining his essence. It was natural, therefore, for him to identify himself with Jacob, who also took the measure of immortality.

Unamuno also realized that his name—Miguel, Michael—was the Hebrew equivalent of "Who is like unto the Lord?" It was a question for which he had his own answer: that he himself was like God, that he wished to be God, and that this was the nature of his struggle. His name, therefore, was very important, for it conveyed the essential meaning of his entire existence: the conflict within him. Moreover, this name gave unity and continuity to the many selves that had been Miguel de Unamuno at one time or another in his lifetime, and which were subsumed under his agonistic essence as soon as that name was uttered. In his later years, he wrote, "I was reviewing my public, historical life . . . . During all of it I have done nothing but strive with the angel, with an archangel of the Lord, asking him: 'Tell me your name!' And I dreamed . . . that this name, the name of the angel with whom I have striven, was my own name, the name which I bear by divine grace, the name of Miguel, which means when uttered, 'Who is like unto God?' " (X, 936). Let us note that the word shift from angel to archangel reveals Unamuno's intention unmistakably. He had used the angel as a symbol of the external God who can only be known by means of struggle. But after learning that this God was within himself, that he became divine because of his struggle, he chose the archangel as a more fitting category.

This word change was quite justifiable in view of the higher level of spiritual achievement that Unamuno enjoyed. Having found God to be part of his inner self, he could be sure that personal salvation was close at hand. His reasoning was that the Christian God was more human and accessible than the Judaic divinity, and that an intimate relationship between God and man prepared the way for salvation. The wrestling scene was just the first stage, symbolizing man's struggle to draw nearer to God, after which he might learn His name. Salvation itself finally came when the divine relationship included God's knowledge of man's name. As Unamuno stated it, "to be saved in the Christian religion means that God always remembers our name, that our name is not erased from the Book of the Living. According to the Scriptures, one asks the Lord, 'Do not forget me!' And when Jacob struggled with the

Lord's angel, he asked him his name. The name is the symbol of personal substance. In the name is included the person" (IX, 910). The name is, therefore, the password that enables us to enter into a relationship with God. It allows an intimate communication to develop that will affect the course of salvation. Moreover, God remembers our merits by recalling our names, since the name is the symbol of personal substance. And to be retained in God's memory, of course, is to be saved forever.

Of the many puzzles inherent to the wrestling episode, the most difficult is the question of why the incident had happened at all. Why was Jacob graced by the angel's visitation? Was it because of God's decision to initiate a dialog, or was it because Jacob was willing and unafraid to seek God out and know him? In other words, was this a matter of divine grace or of human will to power? The second explanation is the more reasonable one from an existentialist point of view, but the fact is that Unamuno did not clarify the issue. It would appear that he was simply concerned with Jacob's experience as a prototype for the struggle to define human existence. Thus, when he found this condition in other men, he praised it, just as he had admired Kierkegaard's "courageous as well as anguished heart, which, a captive of resigned desperation all his life, struggled with the mystery, the angel of God, just as Jacob did years ago" (IV, 426). And yet the question of why the angel appeared at all requires an answer phrased in more theological terms. However, the fact that Unamuno did not bother to provide one indicates quite typically how inattentive he was to religious matters when faced with the drama of an anguished heart. It was Kierkegaard's desperate condition, not his theology, which made the Jacob comparison so appropriate.

Consequently, the struggle with the angel was regarded as a basically internal—and even existential—event. As a result, Unamuno grew more absorbed with the way in which conflicting elements within the individual tended to develop antagonistic values. We have already noted in this book the psychological and ethical forms which this tendency adopted. But Unamuno also found the Jacob myth to be illuminating with regard to that same conflict, and on a level even more profound than the wrestling episode. He saw that the most fundamental struggle in Jacob's life involved his elder brother, Esau, and that the meaning of their rivalry took two directions when viewed in relation to Unamuno's existence. In Unamuno the man, the rivalry illustrated the psychological origin of ideologies. And in Spain the social organism, it characterized the enmity of opposing political factions. Just as Jacob and Esau fought each other within their mother's womb, so too did the national impulse toward civil war suggest the fratricidal relationship between cultural philosophies within the bosom of Spanish society.

Unamuno alluded to this symbolic meaning when, in one of his stories, he spoke of "two brothers who serve contrary causes." This awakened other Biblical associations, "and he even remembered about Jacob and Esau fighting each other right in the womb, where their mother had them together. And he spoke of Cain and Abel fighting" (IX, 398). The womb image allows the national and the personal to be merged into a single concept of struggle, which was why Unamuno seized upon the myth. Whether it is a man divided against himself, or a country similarly divided, the action occurs in the same location: the place where the opponents have been engendered and nurtured. The fragments of one ego, the parties of one nation, and the convictions that contradict each other in both, are all related by their common origin. And so our lives, whether at the individual level or the social, make us "children of contradiction. And intimate, corelike contradiction, that of civil war; and more than civil, domestic; more than domestic, fraternal; more than fraternal, with ourselves. It is no longer the problem of Cain and Abel, the first two brothers who established human fraternity, but that of Esau and Jacob, the twins, who were already fighting in the womb of Rebecca their mother" (IX, 982). More than any other story, the Jacob myth searches the core of the homogeneous matrix which originally produced the dissident elements. Whereas the Cain myth is adequate for Unamuno's analysis of political struggle—although here too the Jacob myth is more faithful to the idea of a "mother Spain"—the rivalry of Jacob and Esau touches the nerve center of personal and cultural psychology.

The fullest exposition of Unamuno's probings into the cause of internecine conflict is found in the essay "Rebecca." Unamuno had always looked behind an author's words to discover the real reason for the man's ideas, and he was ever alert for the seeds of dissidence. He often stated that a writer "felt in his soul the struggle of twin ideas, enemies to each other, that demanded birth and life" (IX, 61). He also believed that writers reflect, on an individual scale, the issues that rage in their cultural milieu. Since life is a solitary condition first, and only then a social situation, the splintered selves of man's consciousness parallel the internal warfare of his nation. This is most frequently the problem of the intellectual, especially when he is, like Unamuno, preoccupied with the fate of his country. For, strange as it may sound, he can alternately adopt the perspectives that vie for national power, and align himself with each one in succession, according to the shifting stage of his inner awareness. The battle of his mind takes place with ideas and values, all purporting to do the same task, and all emerging from the same cultural source. But since they do not occur simultaneously, each successive idea must use whatever means available to gain the approval of the mind that will finally judge the issue. And so, like the fragmentary selves of a divided consciousness, these ideas stand in mutual combat. "Let us imagine," wrote Unamuno, "a nation that feels, like Rebecca, the struggle of brothers in her breast. Yet this is nothing next to the consciousness of an individual that reflects the collective consciousness in the spiritual bosom of a man who concretizes the soul of his people, and who feels within him the prenatal, uterine battle of Esau and Jacob. The latter is born clinging to his brother's heel and is ready to supplant him later, first by deceit, and then by violence" (IX, 61).

This notion is typically Unamunian. The individual absorbs all the elements of his culture, regardless of his conscious ideological beliefs. As a composite of his evolving society, he feels an inner disruption when those cultural forces operate in tension. His personal assimilation of the national heritage ("spiritual bosom") makes him the human concretion of an abstract and eternal set of characteristics known as culture ("concretizes the soul of his people"). This is the meaning of intrahistory, which is truly human because men embody and live their personal versions of the culture they are nourished on. It is also truly eternal, because the issues and traits that appear in historical events are perpetuated throughout the generations as private re-enactments of the public struggle ("reflects the collective consciousness"). When the external balance of tensions is broken, the ensuing unrest reflects the inner competition of ideas and the positions that they each try to justify.

If we could imagine a mythical embodiment of this agitation, it would be Rebecca (motherland) witnessing her son Jacob pitted against the angel as he pleaded for the latter's name (truth). And similarly, Unamuno wondered how she might have explained to herself the "terrible inner struggle, the twins' fight within her breast."

Here the parallel conflicts converge, with the birth of opposite ideas mirroring the fratricidal social order. Did the twin brothers fight to be first in birth, "since they could not, without an absurd contradiction, come out at the same time"? This was the basic question for Unamuno, who knew that the issue of civil war, as well as personal beliefs, depends upon legitimacy, upon the rights of primogeniture. In other words, to be recognized as the first or the eldest is to receive a lawful status, whether the contest is between brothers, princes, or ideas. Two ideas, like two regimes, cannot exist side by side, and since the prestige of priority gives the first-born the right of ascendancy, a battle takes place to decide who will inherit. Unamuno's description of Esau's entrance into the world, restrained by Jacob's hand on his heel, noted the tragedy of this struggle. What was really tragic was the fact that the inheritor later sold his birthright anyway, "and then old Isaac, already blind, blessed Jacob, taking him for Esau. And this is repeated with regard to ideas." The point is that both human perspectives deserve attention, for the intellect cannot see any difference, except in the succession of time, between the geminated products of a single source. The futility of the fight is evident from a logical standpoint as well as a psychological one. And the irony of it all is that both twins have defensible arguments, so that each position is easily surrendered to the other ("Primogenital ideas, red and hairy, fastened to which come others, those that strive at night with the Lord's angel and ask his name. And then those primogenital ideas, strong hunters, one day falter and sell themselves for a mess of pottage!" [IX, 61]).

But what is most pitiful is the fact that the real sufferer is Rebecca, for "the tragedy is in the soul of the one who conceives them" (IX, 62). With this sentiment, Unamuno deposited into the Jacob myth his entire philosophy of paradox and irrationalism, because as far as his cultural and psychological experience went, life was indeed a continual conflict of antitheses and contrary feelings. Thus, Rebecca's tragedy duplicated that of Unamuno and his beloved Spain, and so he exclaimed with vindication: "How easily do those who have never given birth to twin enemies speak of contradictions!" (IX, 62). The philosopher, politician, and cultural anthropologist all require a choice to be made between alternatives, thus indicating that they were free of Unamuno's spirit of contention. For them, the condition involving Jacob and his mother was without relevance. Nor could they see the many-leveled anguish which Rebecca suffered.

Rebecca, like Unamuno's contemplating self, had to witness the spectacle of strife which was her issue and progeny. She learned of the hatred budding within Esau, who plotted to kill Jacob, and she warned Jacob to flee. But the point is that the mother feared for both her sons, for they belonged to her alone even if their values differed to the point of bloodshed. Hence Unamuno's compassion for a woman who was afraid that her children would become killer and victim. As lifegivers, it mattered little to either Rebecca or Unamuno that no agreement could be reached between their fratricidal creations. In truth, as Unamuno viewed himself and Spain, he could only say that "the mother soul, which conceives twin and contradictory ideas, wants all its children to live, wants them alive, not some of them dead and others fratricidal. Let them struggle, let them struggle as they did in the womb before being born. But let them not kill each other! Let them all live!" (IX, 63). And in the perspective of Unamuno's complete works, this is exactly what he allowed them to do.

# 15 THE CAIN MYTH

*Like Jacob* and Esau, Cain and Abel were brothers whose relationship became embittered over events that were beyond their control. However, the Cain myth is more cryptic because it shows God's actions to be entirely unrelated to the efforts of human will. Jacob's determination enabled him to succeed in the end, but Cain's attempt to please the Lord with his harvest offerings failed to win approval. Thus, the mystery of the Cain myth lies in the fact that its version of justice and destiny defy rational explanation. Neither Abel nor Cain show any apparent virtue that might justify the fact that God favored one at the expense of the other, and yet Abel was the chosen one. This strange inequity, not to mention the bloodshed that followed it, prompted Unamuno to raise certain questions about the psychological, axiological, and sociological implications of the myth, particularly as it applied to Spain. For example, he traced the distinction between the descendants of Cain and Abel to historical and economic conflicts on regional and national scales. Then too, in the novel *Abel Sánchez,* he made the secret envy of Joaquín Monegro represent the tragic flaw of the Spanish national character. And in other essays, he drew a parallel between the brothers' competitive struggle for approval and, on a cultural level, a similar competition among divergent principles for control of society.

Unamuno's basic approach to the myth, therefore, was to seek its cultural value. He did this by referring to the social theories which had prevailed during his formative years at the end of the nineteenth century. These ideas, in method more than in substance, served Unamuno throughout his life as criteria for his cultural analysis of Spain. Starting with the notion that a society was as vital an organic body as the living beings that compose it, he went on to view the group as evolving in much the same way that an individual organism does. Like the individual who shows a behavior pattern in keeping with his personality, the social organism displays a collective psychology through its history and institutions. Thus, the traits of an individual Spaniard will have their cultural counterparts in the Spanish national character.

In applying these ideas to Spain by means of the Cain myth, Unamuno began by trying to link envy to the condition of solitude. We saw earlier in the book how central a role solitude plays in the splitting of the self. He found the same divisiveness to be true on a national scale, where Spain's solitary nature sharpened the envious factionalism of her character. In Spain, "solitude is the marrow of our essence, and all of our congregating and flocking together succeeds only in deepening it" (X, 842). This paradoxical statement, let us recall, meant that people not only fail to communicate with each other, but actually drive each other further into their shells when they come face to face. In other words, direct social contact can merely intensify the sense of isolation which each man feels. Such was the case in Cain's life, as well as Joaquín's in *Abel Sánchez*, for each time they confronted Abel, their envy and hatred grew. So too did their loneliness. As for Spain, her solitude was harmful for cultural reasons, since society depended upon interrelationships, not hermeticism, for its growth.

Given this situation, Unamuno could exclaim with conviction, "Where, if not from solitude, our radical solitude, is the envy of Cain born, whose shadow spreads . . . over the solitary desolation of the high Castilian barrenness?" The question is morally loaded, and was intended to awaken definite attitudes in the reader. It linked the arid landscape to the theme of solitude, and demonstrated how the unproductive agricultural life of the central plain roused the envy of the inhabitants. Sterile emotions gripped the territory, with destructive results for the individual and the nation. The land was filled with envy like a fabric saturated with color, and each thread that held the country together was tainted to some degree with this sentiment. Thus, every social activity came to be affected, and eventually the very institutions which directed those activities were also corrupted.

Unamuno did not hesitate to identify some of the tainted institutions. The army and the Church were two structural parts of society which had become defective: "This envy, whose dregs have stirred the present Spanish tyranny, is no less than the fruit of Cainite envy, mainly that of the monastery and the barracks, priestly and military." In these functional areas, and in others, the passion of Cain was symptomatic of more organic troubles. Although envy's external form required an effective counteragent, the institutional malady that lay beneath it also demanded attention and cure. Thus, Unamuno's analysis went deeper than mere social criticism, for he pointed out not only that the color was wrong, but that some of the threads themselves had deteriorated on account of the dye.

Unamuno's cultural analysis succeeded in making clear that the institutions were so organically a part of the social body that they could not be removed without destroying the whole. Hence the fratricidal situation, and the self-envy and resentment within the culture, "which arises when the herd is subjected to petty laws. This inquisitorial envy has made the tragedy of our Spanish history. The Spaniard hates himself" (X, 842–43). Thus, the drama which was externalized between the two brothers in the Biblical myth, is here portrayed within a single organism whose integral parts act to injure each other. But the tragedy of it all is that the struggle had no benefactor. The total defeat of any one element was never achieved, and Spain continued to consume herself in a perpetual cycle of inner conflicts.

Nevertheless, Unamuno did consider certain kinds of struggle to be salutary, even though he despaired at Spain's overall cultural strife. He could conceive, for example, of struggle in the metaphorical sense, where the two combatants stood for a dualism of human action. That is, "if Cain had not killed his brother Abel, he would have perhaps died at the hands of the latter." The point was not to condemn, but rather to recognize the various possibilities of action, since they are all imperfect and carry their moral stigma. Struggle is an unavoidable condition of existence, especially in Spain where various elements constantly seek to gain pre-eminence over one another. In fact, struggle can be viewed as a principle established by divine decree, for "God revealed Himself most of all in war. He began by being the God of hosts." And if it is true that "the purest and most fruitful love embrace" occurs between the combatants at the conclusion of their contest, then this kind of struggle is healthy (XVI, 403).

The difficulty in accepting the foregoing position lies, of course, in the ethical implications of war. And yet it was just this area which Unamuno wished to disregard. He argued that the struggle might be good or bad, depending upon who sustained it, but that in either case it was an existential mode. Indeed, "war is, in its strictest sense, the sanctification of homicide. Cain redeems himself as a general of armies." This means that whereas individual murder is wrong, the same act, when committed collectively on behalf of an idea, becomes justified in the eyes of those who support the idea. Unamuno went even further, and claimed positive results for Cain's misdeed and subsequent flight. His act of dominating and subduing his brother was symbolic of man's impulse to impose himself on the world. And Cain's escape to establish the first city was the beginning of collective—which is to say, cultural—activity: "Cain, the fratricide, was the founder of the State, say the latter's enemies. And we must accept it and transform it for the glory of the State, the child of war" (XVI, 403). Thus, Unamuno found it possible to see good in the midst of evil, and creation in the midst of death. The destructive side of Cain's nature could be redeemed.

This is not to say that Unamuno avoided making value judgments of a moral nature. But his first and last position was that we can never really maintain any judgment for long. He saw that the Cain myth had serious implications for the realm of moral psychology, but that in terms of cultural activity the myth offered only descriptive insights. Consequently, he stated that "no matter how much of a legend a peasant, shepherd people made of Cain—the first killer and founder of the first city, Ur—the truth is that in the course of human civilization, it is quite clear that the Abelites are no better or more humanitarian than the Cainites" (XI, 163). With this observation, Unamuno not only eliminated the ethical problem, but he replaced it with the symbolic apparatus for analyzing Spain's social structure. That is, he devised the antithesis of urbanism versus ruralism-nomadism. Abel and his descendants were shepherds, hence wanderers and enemies of a cohesive society. And in contrast, Cain was a farmer, a man whose life was fixed to one site, and who was later able to found a culture as Unamuno understood the concept: in its Christian and Occidental sense of a city-oriented society. We may, of course, debate Unamuno's interpretation of the relative influence of city and country on culture, especially since the matter is complicated by Cain's ambiguous role as a rural dweller first, and then later as an urbanite. Nevertheless, both phases of Cain's life were stationary, whereas Abel enjoyed the freedom of wandering.

Unamuno translated his antithesis into modern terms by referring to merchants as the descendants of Abel, on the grounds that they were an itinerant group. He said that the image of the merchant as a man who does not produce but only transports, and who therefore has no merit as a creative worker, "is the conception of the merchant held by the farmers, the descendants of Cain" (X, 815). Unamuno also maintained that the Jews, now businessmen in the modern world, were the offspring of the Abelites, who had once been shepherds. The point, however, was not that class antagonisms existed between the two groups, but that the type of work that they chose and the kind of culture they established were incompatible. And as Unamuno exclaimed, relating the myth to Spanish culture, "so much can be drawn for the psychology of the Castilian [from] the fact that his is a herdsman's spirit rather than a farmer's" (III, 158). The importance of this attitude is generally overlooked, because it seems so obvious; but we must remember that Unamuno was the first of the Generation of 1898 to use the myth in this way. He stated the cultural problem in terms of sedentary and wandering societies, and credited the Jews, as shepherds, with first having seen this difference with such profundity, and for devising a concept of history whose basis was the enmity of pastoral and agricultural groups (III, 158).

But there were two points even more basic to the myth than the animosity just described. The first was that it "placed right at the beginning of history the dissension between sedentary farmers and wandering shepherds" (III, 159). This fact meant that at no time in history could society be a bicultural harmony, for the opposing elements within a culture could never tolerate something so intrinsically antithetical to their own nature. The second point was that the myth "blamed the first killing ever committed on earth, not to the struggle for subsistence, but to envy." Since the farmer's fruits were not as pleasing to God as were the shepherd's, the former slew the latter out of instinctive envy. In other words, the roots of conflict within a society were basically psychological and not economic. The Cain-Abel myth did not depict a class struggle, since each man prospered in his own way within the social network of the day. Rather, the myth showed how emotional gratification—in the form of prestige, approval, or satisfaction with having produced something of value—was the reward of God's favor, the denial of which led to violence.

This interpretation was especially suited to Spain, and as Unamuno remarked, "both insights of the Judaic genius are corroborated by our Spanish history and psychology" (III, 159). The implication seems to be that the nation's basic problem was not a political or economic one, but that the latter became problematic because of the people's temperament. Spanish history, therefore, has registered constant fratricidal conflict because of what happens when radically different ways of life confront and reject each other. When one contestant earns the inexplicable approval of a higher authority, the other reverts to destructive emotionalism, thus undermining the entire cultural base.

Unamuno never explored the psychology of the Spanish people very deeply, but he did write extensively on its institutions as a reflection of that psychology. He discussed the techniques of farming, the problems of land ownership and tenancy, the difficulties of land quality, water content, and the distribution of cultivated and uncultivated tracts. Above all, he wondered whether agriculture was not suffering at the hands of a more favored animal husbandry. This was the issue that Unamuno joined to the Cain myth, believing that the persistence of a purely pastoral type was still visible among Spaniards (IV, 1052). As proof, he cited roving herds that seemed to prevail even when times were bad, and he pointed to vestiges of ancient forms of communal property that were still applied to pasture grounds. Thus, the link between the Hebrew Abelites and the Iberian shepherds, although more hypothetical than real, was nevertheless a model of comparative cultural patterns that confirmed the mythic truth of the Cain episode. The myth was a cultural prototype that was repeated elsewhere in time and place.

Again and again, Unamuno turned away from economics and

touched upon what he called the "psychic characteristics of the Castilian people." In one essay, he did so in a manner similar to Renan's treatment of the Hebrews, citing as a focal point "their basically shepherd-like character, a nomadic and still wandering people despite their present sedentariness" (IV, 1053). But he never went too deeply, preferring to describe, in another scene, the somber atmosphere of a Castile haunted first by the shadow of Cain's tragedy, then by solitude, and finally by Abel's sacrificial offering to a heaven that rained hail upon him, killing some of his sheep (IV, 1137–38). The prevailing mood of this scene was one of chastened sobriety at the harsh reluctance with which Nature and God permitted their fruits to be enjoyed by man. Thus, it was not surprising that Cain had lived in envy, just as all peoples of the earth continue to do. Nor was it strange that out of ingenuity or desperation, they turned envy into "one of the mothers of the arts" (IV, 1138).

It is interesting to observe how Unamuno was able to borrow words from the myth to create certain effects. His historical clarity and descriptive realism are somehow immobilized in time and made to sound eternal. For example, a casual reference to Cain's descendant, Tubal-cain, supplies the feeling of the succession of generations; a paragraph devoted to "these stern Abelites," who range the mountains and plains, and who "expelled the farmer, the Moor," in different epochs; and other allusions to the Edenic angel with flaming sword, to the Iberian Abelite's first parents, and to the Canaanite land of promise, all contribute to a sense of timelessness. Thus, Castile is rendered into something more than a landscape, and is seen as a stately and static immensity conceived by legendary vision and focused through a mythical lens with the perspective of history.

The mood-building power of Unamuno's prose dramatizes the lasting value of myth as contrasted to history. This superiority was often alluded to when Unamuno talked about intrahistory, but in this case he declared that "the history of the Iberian Abelite was to struggle against History" (IV, 1138). In other words, the Cain myth set the temporal march of events against the persistence of its own archetype through the various phases of history. This does not mean that the Abelite goes untouched by history, but it does show what the evolution of Spanish culture also shows, namely, that historicity has little value next to the reality of myth. How did this apply to the Spaniard himself, living, as Unamuno would say, intrahistorically? To take one example for an answer, we read that "the Abelite was dragged by his brothers the Cainites to conquer the New World. And there he learned that there is no new world, that it is all old and that History is a nightmare. What was better was the pleasant dream of the Genesiacal legend" which used to fill his hours in the Castilian wilderness (IV, 1139). There is a choice, it seems, and Unamuno suggests that by some intuitive decision the eternal Iberian, who perpetuates the mores and attitudes of the ancient Hebrew pastoral tribes, also senses that it is this condition which assures him of immortality.

Nevertheless, history must also be considered. The same Iberian, living an intrahistoric myth, represents a check on cultural development, which must be measured in terms of historical progress. He is the conservative element in the struggle of the two Spains, the man who scoffs at the advances of the outside world, and who is suspicious and resentful of innovation in his unchanging habitat. As Unamuno asked, why is it that these lands have the type of individual who looks darkly upon such advances in human industry as irrigation, to the point of destroying a canal? "Is it the sad passion of Cain, which bursts from the heart of the bitter nest in which it is lodged and hidden?" There are a number of possible answers. The statement itself suggests a psychologically based explanation. However, the truth might be that he "senses that the curse of work will increase for him" with the advent of modern improvements. And finally, the Iberian has perhaps glimpsed the prospect that this innovation "will uproot him from the cell of his barren plain, next to the dark walls of the forbidden Paradise, and throw him into the fields of economics and history" (IV, 1140).

All of these interpretations contain a good measure of truth, but whatever the reason, the impediment to cultural advances is not removed. Unamuno himself was not categorical about the advantages of its removal. He changed his mind within the dualism of his general philosophy, now advocating a realistic approach to culture as the only assurance for individual and national fulfillment, now scorning practicality by favoring the metaphysics of dream and intrahistory. Much of the time he gave an impartial analysis without seeming to make any value judgments. And yet he was saddened by the Cainite mentality that prevailed in the rural areas, particularly when it aggravated an already intolerable economic situation. Thus, he shifted back once again to making a practical critique. In one case, he explained how the devastation of forests, resulting from a population increase among the poor, led to all kinds of inequalities in natural resources, and finally to conflicts among men: "struggles occur, not of classes . . . but of positions— the farmers of Cain, and the shepherds of Abel—unions, regions, municipal localities, associations, syndicates and proletarian clientele" (V, 90).

This pessimism carried over into the rest of the passage, which quoted Genesis concerning God's commandment to "be fruitful and multiply." Here the economic struggle was not so much between disparate levels of wealth, as between vocations within a single family of financial misery. The internecine situation of Cain applied here, since the masses were not fighting their economic enemies but their vocational ones, all of whom had the same problem. Thus, the split within the Spanish proletariat reflected the country's larger division, and this was Unamuno's point. Fraternal antagonism had been apparent everywhere in Spain at one time or another. Agriculture suffered from its urgent and continual problems, and failures in conservation, along with the neglect of wildlife, led to recriminations and rival controversies. Often, the Spaniards' emotional shortcomings prevented the exercise of proper economic attitudes, and resentment against the landowner and his heavy income was widespread among those with poor investments in non-arable land.

The real inequality is never understood by the Cainite peasant or tenant farmer. All he can do is to chafe at the injustice of having to see his neighbor prosper with fertile soil while he perishes with poor land. The peasants' erroneous remedy is often to ruin their impoverished masters in order to equalize everyone in a common poverty. Of course, the real trouble lies in the unfair distribution of land wealth, a factor beyond the individual wills of the Cainite and Abelite. In fact, just as the original Cain and Abel were victims of a superior design, so too now are their descendants condemned to richer or poorer lands by the forces of political destiny. And so, instead of being able to correct the external structure trapping them, they turn blindly toward each other and commit a tragic internal violence.

Beyond the sociological relevance of the Cain myth was its

transcendental value, nowhere expressed better than in *The Tragic Sense of Life*. Here, Unamuno's materialistic interpretations yielded to man's ultimate desire for immortality. To be immortal was to survive in the memory of others, to triumph over the natural tendency of mankind to forget. From this fervent wish stemmed Cain's murder of Abel, for the crime "was not a struggle for bread, but a struggle to survive in God, in the divine memory" (XVI, 182). The favor bestowed upon the elder brother by God was a symbolic confirmation of divine remembrance. By not being recognized, Cain could not occupy a place in God's mind. Thus, he became jealous, especially since the offerings of both brothers were equally good. Indeed, had it not been for God's intervention and judgment, Cain would have been contented with his labors. Thus, his rage was for the sake of a spiritual, not a material, well-being. "Envy is a thousand times more terrible than hunger, because it is spiritual hunger. If what we call the problem of life, which is bread, were resolved, the Earth would turn into a hell, because the struggle for survival would break out with greater force" (XVI, 182–83). Given the awareness of a superior being, physical competition disappears and men struggle to remain in the eye of that deity. But this effort prompts strong and sometimes ugly emotional responses when the divine memory chooses to retain only some of the images before it. Hence a double tragedy: death, which must come by natural law, and the premature death of the soul by unnatural violence.

# 16 THE GARDEN OF EDEN

Traditionally, the Adam and Eve myth is treated as an allegory of our most fundamental concerns: the nature of man, of sin, of good and evil. These are grave matters, and they have always invited a serious approach in the literary discussions that have dealt with them. Like the writers before him, Unamuno took Adam and Eve seriously; in fact, they are the most frequently mentioned Old Testament figures in his works. Nevertheless, he treated them with more levity than he ever did in discussing the implications of Cain and Jacob. Moreover, what he found to be important in the myth differed considerably from the traditional problems already mentioned. One reason for this difference was the fact that Unamuno approached Biblical figures on a personal level, seeking in their characters and actions a subjective quality that corresponded to his own state of mind. He failed to discover such a correspondence in Adam and Eve, noting that they had much less personality than Cain, Jacob, and Moses. The two innocents in Eden were abstractions, acting out an allegorical narrative instead of being involved as full-bodied characters in the human drama of genuine myth. As a result, Unamuno's allusions to the Garden of Eden story are tinged with distance, and sometimes with an irony that his other Judaic references lack (II, 615; XI, 802 ff.).

This lightness of tone is best illustrated in one of Unamuno's discussions of language, where his intention was perfectly serious without being solemn or grave. Raising the question of whether the written language had evolved independently of the spoken word, he proposed the idea that images or pictures might have existed prior to utterances and words. To support this, he cited Genesis, where God had the animals pass before Adam to be named: "And this happened before Eve was made and when Adam was alone, so that it is hard to comprehend why he would speak, and to whom. But, can we not suppose that things happened some other way? That one day Adam went out into the field with a blackboard and amused himself making sketches from the original beasts and birds. And that when Eve later saw this, she named the sketches, and from here she named the animals depicted in them. Language stemmed from this. One more hypothesis among many" (V, 1116). The passage is a good example of the relaxed manner in which Biblical material was handled by Unamuno, who felt his mythical subject so intimately that his most imaginative recreations were expressed with the offhanded naturalness of a private fantasy.

Unamuno's casual manner did not detract from the intellectual weight of his discussions. Even the preceding quotation bears a close resemblance to one of his favorite ideas: that words and names are the most important factors in our relationship with the concrete world (VII, 1078). We saw this concept at work in the Jacob myth, and now we find it in a different form, applied to Unamuno's vision of reality. Basically, the idea holds that an object eludes our grasp, figuratively speaking, as long as we are ignorant of its name. To know an object is to be able to evoke it, to summon it from the sea of anonymity where it floats namelessly with other unnamed objects in the world. This naming is a symbolic act of possession, for it enables us to control our reality by placing things in order, according to titles and classifications. It also raises the object to a state of human relevance, giving it validity for the world of men as well as for the realm of inert matter. Thus, "to say a thing, to name it, is to make it ours, to humanize it, or rather, to make it divine. The Adam of Biblical legend took possession of the world by giving names to things. To know is to possess—and to love—and to know is to name" (VII, 431). As we can see, the process of humanization means that spirit must be infused into the physical world. Words belong to the realm of spirit, and when they are made to designate material objects, they bring together two antithetical realms. Spiritual and materialistic spheres are joined by an act of possession through words, which we call knowledge.

Unamuno's reasoning may seem to be metaphysical, but he used Adam as a concrete case: "Adam's act of giving a name to all the beasts of the field . . . was to take possession of them, and even today we take intellectual possession of things by naming them" (II, 592). In stating this, Unamuno assumed that there was a supremacy of idea over matter. Indeed, he reminds us of how the universe came into being, as told in Genesis: " 'And God said, Let there be light; and there was light,' thus creating it with His word." Moreover, he quotes the Gospel's affirmation that "in the beginning was the Word." By these quotations, Unamuno established the existence of a concept in God's mind prior to its taking form in the physical world. This demonstrated the power of spirit to be absolute. Man, in contrast, has only limited control over the spiritual realm, for he has no power to take ideas and turn them into concrete forms. What he can do is to dominate the physical world by recognizing, selecting, distinguishing, or even ignoring all the things in that world, simply by handling their names. It is true that he has only a nominal power, but this does not matter. From a mortal standpoint, such power is a very effective kind of control, because without knowledge man is completely cut off from phenomena, neither understanding them nor being able to arrange their occurrence with any sort of order. Without names, his world is chaos.

Having justified the concept of spiritual possession, it was left to Unamuno to determine its exact nature. Aside from its basic meaning of "intellectual grasp," the nature of this possession depends upon the function of the word or name. The name of an object is not equivalent to the object itself, which exists in the world independently of man. The name resides with man, is invented by him, and is conferred upon the object by his own will. The naming of an object, therefore, is a contributory act, a supplementary creation which endows that object with a singularly human quality. Thus, although objects are not changed materially by names, they are transformed in the human mind from a meaningless and undifferentiated mass into unique and comprehensible phenomena. "The name is the human essence of each thing. Any natural object . . . becomes human, is humanized, and is even domesticated when a man, in any human language, gives it a name. According to Genesis, Adam became master of all the animals by giving them names.

And this is why men fight for names more than for things, since a thing without a name is not human" (X, 935).

Not only is a nameless world inhuman, but it has no meaning when it stands independently of man. This is the key to man's power, because it is only when he chooses to confer meaning through words that things become defined. His spirit recreates matter, "the human essence of each thing." This is why the naming of the animals was a momentous event to Unamuno, who saw "Adam growing ecstatic before them, at the dawn of humanity. To name!" (II, 764). Unamuno felt the same exaltation, and was moved to convert it into a semi-religious sentiment. Therefore, he imagined that Adam's ecstasy was also the occasion for a song which praised the greatness of God's name for His having delivered the world into the hands of man. And Unamuno said, in reference to the daily sanctification by millions of people, "if we knew how to give God an exact, poetic name, a creative name, it would be the culmination of lyricism, like an eternal flower" (II, 765). But at this point, Unamuno turned away from philosophy to enter a more religious framework of discussion, where we cannot follow.

All of this emphasis on names is part of a much larger theme which Unamuno thought to be fundamental to the Eden myth. This was the idea of a reverence for communication. Noting that the naming of the beasts occurred before woman was created, Unamuno concluded that "man needed to speak even when alone, to speak to himself, that is, to sing. And his act of giving names to beings was an act of lyric purity, of perfect disinterest" (II, 766). In other words, Adam bestowed names in order that he might have, in return, the exhilaration of lyrical pleasure. He had no other motive for using language, least of all the pursuit of knowledge. But once he did sing, or utter words that distinguished objects, he sensed that he needed someone to whom he could communicate his feelings. The discovery of language and lyric revealed to Adam the possibility of conveying meaning from himself to another human being. Indeed, his knowledge that each animal was distinct opened his eyes to the fact that he too was an individual, and an isolated one. Thus, the general need to communicate his knowledge—and to share his power—led to the creation of Eve from his own rib.

The Eden myth posed a second problem which stemmed from man's communication with reality. How was his knowledge of reality related to the progress made by himself and his culture? That is, did knowledge function as a method of self-improvement and cultural progress? Unamuno's answer was, predictably enough, affirmative, although his reasons were less obvious. Basically, he felt that the original sin committed by Adam and Eve marked the first step along the road of human progress. As a corollary, he also felt that the punishment of this sin—work and pain—were the instruments by which that progress was achieved. Let us not forget that Unamuno constantly wavered between his desire for material cultural advancement and his religious idealism. In this case, then, it is significant that he ignored the theological implications of original sin. On the contrary, he concluded that when Adam ate the forbidden fruit of knowledge, mankind was free to rise from the underdeveloped state in which it had existed since Creation.

At the same time, Unamuno also deduced a principle of action from the forbidden fruit episode. This was the idea that no misdeed was without its saving feature. Despite the suffering and exile that swiftly followed the transgression of God's law, the fruits of man's labors were sweet. In this connection, Unamuno spoke of Eve's punishment—painful childbirth—and wrote that "when one has tasted the most intoxicating fruit, that of discovering a new truth, of making oneself—which is to become a man—one always returns to it, in spite of all the pain" (IX, 82). By this, he did not mean to condone disobedience, but rather, to affirm his faith in man's existence. For Unamuno, the lesson of the Adam and Eve myth was that man's spontaneous impulse turned him toward life regardless of pain and punishment.

While admitting that sin and punishment were the central issues of the Garden of Eden drama, Unamuno was also interested in why the Temptation ever succeeded in the first place. His reconstruction of the Fall was not systematic, but it is worth examining because of several related ideas which were derived from it. To begin with, he considered the original sin to have occurred under conditions of usufruct. Adam and Eve did not own Eden, but they could use it with God's permission provided that they avoided the tree of knowledge. This prohibition was their downfall, because the tempter's seduction was based on the promise that they would know "the reasons for things," namely, good and evil. Therefore, they ate the forbidden fruit, "and from this stem all our ills, among them, foremost and gravest of all, what we call progress" (II, 610).

But, although progress was the gravest of ills, it was also the most valuable, and Unamuno would have been the last man to deny this. If he judged progress so pessimistically, it was because he also perceived the mythic tragedy of Paradise. This consisted of the fact that Adam and Eve, after living in perfect health and innocence, fell "subject to all illnesses and their crowning end—death—and to work and progress" (XVI, 146). And yet this illness led to health, just as sin leads to salvation, not by necessity but because of man's inner excellence. Indeed, the very human qualities which brought about man's downfall would also save him: "Eve's womanly curiosity, which held her so fast to organic needs and preservation, was what led to her fall, and with the fall, to redemption." Unamuno's implication was that Eve had been compelled by an inner requirement to sin. Her "organic" impulse to know was a natural part of her human makeup, although curiosity was, admittedly, a lesser form of the desire for knowledge.

This explanation of original sin led Unamuno to analyze the nature of knowledge, and to seek its relationship to the paradox of Fall-Redemption, or pain-progress. He distinguished between two kinds of knowledge, "the desire or appetite for knowing . . . out of love of knowledge itself"—which was the desire to taste the forbidden fruit—and, in contrast, "the need to know in order to live" (XVI, 149). The latter form of knowledge was instinctual and spontaneous, whereas the former, although equally inherent in man, is what sets him apart culturally from the beasts. This higher form appears only after the basic desire to know in order to survive is satisfied. In other words, Eve's curiosity was a product of idleness, not need, and she wished to have pleasure in knowledge for its own sake.

Unamuno believed, however, that the desire for pure knowledge had been perverted by rational man, who allowed it to be taken over by his many needs. Thus, whenever man suffers anguish and doubt, he relieves them by making use of his knowledge and reason, molding the latter to suit his irrational ends. As a result, instead of delighting in pure knowledge, he suffers and searches his mind for relief. Pain, therefore, becomes a motive behind the desire to know, and it can, by extension, be a source of creativity, as well as a form of punishment, as it was in Eve's case. Unamuno summed this idea up by observing: "When you find wisdom in a work of knowledge, have no doubt that it was inspired by an emotion, a painful emotion much deeper and more essential than that miserable curiosity for finding out the why of things. 'You will be like gods, knowing good and evil,' tempted the serpent when Adam and Eve were languishing in the fatal felicity of Paradise, free of pain" (IV, 506).

But since pain is a psychological characteristic of contemporary man, this was not intended to be an adverse judgment of the wellsprings of knowledge. On the contrary, the sorrow afflicting Adam and Eve represented their first experience as mortals, and this condition was Unamuno's point of departure. His first principle of action was that man must strive to transcend himself "by taking strength from his weakness, turning his degradation into glory, and making sin the foundation of his redemption" (IV, 112). This idea was not simply the source of consolation to a suffering humanity. It was also Unamuno's definition of heroism and the justification for his apotheosis of Don Quixote. That is, a man is fully a man only when he wants to be more than just a man, when he is not content with being merely what he is ("You are lost unless you awaken the Adam deep within you, and his fortunate guilt, the guilt which has warranted us our redemption. For Adam wished to be like a god, knowing good and evil, and to become one he ate the forbidden fruit of the tree of knowledge. And his eyes were opened and he found himself tied to work and progress. And since then he began to be more than a man" [IV, 112]).

Thus, if man's first experiences after falling from grace were pain and shame, the rules which guided his later conduct were progress and work. Once again an exegesis of the Eden myth helped Unamuno to explain the role of work, as of all creativity, in terms of an existential imperative. He cited contradictory passages in Genesis 2:5, 15 and 2:17, to clarify an apparent conflict of statements. The first text states that before Adam's creation, there was no one to tend the Garden of Eden, and that Adam was placed there for this reason. This would seem to classify work as a special favor bestowed by God, a gift which opened the door to Paradise. And yet later on, Adam's punishment consists of being condemned to till the land. How, then, should work really be classified? Unamuno's explanation is the traditional one. That is, before the Fall, work was spontaneous and joyous, a "natural expansion of creative activity," whereas afterward, it became genuine labor, "in the economic sense of painful effort, directed more at earning a living than enjoying life" (XI, 429). Thus, Unamuno established two concepts of work, just as earlier he did so with regard to knowledge. One concept belonged to an "instinctive" category, a natural activity, while the other is acquired secondarily. And in the case of both work and knowledge, the later form characterized man as a cultural animal.

With this interpretation, Unamuno added the Eden myth to the previous two Judaic myths which could be applied to the analysis of Spanish culture. If Adam and Eve were not as dramatically human as the other figures in the Old Testament, they at least represented philosophical issues which the other two myths did not. What Cain and Jacob lacked in abstract speculation, the pale allegory of Eden supplied. All three of the Biblical episodes served Unamuno's secular purpose, since they were full of social, moral, and psychological implications. But as far as a theoretical approach was concerned, the Adam and Eve myth was the most useful for the analysis of cultural history.

# 17 HEBRAISM AND CHRISTIANITY

In the prolog to the third edition of *Mist*, written a year before his death, Unamuno returned to the problem of immortality which the novel posed so dramatically. Like the hero Augusto Pérez, Unamuno knew that he was going to die, and he thought of himself in relationship to God in the same way that Pérez had thought of himself when he confronted the author. Both men faced their creators with the determination to keep their freedom and individuality. As he wrote in 1935, it seemed natural for Unamuno to have thought of Jehovah as his Creator, and not Jesus, since the former had much more of a paternal image, as we have seen. Nevertheless, he went beyond Jehovah in his definition of immortality, and conceived of a "creative, dreaming word" which would remain after everything else disappeared. Unamuno was referring to the song of a "gigantic cock, taken from a Targum paraphrasing of the Bible," which reputedly told of the universe's final dissolution. He rejected this prediction, asserting instead that "the wild cock's crow will remain, and God's whisper with it. The Word, which was the beginning and will be the end, will remain" (II, 803). In other words, Unamuno knew that, as a creator, he had the power of life and death, a fact demonstrated by the fate of Augusto Pérez. However, he also realized that creators must also die, and this other fact prevented him from believing in God's immortality. What was left, therefore, was this variation of the Targum legend, a communal dream by conscious men which was perpetuated forever through words.

This was the metaphysical foundation which helped Unamuno to justify his vast store of ideas about civilization and human conduct. Some of them were contradictory, but as a total philosophy, their nature was what we might call markedly Hebraistic, as opposed to Hellenistic, in content. These categories, which Matthew Arnold defined as cultural forces in *Culture and Anarchy*, are very useful in understanding the role that Judaism played in Unamuno's thought. Briefly, Arnold defined Hebraism as strictness of conscience, an attitude toward culture in which duty, action, self-control, and obedience to God's will are what shape the conduct of man. This he opposed to the spontaneity of conscience which is Hellenism, an attitude wherein reason, flexibility, knowledge, and beauty are motivating forces. Although no modern secular thinker can be exclusively one or the other, the general bent of Unamuno's observations indicates that he was a Hebraist, as Arnold would have used the term. This is especially true in his concept of action being superior to contemplation. Unamuno praised the man whose reliance upon himself revealed a "faith that was lacking in arrogant contemplative men." His was a self-confidence in action, which "stemmed from his life's plenitude." For this type of man, as well as for Unamuno, the only value was to work, to "engender, gestate, and give birth to live thoughts, because, like Rachel, he felt that without children he would die" (III, 819).

At the same time, the will to action was more than just a desire to perform deeds. It also embraced the yearning for immortality, which it sustained by the very enormity of man's desire. Unamuno's wish ("If only I could lead this other life and do these and other things which I cannot do today!") had a Hebraic root: "The Jews, on leaving Egypt, yearned for the promised land, and once there, sighed for Egypt. They wanted both lands at the same time, and man wants every land and every century. He wants to live in all of space and time, in infinity and eternity" (III, 1041).

In fact, Unamuno saw a profound relationship between the will to action and gaining immortal life. In *The Life of Don Quixote and Sancho*, he asks the lethargic squire, "How, Sancho, can you wish Adam to live in paradise without working? What kind of paradise can it be if there is no work?" In truth, there could be no true paradise without some element of work present, and, even more, we learn from the Book of Genesis "not that God condemned man to work, for it says that He put him in paradise to till and care for it (2:15), but rather that after Adam sinned, He condemned him to the hardship of work . . . to eat from the earth in pain" (IV, 275). The paradise that was Adam's, and for which man now strives, was graced by personal immortality, to be sure, but it also represented the very state of perfection which had later become the major goal of cultural activity. The question now, therefore, was how to achieve this perfection. One of Unamuno's solutions was to have hope in the emergence of a hero. Whatever description fitted this hero—collective, individual, genius, or ingenuous—his destiny was to follow his inner impulses and lead the rest of his people to a better life. This will to action was a basic requirement. As Unamuno suggested while praying that Spain's youth would yearn for a cultural messiah, each man had to make this demand upon himself and upon his milieu. In other words, by trying to be in fact a precursor of the redeeming genius, the "Prince of youth," it was conceivable that the latter might some day arrive. The situation was equivalent to the Biblical episode where "the Envoy came, but he came to Rachel's village, the [same] Rachel who said to her husband Jacob: 'Give me children, or else I die,' (Gen. 30:1). And he gave them to her" (III, 735).

Desire, therefore, was the first step to fulfillment. Unamuno was so intent in realizing this aspect of will that in one passage he overstated his argument for the cultural hero. He rightly affirmed that to await the genius' arrival would, far from tranquilizing the people into passiveness, move them to action instead. But then he said that this was "like waiting for the Messiah, [which] roused the Jewish women from their voluntary sterility and made them yearn for maternity." He believed that "waiting for the Messiah is what keeps that marvelous people still alive and active," and for that reason "every Jewish maiden ardently desired the arrival of the man who would make her womb blossom, in the hope that its fruit would be the promised Messiah" (III, 726). Despite the exaggeration, Unamuno was writing seriously, and his intention can only be construed as wanting to document his assumption with supposed Jewish folklore. Given the prominence of the maternity theme in his works, and his allusion to Mary in connection with Messianic genius (III, 735), it is easy to see why Unamuno found the fiction useful.

But legend is only the anecdote of cultural philosophy, not its precept. If Unamuno found action to be one of the precepts of Hebraism, he saw it as the expression of obedience as well as of individual freedom. When a hero is inspired by a great and terrifying mission, how can he disobey, "having heard in the recesses of the soul the silent voice of God, which says, 'You must do this'" (IV, 110)? In order to complete the task, whether imposed by God or by social necessity, the heroic temper had to exercise a strong degree of self-discipline. And yet the hero's responsibility is more difficult to bear because he has no one to share the burden with. His alliance is with a secret and transcendent power that demands obedience of him. He is "the only one who hears and knows it, and since obedience to the mandate and faith within him is what makes him over into a hero, [then] to be the man that one is can very well mean: 'I know who I am, and only my God and I know.'"

However, this kind of a self-assertion is only possible when it is fortified by a strong sense of duty. In this regard, Unamuno was reminded of Abraham, "the hero of the faith," when he was put to the test on Mount Moriah (IV, 110–11). If Abraham had been guided by a Hellenistic spirit, he would have restored a rational balance to his mission. Instead, he pushed to one side every consideration except the one which God's commandment dictated. Unamuno also remembered Don Quixote in this connection, interpreting the knight's adventure with the lion as an episode of "consummate obedience and perfect faith" (IV, 248). God had caused the lions to appear so that the knight would attempt to engage them. God tried to "test the faith and obedience of Don Quixote as He had tested Abraham's, commanding him to ascend Mount Moriah to sacrifice his son" (IV, 249). Neither of the two events revealed any virtue in moderation or reason, and still less in the motive of self-interest. Heroic values, therefore, could be defined according to the Hebraic tradition of self-sacrifice, a surrendering of the material world to a higher spiritual good.

As a cultural historian, Unamuno was very conscious of what Arnold called the more spiritual development of Hebraism: the transition which Christianity had made from obedience to the law to its subsequent self-abnegation. Since it was sinful to transgress the law, everything worldly that might lead to transgression was subjected to the interests of moral asceticism, and even in the Old

Testament, one could cite Ecclesiastes as a forerunner of negation. Although Unamuno rejected the literal meaning of "vanity of vanities" (III, 768–69), he accepted the metaphorical value of its pessimism. The Preacher's vision of life's tragedy caught the essential fact that everything is a dream. This "breath of Solomonic wisdom" was infused into the Spanish mentality, along with "a certain cult of vivifying death" (IV, 1082). The result was a kind of popular philosophy, whose central idea was "the sense of the nothingness of everything temporal before the eternal," a notion which "gives to our people a fortitude that shields them against the attacks of life."

Since the Spanish nation had suffered a series of severe colonial losses, the case for considering the world as a vanity was strengthened. Spain lived in what Unamuno called a "quiet submissiveness to Destiny, which is our greatest resisting strength." This resignation, however, far from being sluggish apathy, would serve to quicken Spain's incentive for progress. Her action would be based on the regulatory effect of the vanity motif: "The core of the lesson on 'vanity of vanities,' which we take so much to heart, will be our best aid in cultivating that same, indispensable vanity; to dream of a fleeting life" (IV, 1082–83). The spontaneity that had consumed Spain's energy in the past would now be controlled, its impulse modified by the sober appraisal of action that prophetic moralizing brings.

There was still one more Old Testament patriarch who represented the qualities of the Hebraism which we have been discussing. For Unamuno, the paragon of all Hebraistic values was Moses, the sage who codified the Law and gave it to his people to be obeyed. Unamuno wrote an essay on the solitude of Moses that was inspired by the civil and spiritual preoccupations which he shared with the prophet (VIII, 995). Moses was also a model for action in the life of Unamuno's fictional martyr, Saint Emmanuel the Good. As a result, the essay's main theme was the prophet's solitude, a condition which began when the infant was abandoned among the bulrushes. This initial event, in which Unamuno admitted having an obsessive interest, symbolized the helplessness of the man whose life would be a continual spiritual isolation. Tracing the incidents that illustrated Moses' solitary condition, Unamuno led up to the fact that this was the only Hebrew prophet who saw God's face, and who then died on Pisgah of Nebo near Jericho, names which "arrive scented with the perfume of desert flower memories" (VIII, 997).

Why should Unamuno have concentrated more on this aspect of Moses' life than on its religious or social implications? The answer depends upon how we understand the concept of solitude. In this essay on Moses, Unamuno was really concerned with the problems of freedom and obligation which the prophet's solitary condition imposed upon him. These concerns had, as we saw on other occasions, personal and collective aspects to them. Unamuno describes Moses as an old man with a tremendous responsibility, and without anyone to help carry it out. As an added burden, he had to contemplate the approach of death, and it was "a terrible thing to find oneself in the vanguard of the army advancing toward death!" Thus, Unamuno sensed the feeling of "abysmal solitude" that occurs when the awareness of time isolates the leader from his people and undermines his sense of duty. Moses was "at the head of his people, and since he saw no men in front of him, and could not look back over his shoulder at his people, he found himself alone" (VIII, 997). Moses' responsibility for the group automatically cut him off from the latter without reducing his sense of obligation. This was remarkable, since the Israelites were a nation to which Moses scarcely belonged. Indeed, the duty which God set upon him had in effect separated him from the people. And yet the ensuing solitude had merely strengthened his moral sense. Therefore, Moses curtailed his range of individual freedom in the manner of the Hebraist mode of behavior, in obedience to the decrees of God and cultural destiny.

In addition to what we have said, the delicate balance between personal and public roles was fully articulated within a Judaic context. Unamuno held, for example, that a man was of historical importance only when he was inwardly aflame with the passion of individual action. At first glance, it would seem that when the thread of life was consumed, nothing would be left besides a few scattered filaments of his life history. But the truth was that Unamuno found the flame to be constantly renewed, in the same way that the burning bush was found to be unconsumed (IX, 933). Thus, the life of genuine heroism required the inward fire of

human will, as well as the external heat of action. And above all, it
needed to be illuminated by introspection (IX, 838, 862).

Unamuno's constant faith in the principle of self-knowledge was
as important in this area of personal action as it was anywhere. One
of the lessons he learned from Genesis was the truism that "God
created Man in His image and likeness," which was to say that "He
created him as a mirror to see himself in, to know himself, to create
himself" (X, 862). When man learns to know himself, he can
control the demands of his own spontaneity and his duty to the
law. Moses was able to accomplish this, becoming a hero in an
individualistic sense, and at the same time a self-sacrificing patriarch
who discharged his responsibility to his people and God.

In this regard, Unamuno was sometimes fond of citing the her-
oine Abishag, the Shunammite who gave herself to the dying King
David and forfeited thereby her hope for marriage. Her example
tragically represented the soul of any individual or group that
sacrificed self-interest out of love for God. Abishag became the
symbolic mother of David, and yet she might have become a
genuine mother had she married Adonijah. But the outcome was
not a loss, at least not in Unamuno's eyes, since "they were both the
same thing, the mother of action and of contemplation" (X, 535).
The ability to see oneself objectively placed the other, sacrificed
self in perspective. In fact, it might even show that one interest can
be served by another, in the same way that a willing service to God
can also benefit the self.

The individual, therefore, contributes to his own transcendence
as well as that of his culture by placing his self-knowledge at the
service of moral action. One of the purposes of this is to acquire
truth, especially because it enhances personal freedom. Unamuno
spoke of the prophet as "he who speaks (*phet*) before (*pro*) the
people, he who does not silence what his spirit, which is
Truth—and Life—inspires in him" (XI, 466). When culture is in a
state of decline, this love of truth is perhaps the most immediate
objective. Thus, when Jeremiah spoke during Israel's period of
captivity, he was not so much the prophet of lamentation as he was
the sage who "told his people the most medicinally bitter truths:
why they deserved the bondage which they were bemoaning."
Unamuno went on to quote from the Book of Lamentations, sug-

gesting that Jeremiah's personal vision of the cultural situation was a necessary statement that obeyed the imperative of truth-seeking. The prophet had said that he who sought truth would be saved, and according to Unamuno, "it was the truth that Jeremiah sought, and if truth [seemed] to justify his people's slavery, he spoke it. Because truth and only truth liberates" (XI, 466). This, then, is the final law that must be obeyed in a culture's evolution toward its own perfection, a precept whose Hebraistic force, as both Arnold and Unamuno would define it, ties man to a destiny greater than himself.

# CONCLUSION

*No single* study of Unamuno can ever present his complete philosophy. The most that may be hoped for—and what he himself desired—is that within the critical perspective chosen, "the intelligent reader will supply the missing method and fill in the gaps" (III, 303). This is a difficult task, because Unamuno's dialecticism and irony are always pulling the critic in different directions, and they sometimes end by pulling his leg. Nor are Unamuno's grammar and style always assets in helping to determine his meaning. But of all the hurdles, the least surmountable is his spirit of contradiction.

It is clear that Unamuno's main preoccupation was the study of man, and yet he dealt with mortal man and the social condition on the one hand, and with man's aspirations to immortality on the other, two antithetical, if not incompatible, concepts, as *The Agony of Christianity* shows. And since his psychological disposition led him to axiological ambiguity, he assumed an ironic outlook whose styles took the form of paradox and contradiction. Thus, Unamuno seems to be resolving many issues at the same time, and not always on the same level. What do remain constant, however, are the structures of experience, be they in the psychological realm or in culture. Related subjects such as personal and collective destinies, the Cain myth, Don Quixote, and Jesus, are all thematically bound to each other while serving to link areas as distinct as the individual and the group, temporality and eternity, humanism and Christianity. Hence the usefulness of the Judaic tradition as a method of cultural analysis, for both its myths and its history deal with the same problems. In the cultural experience of both the Spaniard and the Jew, the sacred and the profane become two sectors of the same existential sphere, and whether in the collective memory of the Bible, or in the private theater of Unamuno's consciousness, there was the same thirst for an immortal spiritual identification.

The origin of this quest occurs in the self-awareness of the individual. For Unamuno, man transcends the world of phenomena to the realm of spirit through consciousness. This idea is the rationale behind the cultivation of the existential personality, which, for all of its divisiveness, is the only means of acquiring life's plenitude. Moreover, in the final stage of psychic integration, personality becomes the instrument of spirit. Once the individual harmonizes the fragments of his personality, he may enter into a more profound spiritual experience. His effective control of the marginal components of his self will strengthen the bond of communication between the real permanent self and the outer world, precisely because these elements are the creations of both realms. But at the same time, existence is more than just a participation in exterior and inner realities. All of life is a continual becoming. The psychological mechanisms of personality are less important than the imperative to "become." Nevertheless, these factors determine the self to be willed, and in fact, once this desired self is realized, it will be as valueless as any other present self which the will is supposed to transcend. The heart of Unamuno's thinking lies in just this paradox. Man is to be himself and yet to keep becoming. Thus, the key to Unamuno's general philosophy is found in his ideas on psychology.

At this point, it grows evident that the structures of psychological and cultural experiences are the same. For example, in the concept of the "satanic self," the antagonistic split within the self is comparable to the struggle in society between separate individuals or factions with opposing values and impulses. This was the problem of Spain, and as a Spaniard Unamuno felt himself torn precisely because he could adopt, as he did with his own personality, all points of view. Consequently, he took the mythic form of the Cain episode to elucidate both his private and his Spanish conditions. In the myth, the brothers' roles are reversible, just as in each human being the characteristics of both men are found in equal proportion. In fact, Unamuno offered a new ethical perspective based on the Cain myth: that behind every gain there is someone else's loss, and behind every evil is a compensating good dependent on it. But this reversibility depends on the ulterior Christian motive of love. Similarly, the notion of "the Other" illustrates both Unamuno's idea of personality structure and his psychological approach to the theory of values. He spans the gulf between his own self seen as an object, and another object which is the self of his neighbor. Thus, the concept of the Other is extended to include the ethical relationship between the individual and a different Other.

With respect to this kind of value formation, Unamuno's attitude toward Nietzsche is highly relevant, not because he responded often to the German, which he violently did, and not because they both belong to the same branch of existentialism, which they do. More important is the fact that the two men gained the identical insight into the relationship between psychology and morals, and reacted differently. In both philosophers, their self-contemplation eventually led to an ironic viewpoint. But whereas Nietzsche sought to be serious, Unamuno maintained his secret irony. If the terms good and bad faith were used, it would be fair to say that Unamuno acted in bad faith, because he "sincerely" lived, in turn or alternately, all of his contradictory selves, which meant, ultimately, that he found nothing serious within himself except his irony. Nietzsche, on the other hand, acted in good faith, because he overcame the personality split with the rejection of all psychological standards other than the unconscious impulse. And thus he passed beyond good and evil. Unamuno could not take this last step, and the result was an irrationalist approach to valuation, and a methodology that dispensed with logic in favor of antithesis. He knew that there was no unequivocal idea or answer to an issue. He therefore allowed himself to entertain opposing and even contradictory statements where all elements were recognized to be true. No effort to synthesize or reconcile opposites had to be made, because life itself was "bound by antitheses and antinomies."

Unamuno's deep interest in value formation was intensified by the knowledge of his own inner fragmentation and the hypocrisy which was its product. But these very faults led him to affirm love as the supreme value, and to seek a divine power to support him in his weakness. Here, then, is Unamuno's existential contribution. He showed that the return to God is polarized on an intellectual knowledge of ethical and psychological failure, and on an emotional need in spite of disbelief. He is not interested in God per se—which explains his distaste for theology—but only insofar as He will love and make man immortal too. Thus, the Mosaic God is humanistically useless, for His love is less than man's self-love and desire to live forever. The concept of God becomes valuable only to the extent that the Deity reflects man's existential concern. And the image of Jehovah rises in esteem as it becomes transformed into an anticipation of Christ the *man*.

The prototype of this search for God and the struggle to believe was to be found in Jacob, in whom Unamuno saw the first "man of flesh and bone" whose spiritual awareness springs from a problematic human condition. Beyond this, the Jacob myth unified the three sectors of existence outlined in this book: personality, valuation, and culture. In Unamuno the man, it illustrated the psychological origin of ideologies, and in Spain the social organism, it characterized the enmity of opposing cultural factions. The fragments of one ego, the convictions that combat each other, and the parties of a single nation are all related to one another by genetic origin. Our lives on both the personal and social levels make us "children of contradiction," not just in the mythic sense of Cain's and Abel's fraternal and domestic context, but like Jacob and Esau, biologically and in the womb: the one common matrix of dissident elements within a single organic body. Unamuno's unceasing spiritual schism was due to his quest for identity within the tensions of his existence. His self-definition was partly achieved through a state of discord which was itself a prime requisite of his existence. But the latter's full meaning had also to include the nature of divine essence, since the self's ultimate goal was to become immortal like God. Hence Unamuno's interest in the Jacob myth, which exteriorized the internal conflict of all agonistic figures.

Thus the interlocking chain of themes joins itself at each end and becomes a complete circle. The existentialist's dilemma is measured in terms of mortal dimensions, but is set against the backdrop of eternity. It is conceived in the arena of human awareness, but is then projected upon a divine consciousness. His problem is that there is no knowledge of objective reality, not even of man's own nature. Nevertheless, the pattern of psychological and moral activity that takes place on an individual basis occurs in similar form in society, and both structures are represented in the great socio-religious Judaic myths which provide a mirror for analysis. The continuity which each personality achieves for itself in the psychochronic self has its parallel in the historic memory of a people, but any attempt to know either personality or people results in a series of dichotomies, all parts of which are valid. At the same time, the rivalry among fragmentary selves produces an ethical ambiguity wherein all values may appear to be justifiable, while the comparable struggle of diverse cultural tendencies within one social organism will reveal all positions to be defensible, according to the point of view adopted. The initial result is a dual form of absurdity, in which the individual's relationship to society is deprived of any consistent valuation criteria, and in which the elements of society itself become mutually destructive.

Only the power of love can effect the integration of cultural parts, and only a commitment to this culture can restore the psychic wholeness eroded by the demoralization of the social self. Man strives for a psychological equilibrium, just as a nation does for cultural harmony. And man aspires to spiritual immortality, just as a nation does to utopian permanence. Unamuno found his private war duplicated and enlarged in his country's historical condition, and he described the task of both man and nation as the identical need to reconcile incompatible value systems. If the initial outcome of the struggle was absurdity, the second result was the creation of Unamuno's final mask: the face of the Spaniard.

*Reference Matter*

# APPENDIX

*List of Works Cited from the* Obras completas,
*with Date of Composition*

I,    179–84:    "Del Arbol de la Libertad . . ." (*De mi país*). 1891.

I,    484–93:    " 'La gloria de Don Ramiro' " (*Por tierras de Portugal y de España*). 1909.

I,    504–12:    "Excursión" (*ibid.*). 1909.

I,    534–41:    "Grandes y pequeñas ciudades" (*ibid.*). 1908.

I,    578–87:    "Trujillo" (*ibid.*). 1909.

I,    623–32:    "Ciudad, campo, paisajes y recuerdos" (*Andanzas y visiones españolas*). 1911.

I,    686–93:    "Por capitales de provincia" (*ibid.*). 1913.

I,    711–17:    "En la Peña de Francia" (*ibid.*). 1913.

I,    718–26:    "Salamanca" (*ibid.*). 1914.

I,    792–98:    "La Torre de Monterrey . . ." (*ibid.*). 1916.

I,    822–26:    "En Palencia" (*ibid.*). 1921.

I,    838–43:    "Paisaje teresiano" (*ibid.*). 1922.

I,    956–59:    "Callejeo por la del Sacramento" (*Paisajes del alma: Madrid*). 1932.

I,    1079–82:    "En San Juan de la Peña" (*Paisajes del alma: Aragón*). 1932.

I,    1103–6:    "País, paisaje y paisanaje" (*Paisajes del alma: España*). 1933.

II,    71–417:    *Paz en la guerra*. 1897.

II,    421–585:    *Amor y pedagogía*. 1902.

| III, | 718–36: | "Almas de jóvenes." 1904. |
| III, | 737–52: | "Sobre la filosofía española." 1904. |
| III, | 753–70: | "¡Plenitud de plenitudes y todo plenitud!" 1904. |
| III, | 806–20: | "Sobre la soberbia." 1904. |
| III, | 821–41: | "Los naturales y los espirituales." 1905. |
| III, | 842–60: | "¡Ramplonería!" 1905. |
| III, | 881–901: | "Soledad." 1905. |
| III, | 902–25: | "Sobre la erudición y la crítica." 1905. |
| III, | 957–74: | "Sobre el rango y el mérito." 1905. |
| III, | 992–1009: | "¿Qué es verdad?" 1906. |
| III, | 1027–42: | "El secreto de la vida." 1906. |
| III, | 1043–64: | "Sobre la consecuencia, la sinceridad." 1906. |
| III, | 1065–1104: | "Algunas consideraciones sobre la literatura hispano-americana." 1905–6. |
| III, | 1105–26: | "Sobre la europeización." 1906. |

| IV, | 65–384: | *La vida de Don Quijote y Sancho.* 1905. |
| IV, | 387–94: | "Verdad y vida" (*Mi religión y otros ensayos*). 1908. |
| IV, | 402–7: | "El Cristo español" (*ibid.*). 1909. |
| IV, | 417–25: | "La envidia hispánica" (*ibid.*). 1909. |
| IV, | 433–40: | "Los escritores y el pueblo" (*ibid.*). 1908. |
| IV, | 491–96: | "A un literato joven" (*ibid.*). 1907. |
| IV, | 503–8: | "El pórtico del templo" (*ibid.*). 1906. |
| IV, | 557–66: | "Conversación segunda" (*Soliloquios y conversaciones*). 1910. |
| IV, | 592–99: | "Divagaciones de estío" (*ibid.*). 1908. |
| IV, | 608–15: | "El escritor y el hombre" (*ibid.*). 1908. |
| IV, | 625–33: | "Confidencias" (*ibid.*). 1910. |
| IV, | 642–49: | "Al señor A. Z., autor de un libro" (*ibid.*). 1909. |
| IV, | 693–701: | "Público y prensa" (*ibid.*). 1908. |
| IV, | 702–10: | "Nuestras mujeres" (*ibid.*). 1907. |
| IV, | 750–57: | "Algo sobre la crítica" (*Contra esto y aquello*). 1907. |
| IV, | 767–75: | "La 'Grecia' de Carrillo" (*ibid.*). 1909. |
| IV, | 801–9: | "Educación por la historia" (*ibid.*). 1910. |
| IV, | 838–44: | "El Rousseau de Lemaître" (*ibid.*). 1907. |
| IV, | 845–53: | "Rousseau, Voltaire y Nietzsche" (*ibid.*). 1907. |

IV,    890–99:    "A propósito de Josué Carducci" (*ibid.*). 1907.

IV,    935–42:    "Literatura y literatos" (*ibid.*). 1908.

IV,    953–1015:    *El porvenir de España.* 1898.

IV,    1075–93:    "España y los españoles" (*España y los españoles. I*). 1902.

IV,    1121–28:    "¡El español . . . conquistador!" (*ibid.*). 1915.

IV,    1129–35:    "De las tristezas españolas: la acedía" (*ibid.*). ¿1916?

IV,    1136–40:    "Junto a la cerca del Paraíso" (*ibid.*). 1916.

V,    72–75:    "La enormidad de España" (*España y los españoles. II*). 1932.

V,    99–102:    "Mandarines y no mandones" (*ibid.*). 1936.

V,    192–96:    "Lope de Aguirre, el traidor" (*Lecturas españolas clásicas*). 1920.

V,    260–67:    "Comentarios quevedianos" (*ibid.*). 1935.

V,    326–34:    "El problema religioso en el Japón" (*Libros y autores españoles contemporáneos*). 1907.

V,    335–42:    "Más sobre el japonismo" (*ibid.*). 1907.

V,    363–71:    " 'Lecturas españolas' " (*ibid.*). 1912.

V,    377–93:    "Sobre un libro de memorias" (*ibid.*). 1913.

V,    418–25:    "Nuestra egolatría de los del 98" (*ibid.*). 1916.

V,    540–44:    " 'Redenta' " (*De literatura vasca*). 1899.

V,    554–62:    "Otro escritor vasco" (*ibid.*). 1908.

V,    603–6:    " 'Fulls de la vida,' por Santiago Rusiñol" (*Sobre la literatura catalana*). 1899.

V,    681–84:    "Más de la envidia hispánica" (*ibid.*). 1934.

V,    869–76:    "La feliz ignorancia" (*La vida literaria*). 1907.

V,    877–84:    "El trashumanismo" (*ibid.*). 1909.

V,    929–34:    "De antruejo" (*Ensayos erráticos o a lo que salga*). 1901.

V,    1103–6:    "La escalera de vecindad" (*ibid.*). 1922.

V,    1115–17:    "Escritura y lenguaje" (*ibid.*). 1922.

V, 1187–1218:    *Aforismos y definiciones* (inédito, 1923).

VI,    503–8:    "Mayúsculas y minúsculas" (*En torno a la lengua española*). 1901.

VI,    613–17:    "La firma" (*ibid.*). 1918.

VI,    629–34:    "Cosas de libros" (*ibid.*). 1918.

VI,    643–45:    "Metáforas" (*ibid.*). 1923.

VII,        139:    *Prólogo* al libro de José Balcázar y Sabariegos *Memorias de un estudiante de Salamanca*. 1894.

VII,    242–64:    *Prólogo* a la versión española del libro de Benedetto Croce *Estética*. 1911.

VII,    308–26:    *Introducción* al libro *Simón Bolívar*. 1914.

VII,    334–51:    *Prólogo* a la versión española del libro de Gabriel Hanotaux *Historia ilustrada de la guerra*. 1915.

VII,    352–58:    *Prólogo* al libro *Yo acuso*, por Un Alemán. 1916.

VII,    429–33:    *Prólogo* al libro de Victoriano García Martí *Del vivir heroico*. ¿1925?

VII,    434–37:    *Prólogo* al libro de Ariel Bension *El Zohar en la España musulmana y cristiana*. ¿1931?

VII,    473–92:    "Sobre el estudio de la demótica," conferencia. 1896.

VII,    547–62:    Conferencia en el teatro Principal, de La Coruña. 1903.

VII,    568–88:    Conferencia en los Juegos Florales de Almería. 1903.

VII,    697–714:    Conferencia en el Círculo Mercantil, de Málaga. 1906.

VII,    715–28:    Conferencia en el teatro de Novedades, de Barcelona. 1906.

VII,    786–809:    Discurso en el homenaje a Darwin. 1909.

VII,    824–30:    Discurso en el Ateneo de Vitoria. 1912.

VII,    1076–91:    Oración inaugural del Curso académico 1934–1935 en la Universidad de Salamanca, al ser jubilado como catedrático.

VIII,        69–75:    "Carta abierta a Casimiro Muñoz" (*Letras hispanoamericanas*). 1899.

VIII,    173–86:    "Sobre varios libros americanos" (*ibid.*). 1902.

VIII,    199–205:    "Entremés justificativo" (*ibid.*). 1903.

VIII,    222–30:    "Impresiones viajeras de Amado Nervo" (*ibid.*). 1903.

VIII,    241–44:    "Anales argentinos: *Mi año literario*, por Arturo Reynal O'Connor" (*ibid.*). 1904.

VIII,    474–81:    "Sobre la continuidad histórica" (*ibid.*). 1913.

VIII, 491–95: "La escala de Jacob" (*ibid.*). 1914.

VIII, 585–90: "Mi libro" (*ibid.*). 1919.

VIII, 657–61: "El esteticismo d'annunziano" (*Letras italianas*). 1918.

VIII, 707–11: "Andología" (*ibid.*). 1934.

VIII, 717–21: "La afanosa grandiosidad española" (*ibid.*). 1934.

VIII, 859–63: "La nube de la guerra" (*Letras de la antigüedad clásica*). 1914.

VIII, 995–98: "La soledad de Moisés" (*Letras francesas*). 1922.

VIII, 999–1004: "La fe de Renan" (*ibid.*). 1923.

VIII, 1095–99: "Uebermensch" (*Letras alemanas*). 1914.

VIII, 1100–1109: "Algo sobre Nietzsche" (*ibid.*). 1915.

VIII, 1110–20: "Sobre el paganismo de Goethe" (*ibid.*). 1915.

VIII, 1133–37: "¿Para qué escribir?" (Comentarios al *Epistolario inédito* de Nietzsche) (*ibid.*). 1919.

IX, 59–63: "Rebeca." 1914.

IX, 76–80: "El contra-mismo." 1918.

IX, 81–85: "Fecundidad del aislamiento." 1918.

IX, 95–100: "Una vida sin historia: Amiel." 1923.

IX, 146–49: "El lego Juan." 1898.

IX, 194–201: "El que se enterró." 1908.

IX, 284–88: "Artemio, heautontimoróumenos." 1918.

IX, 289–92: "Robleda, el actor." 1920.

IX, 305–8: "La sombra sin cuerpo." 1921.

IX, 355–62: "Querer vivir" (inédito).

IX, 379–409: *Tulio Montalbán y Julio Macedo.* 1920.

IX, 413–23: "Prólogo" (*Tres novelas ejemplares*). 1920.

IX, 526: *La tía Tula*, Ch. I. 1921.

IX, 642–49: "Hay que hacerse niño" (*Monodiálogos*). 1902.

IX, 650–56: "De la vocación" (*ibid.*). 1900.

IX, 687–714: "Diálogos del escritor y el político" (*ibid.*). 1911.

IX, 715–18: "La idea y el palo" (*ibid.*). 1911.

IX, 732–36: "Cuestiones de momento. Intermedio lírico" (*ibid.*). 1913.

IX, 737–42: "Del dolor, de la soledad y de la lógica" (*ibid.*). 1913.

IX, 743–51: "Conversación" (*ibid.*). 1913.

IX,    758–63:   "Cuestiones de momento. Cobrar conciencia" (*ibid.*). 1913.

IX,    773–79:   "Al borde" (*ibid.*). 1913.

IX,    822–26:   "Sobre el gran Roque Guinart y su imperio" (*ibid.*). 1915.

IX,    837–42:   "¡Ensimísmate! Una vez más" (*ibid.*). 1915.

IX,    848–51:   "Sobre la necesidad de pensar" (*ibid.*). 1915.

IX,    852–59:   "El que se vendió" (*ibid.*). 1916.

IX,    893–97:   "El talento de hacer artículos" (*ibid.*). 1917.

IX,    898–902:  "Nuestro yo y el de los demás" (*ibid.*). 1917.

IX,    907–11:   "Daoíz y Velarde" (*ibid.*). 1918.

IX,    931–34:   "¿De nuevo? ¡Ni el hilo!" (*ibid.*). 1919.

IX,    949–52:   "Educación e instrucción" (*ibid.*). 1920.

IX,    965–68:   "La telaraña" (*ibid.*). 1920.

IX,    981–86:   "Monodiálogo" (*ibid.*). 1922.

IX,    1015–18:  "Pan y toros" (*ibid.*). 1932.

IX,    1045–48:  "Nuevas contemplaciones" (*ibid.*). 1935.

X,     77–80:    "Un artículo más" (*De mi vida*). 1899.

X,     85–94:    "La leyenda del eclipse" (*ibid.*). 1900.

X,     95–97:    "Darwin" (*ibid.*). 1901.

X,     98–102:   "Por una pajarita" (*ibid.*). 1902.

X,     110–13:   "Autorretrato" (*ibid.*). 1902.

X,     132–38:   "Del primer firmante. Voto explicado" (*ibid.*). 1905.

X,     236–42:   "Días de limpieza" (*ibid.*). 1913.

X,     262–66:   "El círculo vicioso teatral" (*ibid.*). 1914.

X,     355–67:   "Nada de pretensiones" (*ibid.*). 1916.

X,     373–78:   "El morillo al rojo" (*ibid.*). 1916.

X,     433–35:   "Desde la cama" (*ibid.*). 1920.

X,     510–12:   "Yo, individuo, poeta, profeta y mito" (*ibid.*). 1922.

X,     529–35:   "Nuestros yos ex-futuros" (*ibid.*). 1923.

X,     536–40:   "La lanzadera del tiempo" (*ibid.*). 1923.

X,     577–80:   ["Aprende a hacerte el que eres"] (*ibid.*). 1924.

X,     649–50:   "Jueves Santo" (*En el destierro. Fuerteventura*). 1924.

X,     694–97:   ["Extracciones fotográficas"] (*En el destierro. Aspectos de París*). 1924.

X,  774–81:  "Noche de huracán" (*En el destierro. Desde Hendaya*). 1926.

X,  813–16:  "El mercado de los sábados" (*ibid.*). 1925.

X,  827–923:  *Cómo se hace una novela.* 1927.

X,  934–36:  "Miguel, o '¿quién como Dios?' " (*Ultimos escritos*). 1931.

XI,  68–70:  "Afrancesamiento" (*Inquietudes y meditaciones*). 1899.

XI,  105–12:  "Sobre eso del vino" (*ibid.*). 1902.

XI,  168–74:  "Divagaciones sobre la resignación y el esfuerzo" (*ibid.*). 1911.

XI,  175–80:  "Ganas de escribir" (*ibid.*). 1911.

XI,  319–23:  "La lucha con el oficio" (*ibid.*). ¿1914?

XI,  329–33:  "El cuarto de Juan y la última España" (*ibid.*). 1914.

XI,  366–70:  "La victoria metafísica" (*ibid.*). 1916.

XI,  393–98:  " 'En un lugar de la Mancha' " (*ibid.*). 1917.

XI,  429–32:  "Arte y trabajo" (*ibid.*). 1920.

XI,  441–44:  "Lujuria de dolor" (*ibid.*). 1921.

XI,  453–56:  "La hora de la resignación" (*ibid.*). 1922.

XI,  465–67:  "El deber del profeta" (*ibid.*). 1923.

XI,  511–16:  "De vuelta de teatro." 1913.

XI,  536–40:  "Hablemos de teatro." 1934.

XI,  587–97:  "El Greco." 1914.

XI,  609–14:  "La labor patriótica de Zuloaga." 1917.

XI,  615–19:  "En el Museo del Prado." 1919.

XI,  739–48:  "Aprender haciendo. (Conversación.)" (*A propósito del estilo*). 1913.

XI,  795–98:  "Hombre, persona e individuo" (*Alrededor del estilo*). 1924.

XI,  802–4:  "Traje y estilo" (*ibid.*). 1924.

XI,  820–23:  "Lenguaje y estilo" (*ibid.*). 1924.

XI,  838–41:  "El estilo nos hace" (*ibid.*). 1924.

XII,  228:  *La Esfinge*, acto primero. 1909.

XII,  828:  *El otro*, jornada segunda. 1926.

XII,  859:  *El otro*, epílogo. [n.d.]

XIII,      611:   "A Nietzsche" (*Rosario de sonetos líricos*). 1910.

XVI,   99–113:   "La fe." 1900.
XVI,   117–24:   "Mi religión." 1907.
XVI,   127–451:  *Del sentimiento trágico de la vida.* 1913.
XVI,   455–559:  *La agonía del Cristianismo.* 1924.
XVI,   583–628:  *San Manuel Bueno, mártir.* 1930.
XVI,   832–39:   "La honda inquietud única." 1914.
XVI,   844–47:   "Ley de piedra y palabra de aire." 1919.
XVI,   873–76:   "La ciudad de Henoc." 1933.
XVI,   890–93:   "En la calle: sarta sin cuerda." 1933.
XVI,   898–901:  "Sed de reposo." 1933.
XVI,   911–14:   "La lengua de fuego se pone en la tierra." 1933.

## *Selected Works by Unamuno in English Translation*

*Abel Sánchez and Other Stories.* Translated by Anthony Kerrigan. Chicago: Henry Regnery Co., 1956.

*The Agony of Christianity.* Translated by Kurt F. Reinhart. New York: Frederick Ungar, 1960.

*The Christ of Velazquez.* Translated by Eleanor L. Turnbull. Baltimore: Johns Hopkins Press, 1951.

*Essays and Soliloquies.* Translated by J. E. Crawford Flitch. New York: A. A. Knopf, 1925.

*The Life of Don Quixote and Sancho.* Translated by Homer P. Earle. New York: A. A. Knopf, 1927.

*Mist: A Tragi-Comic Novel.* Translated by Warren Fite. New York: A. A. Knopf, 1928.

*Perplexities and Paradoxes.* Translated by Stuart Gross. New York: Philosophical Library, 1945.

*Poems.* Translated by Eleanor L. Turnbull. Foreword by John A. Mackay. Baltimore: Johns Hopkins Press, 1952.

*The Tragic Sense of Life.* Translated by J. E. Crawford Flitch. New York: Dover Publications, 1954.

*Three Exemplary Novels and a Prologue.* Translated by Angel Flores. New York: Grove Press, Inc., 1956.

# INDEX

sible superman, 180; frees galley slaves, 213; his apotheosis, 263; strives for immortality, 266; adventure with lion, 268; mentioned, 3, 10, 14, 137, 163, 188, 205, 273

*Doppelgänger*, 28

Dostoyevsky, Fiodor, 5, 7

Dreyfus, Alfred, 212

### E

Ecclesiastes, 207, 269

Economics, 248–56 *passim*

Eden, 206, 207, 257–64

Ego: its harmony disrupted, 40; its disintegration, 45; its captivity, 108–9

Egoism: rejected by Unamuno, 12, 22; and self-knowledge, 98; defined, 115; contrasted with egotism, 115, 145; in Nietzsche, 127

Ellis, Havelock, 169

*Ensimismamiento*, 8–9, 36, 49

Envy: of self, 44–45, 95, 137; linked to alienation, 82; by Nietzsche of Christ, 129; monastic, 151, 249; factor in cultural purism, 219; linked to solitude, 248; linked to landscape, 248; and economics, 253–56 *passim*

Esau, 240–45 *passim*, 276

Essence: in Jacob myth, indicated by nominalism, 239–42; in Eden myth, indicated by nominalism, 258–60

Eternal return: solution for immortality, 178; its historical meaning, 188; Unamuno's reaction to, 189–92; mentioned, 127, 128, 129

Eternity: of the self, 23; of the real self, 103–4; and history, 191. *See also* Time

Ethics: reveals will to power, 11; not a behavioral science, 11–12; its criteria, 43; and satanic self, 43; and moral self, 44; its use of alienation, 96–97; neutralized by self-contemplation, 137; Christian, Nietzsche's concept of, 144–45; true moral behavior, 145; of instrumentalism, 149–50; quixotic morality, 159; its formalism, 225, 226; its rationalism, 226; moral asceticism, 268–69

Evil. *See* Good and evil

Evolution, social, 175

Existence: proof of personal, 29; Cartesian proof of, analyzed, 37–38; meaningful human, 73–74; defined as gain or loss of selves, 101

Existentialism: questions raised by, 5; its definition, 5, 6, 7, 9, 10; existential psychology, Unamuno's concept of, 73, 274; its psychological dilemma, 109; the existentialist's dilemma, 276; absurdity, Unamuno's concept of, 277

### F

Faith: its conflict with reason, 16; need for proof, 16, 227; good and bad, 136–37; lack of, in Tirso's play, 159; is blind in masses, 226; its irrationalism upheld, 228; existential, tested, 228–29; agonistic, 229; of Jacob, 237; of mystics, 237; Don Quixote's tested, 268; Abraham's tested, 268

Fear: during loss of self, 32; of death, 128; linked to concept of God, 200–202

Fichte, Johann Gottlieb, 123

Fiction. *See* Myth; Role

France, 119

Frankl, Viktor, 7

Freedom: requires instinct, 12; limits on, 12, 13, 77; in choosing social role, 76; its role in developing self, 116; Nietzsche's need of, 135; from evil in self, 155–57; as tenet of Hebraism, 268, 270; limited in Moses, 270; enhanced by truth, 271

Freud, Sigmund, 25

Fulfillment, 114–15

### G

Ganivet, Angel, 212

Generation of 1898, 14, 119, 169, 215, 251

Genius: his role in society, 174; as cultural hero, 267

Geography. *See* Land; Landscape

Germany, 119, 123, 217, 218, 220

Gideon, 207

God: the absolute superman, 13, 179; of love, 198; of justice, 198, 202; of law, 199; anthropomorphic concept of, 200, 201; fear of, 200–202. *See also*

Jehovah; Jesus Christ

Goethe, Johann Wolfgang von, 14, 166

Good and evil: are relative, 11; beyond, 11, 159–60, 186; in self-contemplation, 42; linked to the Other, 97–98; revaluation of, 142; their mutual dependence, 149; are reversible, 150; do not reflect basic self, 152–53; evil is useless concept, 154–55; evil conquered by action, 155–56; defined by motivation, 156–57; to do and to be, their difference, 158; limitations of, in Phariseeism, 224–25; in Eden myth, 261–62. *See also* Innocence; Sin

Grace, 13, 185

Group. *See* Masses

### H

Hegel, Friedrich, 121, 123

Heidegger, Martin, 4, 5

Hellenism, 214, 223, 230, 266, 268

Heredity: collective, 217

Hero: linked to human salvation, 13; exempt from traditional values, 137; repressed by mediocre men, 163; his desire for immortality, 163; is sacrificed for masses, 170; defined, 171; his cultural destiny, 267; heroic values, 268; as tenet of Hebraism, 268; Moses as, 270–71

Hirsch, Baron Moritz, 217

History: confused with legend, 77, 192; as lived by hero and masses, 174; and intrahistory, 174, 244, 253–54; concepts of, Unamuno's and Nietzsche's compared, 185; and the eternal return, 188; and counterhistory, 191; as concept in Judaism, 204, 231–32; as concept in Christianity, 231–32; as nightmare, 254

Humanism, 214

Humanity: salvation of, 181–82; its struggle with Nature, 193

Humanization, 258

Husserl, Edmund, 7

Hypocrisy: defined, 10, 71, 78–79; relation to personality, 71; when unconscious, 80–81; attributed to Nietzsche, 130; of the virtuous, 147–48

### I

Idealism: contrasted with spiritualism, 170–71; in Christianity, 213

Idealization of self, 76

Identity, 100, 101

Immortality: and the superman, 13, 179; of the self, 103–4; basic goal of man, 162–63; the will to, 177; and the eternal return, 178, 189; role in Judaism, 204, 231–32; of society, 230–31; role in Christianity, 231–32; reflected in Cain myth, 256; the creator's power of, 265; as tenet of Hebraism, 266–67

Individualism: and the superman, 168–69; its relativity, 172

Innocence: animal, 12, 155–57. *See also* Good and evil; Motivation; Sin

Inquisition, 211, 212

Instinct: crippled by intelligence, 12; manifests will to power, 12; and sincerity, 12, 145; in Nietzsche, 132–33; for survival, 177

Instrumentalism: in ethics, 149

Intention. *See* Motivation

Interiorization: of social self, 68

Intimacy: destroyed by memoirs, 84–85

Introspection: discussed, 20–22, 24; leads to nothingness, 36, 53; rejected by Unamuno, 48; creates sociability, 54; rejected by Nietzsche, 133; in life of Moses, 270–71

Inverse reasoning, 141–43. *See also* Antithesis

Inversion: of values, 150

Irony: toward social self, 8, 83–84; and sincerity, 10; a method of mental health, 45–46; its pervasiveness in life, 88; secret, 136–37; as philosophical method, 140

Isaac, 245

### J

Jacob: myth discussed, 234–46; mentioned, 95, 96, 98, 194, 257, 267, 276

Jaspers, Karl, 4, 5, 14

Jehovah, 16, 198–205, 231. *See also* God

Jeremiah, 209, 271, 272

Jesus Christ: rejected by Nietzsche, 12, 121, 178; compared to superman, 12,

—self-willed impulse, 114–16
—social: analyzed, 54–55, 74–75; in Nietzsche, 134, 135
Selfness: its degrees of fullness, 92; and sameness, 98, 100
Semitics, 198
Senancour, Etienne de, 124, 179
Seneca, 189
Sin, 147, 164, 261–62. *See also* Good and evil; Innocence
Sincerity: problem of, 10; when destroyed, 41, 43; and hypocrisy, 44; analyzed, 78–90; and spontaneity, 145
Skepticism: in religion, 228
Slave morality, 144–45
Sociability: and solitude, 49, 53–57 *passim;* and self-knowledge, 52; true and false, 66–67; and others, 74
Social action. *See* Action
Social self. *See* Self
Society: within the self, 54; its welfare, 171; evolution of, 175; its progress, 180; and religion, 186; its salvation, 230; and civil conflict, 243–46 *passim,* 274; its psychology, 248; its origin, 250
Socrates, 130, 145
Solomon, 269
Soul: related to self, 20, 21; of individual and of society, 230–31
Spain: as "a problem," 14; her self-hatred, 249; her destiny, 269
Spectator: to oneself, 74, 82–84; as judge of sincerity, 81–82. *See also* Contemplation
Spencer, Herbert, 121, 169, 170, 193
Spirit: linked to personality, 9, 62, 109–10, 274; its definition, 19; and matter, 19, its effect in man, 51; its privacy, 171; related to society, 230; concept of, in Jacob myth, 237; and nominalism, 258–60
Spiritual naturalism, 238
Spiritualism: contrasted with idealism, 170–71
Spirituality: inner, 8; contrasted with individuality, 60
Spiritualization: contrasted with naturalization, 111
Stirner, Max, 169

Strength: in Nietzsche, 10–11, 128, 138; against weakness, 137, 144–45; hated by the virtuous, 152; and the superman, 168, 176–77; its use of violence, 172; and the search for immortality, 178; Unamuno's definition of, 184, 194
Struggle: for survival, 145, 176–77; to impose the self, 146; and the eternal return, 178; between man and nature, 193–94; in Jacob myth, 236–37, 239–42; in society, 243–46 *passim,* 274; between ideas, 244–46; within Spain, 249–50; as an existential mode, 250; in Cain myth, 250; is beyond moral judgment, 250; and satanic self, 274
Style, Unamuno's, 13–14, 28, 110, 141, 229–30, 257
Subject-object: in self-contemplation, 92–93; in self and non-self, 111–13
Subjectivism: in moral values, 145
Sublimation, 25
Submergence into the self, 8–9, 36, 49
Substance. *See* Reality; Spirit
Substantiality: of the self, 20; its limits, 35–36; its transcendence, 63; in Jacob myth, 239–40, 242

*T*

Targum, 265
Teresa, Santa, 206, 236
Theater: and personal farce, 8; and personality, 63–65; of consciousness, 64; in private life, 67–68; in public life, 67–68; and existence, 69; private self dramatized, 81; philosophy as, 140–41
Theology: moral, attacked by Unamuno, 145
*Three Exemplary Novels,* 46
Time: awareness of, 9; the self revealed in, 23; defines personality, 99; gives authenticity to the self, 99–100; and potential selves, 100; and future, 101; and memory, 101; and the superman, 167–68; and eternal return, 191; vanity and sin of, 268–69
Tirso de Molina, 159
Tolstoy, Leo, 124
*Tragic Sense of Life, The,* 3, 5, 16, 36, 139, 203, 256